ROTH FAMILY FOUNDATION

Imprint in Music

Michael P. Roth
and Sukey Garcetti
have endowed this
imprint to honor the
memory of their parents,
Julia and Harry Roth,
whose deep love of music
they wish to share
with others.

The publisher and the University of California Press Foundation gratefully acknowledge the generous support of the Roth Family Foundation Imprint in Music, established by a major gift from Sukey and Gil Garcetti and Michael P. Roth.

Additional support for this book was generously provided by the General Fund of the American Musicological Society, supported in part by the National Endowment for the Humanities and the Andrew W. Mellon Foundation.

An Eternal Pitch

PHONO: BLACK MUSIC AND THE GLOBAL IMAGINATION

This series is a dynamic collection of work that explores and documents the long-playing histories of Black musical innovation. The title is a nod to the grooves, play, tactility, and archives produced by the phonograph, which serves as inspiration for a complex series of musical concerns and possibilities. The series title indexes how Black sound, performance, and musical idioms are inscribed in the acoustics of everyday Black life, both local and transnational.
Shana L. Redmond and Tsitsi Jaji, Editors

1. *Who Hears Here? On Black Music, Pasts and Present,* by Guthrie Ramsey
2. *An Eternal Pitch: Bishop G. E. Patterson, Broadcast Religion, and the Afterlives of Ecstasy,* by Braxton D. Shelley

An Eternal Pitch

BISHOP G. E. PATTERSON, BROADCAST RELIGION, AND THE AFTERLIVES OF ECSTASY

Braxton D. Shelley

UNIVERSITY OF CALIFORNIA PRESS

University of California Press
Oakland, California

© 2023 by Braxton D. Shelley

Library of Congress Cataloging-in-Publication Data

Names: Shelley, Braxton D., author.
Title: An eternal pitch : Bishop G. E. Patterson, broadcast religion, and
    the afterlives of ecstasy / Braxton D. Shelley.
Other titles: Phono (Oakland, Calif.) ; 2.
Description: Oakland, California : University of California Press, [2023] |
    Series: Phono: black music and the global imagination ; 2 | Includes
    bibliographical references and index.
Identifiers: LCCN 2023013777 (print) | LCCN 2023013778 (ebook) |
    ISBN 9780520387133 (cloth) | ISBN 9780520387140 (paperback) |
    ISBN 9780520387157 (ebook)
Subjects: LCSH: Patterson, G. E. (Gilbert Earl), 1939-2007. | Church
    music—Pentecostal churches. | Pentecostal churches—Liturgy. |
    Musical pitch—Religious aspects. | Religious broadcasting—
    Christianity. | Church of God in Christ.
Classification: LCC ML3178.P4 S54 2023 (print) | LCC ML3178.P4
    (ebook) | DDC 781.71/994—dc23/eng/20230531
LC record available at https://lccn.loc.gov/2023013777
LC ebook record available at https://lccn.loc.gov/2023013778

32 31 30 29 28 27 26 25 24 23
10 9 8 7 6 5 4 3 2 1

For Joyce

Contents

List of Illustrations		ix
Author's Note on Media Files		xi
Acknowledgments		xvii
Prologue		xxi
	Introduction	1
1.	Broadcast Religion	37
2.	Broadcast Medium	70
3.	Broadcast Grammar	96
4.	Broadcast Frequency, or The Politics of Key	120
5.	Broadcast Ensemble: The Logic of the Prayer Cloth	147
	Eternal Life: An Epilogue	177
Notes		193
Bibliography		209
Index		219

Illustrations

MUSICAL EXAMPLES

1.	Eternal song in F major, 2006	2
2.	Eternal song in E major, 2006	3
3.	Eternal song in A♭ major, 2002	64
4.	Eternal song in A♭ major, 2001	87
5.	Eternal song in E major, 2006	88
6.	Eternal riff in G♭ major, 1993	91
7.	Eternal song in E major, 2006	117
8.	Eternal song in A♭ major, 2003	126
9.	The eternal pitch	140
10.	Eternal song in G major, 1995	158

ILLUSTRATIONS

FIGURES

1. Greeting published in International Youth Congress of the COGIC, Souvenir Book and Official Program, 1966 — 41
2. Greeting published in Sixty-second Annual Holy Convocation of COGIC, Souvenir Book and Official Program, 1969 — 42
3. *TV Guide* advertisement demonstrating Bishop Patterson's appearance on WMKW-TV30, 1980 — 44
4. Screenshot of Jonah 2:10 from Bishop Patterson's "The Hope of Our City," 2000 — 55
5. Screenshot of Bishop Patterson, robe bathed in red lights, from "Vicarious Victory," 2005 — 61
6. Screenshot from the *Bountiful Blessings* broadcast, 2020 — 68
7. Screenshot of 1 Peter 5:7 from Bishop Patterson's "He Cares for You," 2005 — 136
8. Announcement published in COGIC's Holy Convocation souvenir book about the establishment of radio station WBBP 1480 AM, 1991 — 143
9. Instagram post by Linwood Dillard, depicting Dillard ministering in a robe worn by Bishop Patterson, 2015 — 148
10. Folded card included in a package from Bountiful Blessings, Inc. containing three of Bishop Patterson's neckties, 2022 — 156
11. Members of Trinity Temple COGIC's congregation gathered beneath a banner with Patterson's exhortation: "Be Healed, Be Delivered, and Be Set Free," 2018 — 165
12. A YouTube user's annotations and time stamps of Bishop Patterson's "The Purpose of the Four Gospels," 2016 — 170
13. Instagram users' comments depicting Bishop Patterson's eternal flame, 2020 — 185
14. Instagram users' comments depicting Bishop Patterson's eternal flame, in response to a post by @Preachernation, 2022 — 186

Author's Note on Media Files

This book references a number of video examples, which are available for viewing as a YouTube playlist accessible at ucpress.edu/go/an-eternal-pitch. While the manuscript details Bishop G. E. Patterson's words, describes their form, and interprets their meanings, these media files offer an invaluable opportunity to hear the sounds of these messages.

Video examples are named and numbered by chapter using an abbreviation of the chapter title, as defined in the list that follows. Files are signaled in the text by the "play" icon (▶) and a boldface callout enclosed in square brackets. For instance, the first video example in Chapter 1, "Broadcast Religion," is called out in the text as [▶ **Video Example BR1**]. Descriptions for these videos are below.

INTRODUCTION (INT)

INT1: Bishop G. E. Patterson, "Jehoshaphat's Prayer and God's Answer," at Ninety-ninth Annual Holy Convocation of the Church of God in Christ, Memphis, Tennessee, Sunday, November 12, 2006.

INT2a–c: Bishop G. E. Patterson, "Acts 2:1–4," Memphis, Tennessee, Pentecost Sunday, May 23, 1999.

AUTHOR'S NOTE ON MEDIA FILES

CHAPTER 1: BROADCAST RELIGION (BR)

BR1: Bishop G. E. Patterson, "Prayer in *Singing the Old Time Way, Vol. 2*," Memphis, Tennessee, released March 28, 2006.

BR2: Bishop G. E. Patterson, "The Gospel According to John," Memphis, Tennessee, Christmas, Monday, December 25, 2006.

BR3a–b: Bishop G. E. Patterson, "Hold On! Help Is on the Way," Memphis, Tennessee, Sunday, November 14, 1999.

BR4: Bishop G. E. Patterson, footage from "G. E. Patterson, the early years 1," uploaded by NewLifeMinistry1990, January 23, 2014, https://youtu.be/whl-1ochWL0.

BR5a–b: Bishop G. E. Patterson, "The Hope of Our City," New York, Sunday, May 14, 2000.

BR6: Bishop G. E. Patterson, "All We Need Is at Home," Memphis, Tennessee, Sunday, May 8, 1983.

BR7: Bishop G. E. Patterson, "Victory: The Departed Glory Shall Return," Memphis, Tennessee, Palm Sunday, March 20, 2005.

BR8: Bishop G. E. Patterson, "It's Time for You to Sing Your Song," Memphis, Tennessee, Sunday, December 15, 2002.

CHAPTER 2: BROADCAST MEDIUM (BM)

BM1: Bishop G. E. Patterson, "Discouraged?" Memphis, Tennessee, Sunday, December 3, 2000.

BM2: Bishop G. E. Patterson, "Altar Call (Is Your All on the Altar), in *Singing the Old Time Way, Vol. 2*," Memphis, Tennessee, released Tuesday, March 28, 2006.

BM3: Bishop G. E. Patterson, "There's Power in the Blood," Memphis, Tennessee, Sunday, October 21, 2001.

BM4: Bishop G. E. Patterson, "The God of All Supply," Memphis, Tennessee, Sunday, August 27, 1989.

BM5a: Bishop G. E. Patterson, "The Healing of King Hezekiah," California Northwest Jurisdiction's Forty-seventh Holy Convocation, Los Angeles, California, Friday, June 11, 2004.

BM5b–c: Bishop G. E. Patterson, COGIC's Ninety-seventh Holy Convocation, Memphis, Tennessee, August 9, 2004.

BM6a:	Bishop G. E. Patterson, "The Power of the Word," Los Angeles, California, West Angeles COGIC, Sunday, May 16, 2004.
BM6b:	Bishop G. E. Patterson, "The Healing of King Hezekiah," California Northwest Jurisdiction's Forty-seventh Holy Convocation, Los Angeles, California, Friday, June 11, 2004.
BM7:	Bishop G. E. Patterson, "The Password," Memphis, Tennessee, Sunday, August 5, 2001.
BM8:	Bishop G. E. Patterson, "Dealing with Life's Battles," Memphis, Tennessee, Sunday, August 26, 2001.
BM9:	Bishop G. E. Patterson, "Focusing Your Eyes upon the Lord," Memphis, Tennessee, Sunday, November 5, 2006.
BM10:	Bishop G. E. Patterson, "Jehoshaphat's Prayer and God's Answer," COGIC's Ninety-ninth Annual Holy Convocation, Memphis, Tennessee, Sunday, November 12, 2006.
BM11:	Bishop G. E. Patterson, "Neither Were They Thankful," Memphis, Tennessee, Sunday, November 25, 1993.
BM12:	Bishop G. E. Patterson, "The Faith of Strangers," Memphis, Tennessee, Tuesday, August 17, 1999.
BM13:	Bishop G. E. Patterson, "The Power of the Word," Los Angeles, California, West Angeles COGIC, Sunday, May 16, 2004.
BM14:	Bishop G. E. Patterson, "A Compassionate Father," Memphis, Tennessee, Sunday, June 19, 2005.
BM15:	Bishop G. E. Patterson, "Will You Dare To Be Different," Memphis, Tennessee, Sunday, February 13, 2005.
BM16:	Bishop G. E. Patterson, "Philippians 2:5–11," Memphis, Tennessee, Sunday, September 3, 2006.
BM17a–b:	Bishop G. E. Patterson, "After the Dust Settles," Memphis, Tennessee, Sunday, June 11, 2006.
BM18:	Bishop G. E. Patterson, "The Gospel According to John," Memphis, Tennessee, Christmas, Monday, December 25, 2006.
BM19:	Bishop G. E. Patterson, "It Is Time to Recommit to Our Lord," COGIC's Ninety-fourth Annual Holy Convocation, Memphis, Tennessee, Sunday, November 11, 2001.

CHAPTER 3: BROADCAST GRAMMAR (BG)

BG1: Bishop G. E. Patterson, "I Can't Keep It to Myself," Memphis, Tennessee, Sunday, July 3, 2005.

BG2: Bishop G. E. Patterson, "Arrow of the Lord's Deliverance," Memphis, Tennessee, Sunday, September 2, 1990.

BG3: Bishop G. E. Patterson, "Arrow of the Lord's Deliverance," Memphis, Tennessee, Sunday, August 18, 1996.

BG4: Bishop G. E. Patterson, "Arrow of the Lord's Deliverance," Memphis, Tennessee, Sunday, November 19, 2006.

BG5: Bishop G. E. Patterson, "A Compassionate Father," Memphis, Tennessee, Sunday, June 19, 2005.

BG6a–b: Bishop G. E. Patterson, "Call His Name," Memphis, Tennessee, Sunday, December 17, 2000.

BG7a–b: Bishop G. E. Patterson, "Saint's Remedy in Times of Trouble," Memphis, Tennessee, Sunday, November 15, 1998.

BG8: Bishop G. E. Patterson, "The Departed Glory Shall Return," Memphis, Tennessee, Sunday, October 18, 1998.

BG9: Bishop G. E. Patterson, "Focusing Your Eyes on the Lord," Memphis, Tennessee, Sunday, November 5, 2006.

CHAPTER 4: BROADCAST FREQUENCY (BF), OR THE POLITICS OF KEY

BF1: Bishop G. E. Patterson, Ninety-seventh Annual Holy Convocation of the COGIC, Memphis, Tennessee, November 13, 2004.

BF2: Bishop G. E. Patterson, "The Dawn of a New Day," Memphis, Tennessee, Easter Sunday, April 16, 2006.

BF3: Bishop G. E. Patterson, "It's Time for You to Sing Your Song," Memphis, Tennessee, Sunday, December 15, 2002.

BF4: Bishop G. E. Patterson, "David's Day of Thanksgiving," Memphis, Tennessee, Thursday, November 24, 2005.

BF5a–b: Bishop G. E. Patterson, "He Cares for You," Memphis, Tennessee, Sunday, November 10, 2005.

BF6:	Bishop G. E. Patterson, "This Is Your Year of Restoration," Memphis, Tennessee, Sunday, January 2, 2000.
BF7:	Bishop G. E. Patterson, "Cry in Desperation," Memphis, Tennessee, Sunday, February 6, 2005.
BF8:	Bishop G. E. Patterson, "Your Day Will Come," Memphis, Tennessee, Sunday, February 4, 1996.
BF9:	Bishop G. E. Patterson, "Saint's Remedy in Times of Trouble," Memphis, Tennessee, Sunday, November 15, 1998.
BF10:	Bishop G. E. Patterson, "The Gospel According to John," Memphis, Tennessee, Christmas, Monday, December 25, 2006.

CHAPTER 5: BROADCAST ENSEMBLE (BE): THE LOGIC OF THE PRAYER CLOTH

BE1:	Bishop G. E. Patterson, "A Second Touch," Memphis, Tennessee, Sunday, April 1, 1990.
BE2:	Pastor Stephen F. Smith, Dr. Ronald E. Rolfe, Pastor Antonio M. Buckley, and Pastor John Glen Brown, "Remembering Bishop G. E. Patterson," on the *Stephen Smith Show*, March 30, 2014.
BE3:	Bishop G. E. Patterson, "Focusing Your Eyes upon the Lord," Memphis, Tennessee, Sunday, November 5, 2006.
BE4:	Bishop G. E. Patterson, "Jehoshaphat's Prayer and God's Answer," Ninety-ninth Annual Holy Convocation of the COGIC, Memphis, Tennessee, Sunday, November 12, 2006.
BE5:	Bishop G. E. Patterson, "It's Not Your Battle," Memphis, Tennessee, Sunday, August 20, 1995.
BE6:	Bishop G. E. Patterson, "You Can Depend on God," Memphis, Tennessee, Sunday, August 2, 1998.
BE7:	Bishop G. E. Patterson, "Neither Were They Thankful," Memphis, Tennessee, Sunday, November 25, 1993.
BE8:	Introduction to all *Bountiful Blessings* broadcasts.
BE9:	Bishop G. E. Patterson, "The Gospel According to John," Memphis, Tennessee, Christmas, Monday, December 25, 2006.
BE10:	Bishop G. E. Patterson, "Healing Service," Memphis, Tennessee, Sunday, July 23, 2006.

AUTHOR'S NOTE ON MEDIA FILES

ETERNAL LIFE: AN EPILOGUE (EP)

EP1: *Bountiful Blessings* broadcast, first broadcast after Louise Patterson's death, November 27, 2022.

EP2: *Bountiful Blessings* broadcast opening montage, 2007–22.

EP3: Louise Patterson's message to 2005 COGIC International Women's Conference, Atlanta, Georgia, May 30, 2005.

EP4: Eternal Flame outside of Temple of Deliverance Church, Memphis, Tennessee.

EP5: One version of *Bountiful Blessings*'s broadcasts after Louise Patterson's death that announced her passing, 2022.

EP6: Introduction to the rebroadcast of Bishop G. E. Patterson's sermon "Call His Name" (2000), Sunday, December 18, 2022.

EP7: *Bountiful Blessings*'s rebroadcast of communion celebration, January 1, 2023.

All videos are reproduced courtesy of the Estate of Louise D. Patterson. © 1967–2007 The Estate of Louise D. Patterson

Acknowledgments

Like any good sermon, this book is a collective achievement. The interests and curiosities that come to fruition in these pages are almost as old as I am. So, the hands, hearts, and minds that have nourished this project are almost too numerous to name. Despite the insufficiency of the page, I want to acknowledge some of those whose contributions to this project have made possible the publication of the book you now hold.

I wrote the first version of this manuscript during my time as an assistant professor at Harvard University. My scholarly trajectory was transformed by my interactions with the members of this intellectual community, including Carol Oja, Carolyn Abbate, Alex Rehding, Ingrid Monson, Kay Kaufman Shelemay, Kate van Orden, Suzannah Clark, Anne Shreffler, Hans Tutschku, Chaya Czernowin, Vijay Iyer, and Yvette Jackson. When I began working on this project, I benefited enormously from conversations about voice with Carolyn Abbate and archival history with Carol Oja. And, I am indebted to Alex Rehding and Kay Kaufman Shelemay for reading drafts of the manuscript.

Among the many colleagues in the Divinity School, Faculty of Arts and Sciences, and Institute of Sacred Music at Yale University who have enriched my thinking and my life, I am especially grateful to Jonathan

Howard, Laura Nasrallah, and John Durham Peters for reading parts of the final version of this book. Some, like Laura, waded through the same chapter(s) multiple times. I have gained so much from my Yale and broader New Haven community, including Jon Bullock, Kyle Bullock, Lynn Sullivan-Harmon, Willie Jennings, Joanne Jennings, Nathaniel Gumbs, Jonathan Howard, Cami King, Martin Jean, Jamil Drake, Ameera Nimjee, Ian Quinn, Anna Zaruznaya, and Brian Kane. My weeks orbit around Monday night dinners, and the rich intergenerational community that includes Laura Nasrallah, Ann Muench-Nasrallah, Beata Muench-Nasrallah, Marc Muench-Nasrallah, Todne Thomas, and Tashinga Chipmuro.

I am grateful for the skilled editorial staff at the University of California Press: Raina Polivka, senior editor; Sam Warren, editorial assistant; Stephanie Summerhays, project editor; and Amy Smith Bell, copy editor. I also want to thank the series editors Shana L. Redmond and Tsitsi Jaji for inviting this manuscript to be part of the *Phono: Black Music and the Global Imagination* series. I especially thank Shana for the model she casts in her book *Everything Man: The Form and Function of Paul Robeson* of how to take seriously an antiphonal afterlife.

Jacob Sunshine and Alexander Cowan have been wonderful research assistants for the past five years. Alex prepared the musical examples for this volume, while Jacob attended to copy edits and references. Most important, Jacob has compiled, arranged, and formatted a near multitude of media files for the companion playlist that brings this book to life.

In moments of great fatigue, I have been buoyed by the prayers of so many who so frequently remind me that they are "keeping me lifted." This prayer band includes Mary Baldwin, Derensky Cooper, Mary Flounoy, Sandra Harper, Rylan Harris, Karol Harshaw-Ellis, Charletta Hines, Teeshawn Jones, Shaunielle McDonald, Rev. Miriam Phillips-Stephens, Rev. Dewey Williams, Lynne Williams, James Abbington, Yvette Boatwright, Deborah Boston, Richard and Margaret Crandall, Cheryl Townsend Gilkes, Beverly and Johnny Johnson, Annie Lawson, Bishop Eric and Supervisor Jean Leake, Licia and Navarro McDonald, Genna Rae McNeil, Tony McNeil, Lucille Patterson, Emmett Price, Dorothy and Nesbitt Spruill, Lucy Taylor, Jason Thompson, William Turner, Maurice and Pam Wallace, and George Woodruff.

I have also been sustained by a host of meaningful relationships with dear friends in music studies, including Jessica Baker, Jonathan De Souza, Lauren Eldridge, Margot Fassler, Sumanth Gopinath, Bonnie Gordon, Wendy Heller, Loren Kajikawa, Marcus Pyle, Pete Smucker, Gavin Steingo, Michael Uy, Christi Jay Wells, and Christopher William White. Although most of my friends are musicians, there are those to whom I'm certain I'd be close, even if we didn't share this passion: Mycal Brickhouse, Pierce Gradone, Joshua Lazard, Clay Mettens, and G. Preston Wilson Jr.

Evangelist Louise Patterson, wife of Bishop G. E. Patterson, provided crucial support for this undertaking. While I am sad that she passed away before this work was concluded, I will always be grateful for the permissions, for her blessing, and for the neckties I reference in this book's final chapter. And I must thank Leo Davis, whose deep wisdom and infinite Rolodex—in Memphis and across the country—provided vital contacts and context during the beginning stages of this project.

My family played a crucial part in this book, as in every part of my life. For us, as for many, G. E. Patterson was always a household name. I have so many vivid memories of watching his broadcasts on Sunday mornings and Sunday afternoons. To this day, my grandmother insists that Patterson's messages remind her of the way folks preached when her grandfather was alive. In that sense, this book builds a connection to relatives I have not known, even as it sharpens my gratitude for the steady and strong support I glean from Dorothy Shelley Hilton, Jessie Hilton, Brianna Shelley, Lula Ricks, and Lindsay Wright. Lindsay, my most cherished interlocutor, is my partner in life and in thought. I thank her—for love, encouragement, incisive edits, and for listening to me play the same Patterson clips ad infinitum.

Another most important person in the life of this project and its author passed away before it came to fruition. I'm still not over it. Joyce Dawson O'Rourke's contribution to my life resisted categories: she was part godmother, part sounding board, part assistant, part intercessor but mostly friend. Indeed, it was only through her passing that I began to understand all that death is and to more accurately appreciate the meanings of afterlife. This book is dedicated to her memory.

Prologue

A solemn hush filled the sanctuary of the Temple of Deliverance Church of God in Christ, in Memphis, Tennessee, when Bishop Gilbert Earl Patterson's coffin was closed for the last time. Although Patterson's casket had been ceremoniously shut at the beginning of the Thursday and Friday evening funeral services, this moment on Saturday, March 31, 2007, was different: everyone knew this was the last time anyone would see Bishop Patterson in the flesh. Bishops Charles E. Blake and J. Neaul Haynes, the first and second assistant presiding bishops of the Church of God in Christ (COGIC), descended from the pulpit to wait near the casket in recognition of the rite denominational leaders refer to as "the sealing of the bier."

They watched as the adjutants removed the episcopal ring and pectoral cross from the body of their denomination's departed leader and carried these symbols of ecclesial authority to Bishop Patterson's widow, Evangelist Louise Patterson, who was seated on the temple's front row. As Blake and Haynes returned to the dais, the leaders of the denomination's National Adjutancy Corps completed this ritual, a rite designed to signal the sanctity of the late cleric by observing his gradual departure from view: after shrouding Patterson in red and white fabrics, the adjutants fastened the full-couch casket's two oak lids. Then they turned the coffin in a clockwise direction, enacting the Bishop's passage from life into afterlife. Finally, the adjutants draped Patterson's bier in an off-white pall emblazoned with the seal of office of the presiding bishop.

The interworldly kinetics of this threshold moment are worked out in the song that accompanied this mournful act:

> Till we meet, till we meet, till we meet at Jesus's feet.
> Till we meet, till we meet, God be with you till we meet again.
> God be with you. God be with you. God be with you till we meet again.
> God be with you. God be with you. God be with you till we meet again.

Although tenor soloist Elter Lamar Black had sung "Till We Meet Again" in both of Patterson's two preceding funeral services, the emotional weight of this climactic scene was too heavy for Black's lone voice to bear. Just as he became overcome, gospel legends Bettye Ransom Nelson and Timothy Wright picked up the microphone to enlist their instruments in this valedictory selection. But the addition of these two voices suggested the presence of another. As this song and its performance troubled the distinction between speaker(s) and audience, narrator(s) and addressee(s), the hymn invites us to wonder if these vocalists—and the thousands who heard them—imagined themselves to be singing to Patterson, for Patterson, or to be engaging some other preposition, some other relation, some other meeting.

In at least one sense, the duration defined by the preposition "till" turned out to be quite brief. Indeed, very little time passed between the sealing of Patterson's bier and the emergence of his posthumous presence. The very next day—Sunday, April 1, 2007—Patterson's *Bountiful Blessings* broadcast appeared on multiple national TV networks. He was met again as his voice was transmitted on his radio station WBBP 1480, and copies of his sermons were purchased by tens of thousands of listeners and viewers. While the day after Patterson's interment was far from the first time his message enjoyed this kind of dissemination, these broadcasts did have a distinctive significance as testaments to the ongoing power of his voice. In this way, they affirmed one of the most memorable eulogies given during the first of Patterson's three homegoing services: while speaking on behalf of the Memphis Ministers Association, Rabbi Micah Greenstein assured the assembled mourners that Patterson's voice "would not be silenced by death." Although Greenstein's proposal might have been made with reference to any number of prominent public figures, it is hard to imagine a minister about whom these words would have been more fitting. Uttered while standing in a sanctuary that doubled as a cutting-edge recording studio, a cathedral built by the man who led the nation's largest Black Pentecostal denomination, Greenstein's words were somehow equally obvious and prophetic. At that moment, hundreds of thousands of VHSs, CDs, and DVDs of Patterson's sermons and songs were circulating across the country, carrying with them ecstatic declarations about the undying efficacy of the eternal word.

Still, the posthumous reverberation of Bishop Patterson's voice could hardly have been anticipated by those who heard Greenstein's eulogy in person or as broadcast in 2007: Patterson's sermons and songs continue to resound at the intersection of Black music, digital culture, and lived religion. Sixteen years after Patterson's death, his messages still enjoy a weekly national television broadcast. At regular intervals, new videos of his characteristically musical sermons are uploaded to YouTube. Nearly every month, a new follower posts a tribute to one of Patterson's online obituaries. And every day, Facebook, Twitter, Instagram, and TikTok users share some snippet of Patterson's preaching on one or more of these social media platforms. With remarkable consistency, these members of the Bishop's virtual congregation and contributors to his digital catalog claim that Patterson's messages are still efficacious, still able to transmit power from the spirit world into their material conditions. In so doing, these religious broadcasters participate in the nexus of faith, media, and sound that lifted Patterson to the heights of ecclesial power during his life, while laying the groundwork for his uncommon afterlife.

While the digital mechanics of Bishop Patterson's afterlife might have been hard to imagine for a preacher born in 1939, his lifelong pursuit of technologically mediated vocal omnipresence seems to have been in search of precisely this kind of dissemination. Long before YouTube's tempting exhortation to "broadcast yourself" became a motto of participatory culture, Gilbert E. Patterson had built a life and ministry predicated on the very possibility of broadcasting. Upon close inspection it becomes clear that many of the key elements of Patterson's religious imagination—the musical structure of his sermons, the metaphors that convey his theology, and the parachurch infrastructure he indefatigably constructed—are all preoccupied with the methods and materials of mass communication. Raising perennial questions about religious communication and technological possibility, the particular arrangement of these media in Patterson's Pentecostalism is part of what so many gathered to celebrate on that day in 2007.

What thread connects the diverse facets of Patterson's ministry—aesthetic, confessional, and technological? What emerges at the intersection of virtuosic Black preaching and the practice of religious broadcasting? What are we to make of the fact that Patterson was both the first COGIC minister with a national and international television ministry, and the only person to ever unseat the denomination's incumbent presiding bishop? And how do each of these questions get worked out in the musical afterlife of this paradigmatic Black preacher?

An Eternal Pitch: Bishop G. E. Patterson, Broadcast Religion, and the Afterlives of Ecstasy offers a theory of the religious networks that take shape around the voice of Patterson, both during his life and after his death. His technophilic Pentecostalism is a Broadcast Religion. Its logics incorporate far more than the voice alone: the sermon, the song, and the human voice stand on equal footing with microphones, cameras, oil, cloth, television, radio, and the internet as potential conduits of divine power. Patterson's enduring preoccupation with various modes of technological mediation—the condition of possibility for his own unusual endurance—is the link between the numerous domains in which he operated and objects among which his voice circulated. The pervasive practice of religious broadcasting finds new purpose as an essential element of Patterson's Black Pentecostal assemblage, the emerging and evolution of a constellation of "sensational forms" that work together to inculcate intimacy between Patterson's messages, his audiences, and various scenes from scripture. Scripture's ancient events are able to enjoy a "live" presence in the religious experience of contemporary congregants because of a carefully calibrated cycle of remediation. This cycle depends on the dynamic interaction between multiple devotional materialities, none of which is more vital than the voice of this virtuosic preacher. His instrument is the system's defining broadcast medium.

Even as Patterson's Afro-modernist articulation of "old-time religion" carved out a space for him in the devotional practices of those who watched his broadcasts, purchased his recordings, and supported his campaigns, it also sowed the seeds for his ministry's second act. Following Patterson's 2007 death, countless social media users have become participants in his digital remediation, lending his message the same immediacy his voice gave to scripture. Their efforts are motivated by a rhetoric of "Afterliveness"—the sense that these posthumous broadcasts are animated by the same power that brought Patterson's homiletic events into earshot of eternity. While this concern with efficacy and endurance bears witness to many features of Patterson's preaching, Afterliveness is especially indicative of the late bishop's penchant for musical repetition: across decades of Patterson's ministry, and in scores of his sermons, a set of musical gestures recur as sonic channels, bringing an individual sermon into contact with scripture's eternal transmission, turning each of Patterson's messages into an eternal pitch.

Pitch—a productively polysemous word used to refer to both tone and strength, angle and ascent, message and enunciation—gets at the many threads of practice that assemble in Patterson's Broadcast Religion. With regard to Bishop Patterson, "pitch" names both the content of his sermons and the breadth of their dissemination, both the intensity his messages chase and the single sonic destination where this power is so often found. "Pitch," both noun and verb, also refers to one of the chief consequences of these four phenomena: Patterson's staggeringly quick ascent to one of the most prominent positions of religious leadership in the United States— and around the world. This book calls Patterson's pitch "eternal" because of his insistent reiteration of a set of musical devices, the scale at which his sermons were recorded, broadcast, and reproduced, and because of the instructive force of his posthumous remediation—the musical afterlife that clarifies what he was up to all along.

The collective labor undertaken to keep Patterson alive reveals the salience of his articulation of Black Pentecostalism, a fact buttressed by the celebrity and religious authority affixed to Patterson on both sides of the grave. Intervening in a field dominated by white evangelists like Billy Graham and Oral Roberts, while evading the derogations directed at other Black ministers like Frederick (Ike) Eikerenkoetter, Patterson's *Bountiful Blessings* broadcasts braided innovation together with tradition. As the first nationally televised representative of the oldest and largest Black

Pentecostal denomination, Patterson's ministry performed an especially forceful integration of Black aesthetics and institutions into the most widely visible domains of American religious broadcasting. Although Patterson's national television ministry began in 1990, this achievement was built on more than three decades of broadcasting—both in the conventional, technological sense and in the more capacious sense this book intends.

Since the beginning of his ministry in the late 1950s, Patterson's Broadcast Religion has unfolded at the intersection of Black musicality, Pentecostal conviction, and sound technology, producing a set of sonic techniques inspired by the belief that the human voice should become an instrument of divine speech. Although a growing number of music scholars have highlighted the relationship(s) between Black music and sound technologies, none has examined Black Pentecostalism's place in this technopoetic field. Patterson's oeuvre is an ideal place from which to theorize the musical and technological entailments of Black Pentecostalism's fixation with sound—that is, the vocal techniques used to pursue "the baptism of the holy ghost," the distinctive Pentecostal experience whose "initial evidence" must also take a particular sonic, glossolalic form.

Just as Patterson places Black musicality at the center of his religious broadcasting, so too this book grounds its arguments in the sonic details of Patterson's many sermons. This book brings the tools of music analysis to bear on Bishop Patterson's oeuvre because, as much as he was anything else, Patterson was a musician. A gospel organist, bluesy singer, and Holiness preacher, Patterson's sermons bring these facets of his personality into an affective alchemy. This book shows that the sonic elements that scaffold the experience of any single Patterson sermon, and the musical materials that recur in so many of these messages, build connections between decades worth of sermons, between material and spiritual realms, and between Patterson's career and his afterlife. It really does matter that Patterson so often finds his way to a singular sonic destination, his voice resonating at the tenor B-natural, B4, an eternal pitch whose transcendence is demonstrated by its ever-shifting relationships to the rest of a given message's musical ecology. What Patterson believed about the incarnation, the baptism of the Holy Ghost, and the transmissibility of spiritual power is concretized in this solitary pitch. But the repetitive musical gestures at issue in this book are just the tip of the iceberg that is the unusually overt technicity of Patterson's homiletical musicality; these sound techniques and Patterson's preoccupation with sound technologies are mutually reinforcing features of Broadcast Religion.

Written from the scholarly, professional, and personal vantage points of a musicologist, minister, and musician, this book is grounded in an insider's perspective. Although I am not a member of the Church of God in Christ, I have long-standing interest and deep familiarity with the materials and tradition shaped by figures like Bishop Patterson. I have partaken of at least one Patterson broadcast during virtually every week of the past two decades, whether at 8:30 a.m. EST on Black Entertainment Television, at 4:00 p.m. EST on the Word Network, or in the wee hours of the morning, on YouTube, Facebook, Instagram, or TikTok. As a member of Patterson's virtual congregation, I livestreamed the funeral with which this prologue begins. I watched the coffin close and wondered what would come next.

An Eternal Pitch is, in part, an attempt to make sense of all that has happened since that Saturday morning in 2007, to understand the unusual resonance that could not be buried that day, and to grapple with the reasons for his messages' uncommon endurance. One of the key moments in my journey to this book took place on Sunday, August 16, 2020, as I played that week's *Bountiful Blessings* broadcast on the ministry's official YouTube channel. While I had stepped away from the computer to attend to some other task, I hurtled back to my device when Bishop Patterson began to sing, "Praise the Lord for his mercy endureth forever," falling from the tenor A♭ down an octave to A♭3. "That was it!" I thought. That excerpt from the 2001 sermon "Dealing with Life's Battles" was something for which I had long been searching, failing, sadly, to find it anywhere in Patterson's digital archive. Thus the reemergence of this musical fragment was both shocking and familiar.

I remembered watching this sermon nearly twenty years earlier on another Sunday afternoon. I remembered the story of Jehoshaphat and Patterson's maroon suit. But, most important, I remembered this song— the way Patterson made music of this text. This moment was so significant because it was so plural. Through the digital remediation of this homiletic fragment, the living room of my Chicago apartment was palpably commingled with my grandmother's Rocky Mount living room: the place where I first heard Patterson preach. Although I had long imagined undertaking a book-length meditation on Patterson's music and message, this work was not at the top of my list in August 2020. But the broadcast in question proved efficacious: it prompted me to pivot from other projects and to write this book to understand all that is tucked into this ongoing song.

An Eternal Pitch is thus both personal and professional. It focuses on the religious assemblages built around Bishop G. E. Patterson's voice. It also intervenes in many related scholarly discourses. The eclectic theological, aesthetic, and technological elements held together by Patterson's eternal pitch call for an equally eclectic methodological toolkit. As such, this book is in conversation with scholars in media studies, Black studies, music studies, homiletics, religious studies, theology, and liturgical studies. Unfolding in a host of virtual venues, Broadcast Religion iteratively materializes religious authority on multiple digital platforms; this around-the-clock practice of lived religion offers an opportunity to rethink ritual for the digital age. At the same time, the racial politics and musical aesthetics, which are so central to Patterson's religious imagination, occasion the relocation of religion and music closer to the center of Black Study. The musical details of Patterson's many sermons, each of which is a vocal broadcast of biblical events, calls African American religious studies to study sound itself, a medium of great significance to Black religious practice.

Introduction

On Sunday, November 12, 2006, the late Bishop Gilbert Earl Patterson delivered his final message to the Ninety-ninth Annual Holy Convocation of the Church of God in Christ, "Jehoshaphat's Prayer and God's Answer." Near the end of sermon whose title describes an interworldly conversation, Patterson took up the subject of sacred singing's enduring power by reanimating a treasured biblical text, 2 Chronicles 20:4–12 [▶ **Video Example INT1**]. Although this was the last message Patterson would preach to that year's meeting of his Holiness-Pentecostal denomination, his emaciated frame—the visible result of a years-long battle with metastatic prostate cancer—lent the scene an even greater sense of finality. In the face of these terminal possibilities, Bishop Patterson preached about an eternal song. As he told the story of an ancient battle's surprising outcome, Patterson reminded his congregants of the unlikely battle plan given to Jehoshaphat, the king of ancient Judah:

> You would think that if the army came in, you would hide the choir behind the army so that the army could protect the choir. But God did that thing the other way: he said, "appoint some singers, to go before the army."
>
> In other words, the army is not gon' protect the choir, but the choir is gon' protect the army.

Example 1. Eternal song in F major, FedEx Forum, Memphis, Tennessee, November 12, 2006.

Put the army in the back, put the choir in the front. "Well, Lord, what are they gon' sing?" God said, "All they gotta do is sing these two verses." "But, Lord, we haven't had time to rehearse." "But all you gotta do is go out there and say, 'Praise the Lord for his mercy endureth forever.'"

While this part of Patterson's sermon occurred well after he undertook the customary movement from speech toward song, the words "praise the Lord for his mercy endureth forever" heralded yet another movement: from tuning *up* to tuning *in*. Patterson's arrival at this well-known phrase—one that appears more than two dozen times in the Old Testament/Hebrew Bible—prompted him to sing a melody of his own making, a musical fragment that is depicted in Musical Example 1.

This homiletic fragment stands apart from its musical surroundings; temporarily forsaking the recitational character of his sermonic conclusion, Bishop Patterson's falling melody spans a full octave. Through its musical markedness, this brief sermonic moment offered Patterson's audience a gripping invitation into a biblical event, fomenting a transcendent journey that embodies the song's striking assertion that the Lord's mercy endures forever. But the path between Memphis's FedEx Forum and the distant scene in which these words are said to have been sung is not the only traffic that was enacted by this music. Patterson's homiletic articulation of the phrase in question is itself a testament to musical endurance. One week earlier—on Sunday, November 5, 2006—he preached a different sermon from the same text in the pulpit of his own Temple of Deliverance Church of God in Christ in Memphis, Tennessee. Near the end of that day's message, "Focusing Our Eyes upon the Lord," Bishop Patterson made his way to the same moment of unexpected singing, rendering the same melody—this time in E major, that sermon's tonal environment (Musical Example 2).

Example 2. Eternal song in E major, Temple of Deliverance Church, Memphis, Tennessee, November 5, 2006.

Throughout the last decade of Patterson's life, virtually every time he mentioned this scripture during the course of a message, this brief bit of music came into focus, suggesting that each time Bishop Patterson thought about this recorded event, this musical refrain was an essential part of what he heard. As he used this eternal song to draw his various audiences deeper into this ancient scene, he summoned a phonographic conception of scripture, implying that the act of singing could produce a palpable sonic intimacy with what had actually happened on Jehoshaphat's ancient battlefield. Yet if he is not suggesting that this melody was literally sung on Jehoshaphat's battlefield, what, exactly, is being argued? How is this argument strengthened by this melody's recurrence? And what, exactly, is accomplished through these acts of repetition?

Clearly this brief bit of music was central to Bishop Patterson's interpretation of this text. Even if it was not actually sung in the scene detailed in 2 Chronicles 20, it might have been. Thus Patterson's melody lends a contemporary immediacy to that remote occasion, performing a musical exegesis and producing a sonorous intimacy that exhorts multiple audiences to attune their ears to the interworldly reverberation of divine mercy. The persistence of this musical fragment across years of Patterson's ministry is but one thread of a much more expansive story. Patterson's rendering of this eternal song, repeatedly offered during his life, continues to echo through his musical afterlife.

While each of the aforementioned messages can still be found on YouTube, the digital circulation of "Focusing Our Eyes upon the Lord" is especially demonstrative of Bishop Patterson's posthumous resonance: three videos, of vastly differing lengths, were uploaded over a period of five years, more than a decade after Patterson's death. On June 11, 2015, nearly a decade after the sermon's proclamation, one YouTube user uploaded a forty-three-minute video titled "GEP Focusing Our Eyes upon the Lord" onto this online repository.[1] On July 1, 2016, a YouTube account called Official Bishop G E Patterson Channel, managed by Patterson's Bountiful Blessings Ministry, uploaded a two-minute version titled "Bishop G. E. Patterson—Focusing Your Eyes upon the Lord."[2] And, on April 17, 2020, another YouTube user uploaded a sixty-four-minute video titled "GE Patterson Focusing Your Eyes upon the Lord."[3]

Taken together, these videos' inconsistent dimensions and order of appearance clarify that they represent three unique contributions to the ever-expanding virtual archive of Bishop Patterson's sermons. The earliest of these offers an invaluable window into their digital existence, for amid all that happens in this forty-three minute sermon, Patterson's eternal song stands out here too. Nestled between 31:30 and 33:10, this brief bit of music might have been easy to miss. Yet two YouTube users call attention to its emergence, commenting on this video and repeating its lyrics. While one wrote, "Praise the Lord for this mercy endures forever (three hands)," another put the lyrics in quotes, writing, "'Praise The Lord, His Mercy Endures Forever.'" Who is this viewer quoting? Patterson or the ancient choir of which he preached? This question cannot be satisfied in a single sentence. In many ways this is the question that this entire book sets out to answer, investigating the intercalation of Patterson's voice and the sonic rendering of various scriptural scenes—a process that is mediated by recurring musical devices that shape Patterson's vocality on both sides of the grave.

An Eternal Pitch: Bishop G. E. Patterson, Broadcast Religion, and the Afterlives of Ecstasy listens to the still-resounding voice of this archetypical Black preacher, showing how the intimacy audiences enjoy with Patterson's recorded messages and the proximity his sermons give to scripture's distant events both arise from his ecstatic instrumentality. More than fifteen years after Patterson's death, fragments of his characteristically musical sermons circulate across radio, television, and a host of digital platforms, including YouTube, Facebook, Instagram, and TikTok. Likewise, little bottles of Patterson's anointed oil and pieces of his clothing have been seeped and woven into the fabric of countless believers' devotional lives. As they upload, comment, share, extract, and wear pieces of Patterson's archive, a host of believers and social media users becomes a new kind of religious broadcaster. Like radio relays, these articulations of digital participation strengthen and redirect Patterson's homiletic signals, extending the reach of his voice and of the divine mercy about which he preached. In this way religion is broadcast as Bishop Patterson's message travels from telephone to radio, from television to smartphones, enlisting a convergent set of new and old media to enact enduring Christian beliefs about the eternal power of the "word of God."

Not quite a biography of Patterson, not quite a history of Black Pentecostal music-making, *An Eternal Pitch* might be described as a musicological media archaeology that listens to the links between Patterson's mediated afterlife and the forms of religious mediation he practiced throughout his life. This book theorizes Patterson's Black Pentecostalism. In so doing, the project turns the very notion of religious broadcasting on its head. *An Eternal Pitch* defines and explores Patterson's Broadcast Religion, an assemblage of belief, technology, and musicality that carried Patterson to a pinnacle of religious influence while building a media infrastructure that could transmit the message long after the messenger went to sleep. Patterson's life-long preoccupation with various technologies for the reproduction and transmission of sound is inextricable from his distinctive approach to musical preaching. Patterson's technophilic Pentecostalism—one that understands machines like microphones, radios, televisions, cameras, oil, and cloth as channels through which spiritual power can flow—has its basis in the Pentecostal conviction that the human voice should become a channel of unmediated divine speech: glossolalia. As a framework for the patterning of sound, music lends Black Pentecostal instrumentality a set of sound techniques, assembling a network of sound technologies that materialize Black Pentecostal understandings of spiritual power.

As Patterson's voice reverberates within a dialectic of mediation and immediacy—calling attention to faith's technological extensions while asserting the efficacy of its interworldly transcendence—Patterson's Broadcast Religion incarnates Afterliveness.[4] Distinct from notions of "liveness" and "virtual liveness," Afterliveness names the immediacy Patterson's sermons gives to various biblical events, the appeal of his broadcasts during his period of physical animation, and the posthumous power that social media users locate in his recorded messages.[5] Transcending any single sermon's enactment, Afterliveness depends on embodied sound reproduction, effected by Patterson through both the practice of recording and ecstatic acts of musical repetition, a set of recurring musical procedures whose reverberations endow the Bishop's ministry with an eternal pitch.

Through mediation of Patterson's homiletic voices, each message becomes an audible format, enabling numerous scenes from scripture to achieve a contemporary intensity. As these sermonic broadcasts ascend to a pitch that is as climactic as it is familiar, they clarify the inseparability of Patterson's phonographic conception of scripture from his technophilic Black Pentecostalism. Despite growing scholarly attention to encounters between Black sound and sound technologies, Black Pentecostalism remains untouched, even as its defining instrumentality makes it a prime site for such investigation. Combining resources from music studies, religious studies, Black studies, homiletics, and media studies, the project uses Patterson's resonance to intervene in discourses concerning digital culture, lived religion, sound technologies, and voice studies, all the while clarifying the contribution music analysis can make to each of these scholarly conversations.[6] My account also contributes to work on the interrelation of race and technology, a conjunction with deep ties to Black music, both in scholarship and in practice.[7]

This book's concern with the sonic and social links between Patterson's life and musical afterlife necessitates an antiphonal method that listens in two directions simultaneously: always forward and always backward. In the forthcoming chapters, I show that the ways Patterson's voice is deployed after his death clarify much about what he was up to during his life. In this way the posthumous circulation of Patterson's recorded materials—in hard copy and online—affirms literary critic John Guillory's claim that a medium's "full significance is always difficult to see in advance of remediation."[8] During Patterson's life and after his death, these devotional objects—whether recordings, oil, or cloth—have been argued to convey spiritual power across vast distances of space and time. In order to listen to Patterson's message as it acts on both sides of the grave, this book pays particular attention to those moments of performance when an unfolding sermon broke free from boundaries of space and time.

These ecstatic gestures brokered a meaningful homiletic connection between time and time past, between the congregants in twenty-first-century Memphis and the servants of God on Jehoshaphat's battlefield, suggesting the eternal nature of sound. They also provide the sonic links between Patterson's life and afterlife. In these instants Patterson's sonic existence opens out into a form of what writer and interdisciplinary scholar Shana Redmond calls "antiphonal life," which occurs when "the repetition of a call is met by a response in and beyond the time of physical animation."[9] Over the course of Patterson's career, and with increasing intensity in the last decade of his life, as he articulated the pervasive practice of musical Black preaching, his ecstatic project became bound up with three recurring musical devices: the eternal song, the eternal riff, and the eternal pitch. As he pulls these emblems of musical endurance down from eternity into time, Patterson's unfolding sermons draw their audiences into an immersive experience that they believe to be evidence of an eternal presence.

BISHOP GILBERT E. PATTERSON

An Eternal Pitch necessitates that I outline first the crucial features of Bishop Patterson's biography, focusing on his path to ecclesial power and the primary place of religious broadcasting in this trajectory. Gilbert Earl Patterson was born in Humboldt, Tennessee, on September 22, 1939. One of five children of Bishop William Archie Patterson Sr. and Mary Louise Patterson, Gilbert Earl was born into a Church of God in Christ (COGIC) parsonage. He would not stray far from this equally real and metaphorical location. Bishop W. A. Patterson's brother, Bishop J. O. Patterson, married the daughter of COGIC founder Bishop Charles Mason, a union that facilitated substantial contact between the young Gilbert Patterson and the founder of his denomination, to whom Patterson occasionally referred as "Dad Mason."

Pastored by his father, in 1951, Gilbert was "saved" at the age of eleven; in 1956 he received the "baptism of the holy ghost" at age sixteen; and in 1957 he began preaching at age seventeen in Detroit at the New Jerusalem Church of God in Christ. On Tuesday, January 22, 1957, Patterson preached his first sermon, "We Wait for Light, but We Walk in Darkness," taken from Isaiah 59:9. A year later, in 1958, Patterson was ordained by

Bishop John S. Bailey, the same year in which his father was consecrated a Bishop in the Church of God in Christ. In the August 1959 issue of the COGIC's official organ, *The Whole Truth,* Sister Ruth Prince described Patterson's early ministry: "Elder Gilbert Patterson, the son of our pastor, illuminated our souls, lifted bowed down heads and caused the Saints to think deeper and looked up higher when he preached to us on the second Sunday. His subject was: 'Who Hath Bewitched You?'—Gal. 3:1, 1 Samuel 28 and the Lord poured out His spirit upon him. We can truly say that he is following in his father's footsteps."[10]

Elder Patterson must also have been following in the footsteps of his mother, Mary, the long-serving Sunday school superintendent for New Jerusalem COGIC and a former schoolteacher who trained at Tennessee A & I State College (now Tennessee State University). While Bishop W. A. Patterson served as pastor in Detroit, he also maintained oversight of Holy Temple Church of God in Christ in Memphis. After graduating from Detroit's Central High School and studying at the Detroit Bible Institute, the younger Patterson returned to Memphis in December 1961 to attend Lemoyne Owen College and to serve as his father's co-pastor at Holy Temple. He served there from 1961 to 1975, developing a reputation for his ability to attract large crowds—both in person and on the radio. In 1975, after a years-long church and familial dispute between his father Bishop W. A. Patterson and his uncle Bishop J. O. Patterson—Presiding Bishop of the COGIC at the time—Elder G. E. Patterson resigned from Holy Temple, disaffiliating from the COGIC to launch an independent ministry centralized in the church he would pastor until the day of his death: Temple of Deliverance, the Cathedral of Bountiful Blessings. After a thirteen-year hiatus, then Apostle Patterson officially returned to the church in 1988 as a Jurisdictional Bishop, beginning a rapid ascent to the church's highest office: Presiding Bishop.[11]

The theological emphases of COGIC form the backdrop for Patterson's Broadcast Religion; aspects of its history explain these emphases and their impact upon Patterson within his denomination and beyond it. The Church of God in Christ grew from the fertile soils of the African American Holiness movement that swept across the Arkansas Mississippi Delta in the 1890s. Reacting against what they saw as the contaminating influence of fraternal orders and other symbols of material culture, Baptist preachers Charles Price Jones and Charles Harrison Mason founded the Church of God in Christ in 1896 in Jackson, Mississippi. As historian John Giggie contends, although this phenomenon was consonant with the religious reforms of the Wesleyan Holiness movement, the reformation that gave rise to the Church of God in Christ was rooted in Black Baptist traditions. The centerpiece of their theology was the idea that "Christians . . . could suddenly be sanctified and forever washed of sin."[12]

This experience garnered for believers "the promise of salvation" and frequently consisted of "one or more powers that directly recalled the spiritual gifts that Jesus' apostles had received during the Pentecost, such as the ability to heal bodily ills, cast out evil spirits, testify, or prophesy."[13] Although Mason and Jones parted in 1907 over the issue of speaking in tongues—with Mason leading the Church of God in Christ while Jones left to found the Church of God (Holiness)—both leaders retained "sanctification" as the center of their theology. The leaders of the denominational churches did not preclude the possibility of the experience of sanctification, but "most Baptist and Methodist clerics typically insisted that individuals under[go] sanctification only after enduring long periods of prayer, scriptural study, and self-abnegation; that few Christians ever obtained it; and that even when they did, it brought no guarantee of salvation or supernatural power."[14] COGIC's belief that congregants can and should attain routine and transformative access to another world's power motivates the ecstatic character of worship services—the intensive form of songs, sermons, prayers, testimonies, and dance, through which the Holy Spirit's presence produces sonic evidence.

At the time of his death, G. E. Patterson might have been synonymous with the Church of God in Christ. Yet his circuitous route to this position of prominence might never have happened, due to the aforementioned combination of denominational and familial strife.[15] In 1975 his uncle J. O. Patterson Sr., then Presiding Bishop, sought to consolidate power as COGIC's first elected Presiding Bishop. J. O. Patterson Sr. thus resisted the desire of his brother, and G. E. Patterson's father, Bishop W. A. Patterson, to return and serve as the Bishop for the First Tennessee Jurisdiction of COGIC.[16] Referencing the example of Catholic polity, J. O. Patterson Sr. argued that "the Presiding Bishop of the Church of God in Christ should be the Bishop of Memphis just as the Pope is Bishop of Rome."[17]

G. E. Patterson, in conflict, joined the concurrent effort to elevate his father to this jurisdictional position, embroiling himself in this conflict. J. O. Patterson Sr., then Presiding Bishop, supported by the church's General Board, took steps to remove G. E. Patterson and his father from Memphis's Holy Temple Church of God in Christ. Before the removal could be formalized, however, G. E. Patterson resigned from the church and the denomination into which he had been born.

More than a decade later, various COGIC leaders, including Patterson's uncle, sought to bring G. E. Patterson back into the COGIC communion, installing him as the Jurisdictional Bishop for the region of western Tennessee that had been the site of so much discord. After becoming a COGIC Bishop in 1988, Patterson's rising popularity as a preacher and religious broadcaster (a topic more fully discussed in Chapter 1) enabled him to win a seat in 1992 on the denomination's twelve-member General Board. But it was another much-maligned exercise of episcopal power that helped to elevate Patterson to the office of Presiding Bishop. In fact, COGIC's 1996 Presiding Bishop election proved to be highly contentious: it came down to a contest between Patterson and the incumbent, Bishop Chandler Owens, who rose to this position after the deaths of Bishop J. O. Patterson Sr. and Bishop L. H. Ford. In "Divine Worship," a sermon delivered in early 1997, Patterson discussed the campaign's lingering controversy: "And the thing about it, I didn't lose the election. You know. Officially, it said [by] one vote I was edged out, but then there were the forty-some votes that were kicked out of the computer [*sic*] that when they counted those it said I won it. But the fact still remains. I said: I love the church too much. I don't want to divide the body. I don't even want a recount. Let the thing go!"[18]

The election's extremely tight result virtually guaranteed a second contest in the 2000 election. By then, incumbent Presiding Bishop Chandler David Owens had been embroiled in more intradenominational disagreements. As Bishop J. O. Patterson Sr. had done in the 1970s, Bishop Owens referenced the Catholic Church as a reason for his decision to remove Orlando, Florida-based Pastor Derrick Hutchins from his church. While appearing in court as a defendant in Hutchins's lawsuit, Owens stated: "I have the authority to make all of the decisions within the church without any disruption or confirmation. I have a board—a general board—that approves my decisions, but they're still my decisions. Same as the Catholic Church—same identical deal. The pope has the right to send a priest to a Catholic church, and has the right to remove him. I have the same authority."[19] While Hutchins claimed that he was removed from the church because of his support for one of Owens's opponents in the upcoming Presiding Bishop election, Owens argued that he removed Hutchins because he had not kept his promise to leave the pastorate of another church. Although Owens won the trial, his victory unwittingly paved the way for Patterson's triumph in the 2000 Presiding Bishop election.[20]

The fact that Patterson was both the first person in COGIC's history to unseat an incumbent Presiding Bishop and the first COGIC minister with a national television broadcast is far from a coincidence. The denominational path Patterson traveled—his thirteen-year denomination hiatus from 1975 through 1988; his return as a COGIC Jurisdictional Bishop in 1988; his election to the church's twelve-member General Board in 1992; his narrow loss in the 1996 Presiding Bishop election; and two overwhelming victories for the church's highest post in 2000 and 2004—would all have been inconceivable were it not for the remarkable expansion of Patterson's media ministry in the last two decades of the twentieth century. These developments comprised a move to local television in the late 1970s, the launch of radio station WBBP AM 1480 in 1991, and the foundation of Podium Records, his record label, in 1998. These striking, national achievements rested on a decades-long preoccupation with religious broadcasting. From dial-a-prayer technology in the 1960s to streaming internet radio at the turn of the twenty-first century, Patterson was ever ready to enlist new instruments in the service of old-time religion.

In the aforementioned 1997 sermon "Divine Worship," G. E. Patterson made a rare, self-conscious remark about the pervasive presence television afforded him. Responding to those who sought to interpret his itinerant schedule as a reaction against the 1996 COGIC election results, Patterson declared: "Baby, I'm on worldwide television. If I want to get a message out, I can say it."[21] Even if Patterson did not use his television presence to sow doubts about the previous election's outcome, surely his international reputation garnered by his ability to "get a message out" gave him an indispensable electoral advantage. At the same time, this singular prominence made Patterson's Broadcast Religion an extraordinarily influential force in the COGIC denomination. His national television audience provided a platform that proved more powerful than incumbency and denominational history, affirming religion scholar Jonathan Walton's contention that Black televangelists use the medium to "transmit their messages and garner spiritual authority."[22]

When Patterson arrived on national television in 1990, he did so not as a solitary evangelist but as a member of COGIC's General Board; he was an elected official of the oldest and largest Pentecostal denomination in the United States. This fact separated Patterson from most other TV ministers because televangelism and healing revivalism were both fields dominated by religious figures who were exiled or estranged from denominations— even if some have maintained connections to larger religious groups, who could name the denominational affiliations of Jimmy Swaggart, John Hagee, Joel Osteen, Paula White, TD Jakes, Creflo Dollar, Frederick KC Price, or Juanita Bynum? Even the hugely significant evangelist and institution builder Oral Roberts was an outsider to the Pentecostal Holiness denomination he had once served. While megachurches and media empires typically stood in place of denominational structures for many televangelists, Patterson's national broadcasts brought the infrastructure of denomination—a means of distributing religious authority—into conversation with the kind of visibility only television could give, creating a fusion that is a condition of possibility for the afterlife this book studies. As Patterson's national broadcasts shined a bright light on the aesthetics and creeds of the Church of God in Christ, they also received from denominational affiliation a kind of legitimacy and respectability that evaded many other television evangelists.

BROADCAST RELIGION

In numerous publications from the 1990s and 2000s, Bishop Patterson's Bountiful Blessings, Inc. and various news outlets claimed that "an estimated 15 to 20 million watch his Sunday TV broadcast."[23] More significant than the numbers asserted is the implication that lies behind them. Even though the Church of God in Christ has been the largest Pentecostal denomination since its founding at the turn of the twentieth century, it has never boasted more than six million members. Thus Patterson's widespread popularity attests to the fact that more of his audience comes from outside COGIC than from within the denomination. This supposition accords with the anthropologist Marla Frederick's statement that Patterson "gained respect and admiration among Charismatic and non-Charismatic evangelical Christians as the head bishop of the Church of God in Christ."[24] What historian Kate Bowler describes as Patterson's "era of media expansion" punctuates COGIC's century-long progression from the margins of Black Protestantism to its center.[25] The historian Calvin White terms this COGIC's "rise to respectability."[26]

Despite this acclaim, no academic (or) popular monograph or article has been focused on Patterson. This is consonant with a general dearth of studies focused on COGIC.[27] Even as Patterson's denominational affiliation demands a deeper attention to COGIC, his ecumenical appeal prompts two other questions: How best to name the interdenominational collective that takes shape around Patterson's messages on a weekly, daily, and posthumous basis? In what context are these virtual congregants participating? *An Eternal Pitch* answers these questions with the term Broadcast Religion. First, Broadcast Religion names the network of convictions, technology, and aesthetic practices that link Bishop Patterson with audiences during his life and since his death. While COGIC is an important institutional force within Broadcast Religion, so are television networks like Trinity Broadcasting Network (TBN) and Black Entertainment Television (BET), as well as social networking platforms like YouTube and Facebook. All of these systems rely on the belief that something beneficial can take place during a sermon and be subsequently or simultaneously experienced by all those who come into contact with its transmission or reproduction. This belief drives viewership and animates donations, much as it shapes the structure of Patterson's sermons. Second, Broadcast Religion connects Patterson's distinctive practice of religious mediation to Broadcast Religions across the world—from Appalachian Charismatics to Mauritian Muslims. As historian Jill Lepore writes: "However singular a person's life may be, the value of examining it lies not in its uniqueness, but in its exemplariness, in how that individual's life serves as an allegory for broader issues affecting the culture as a whole."[28]

The mechanics that underlie the pervasive interpenetration of belief and technology, confession and infrastructure in a host of religious traditions come into particularly clear relief through close attention to Patterson's Broadcast Religion. This Broadcast Religion emerges from the theories and theologies at work in Patterson's Black Pentecostal practices; these in turn can contribute a sharpened focus on sound in media and religious studies. My focus on Patterson's Broadcast Religion allows me to model a methodology for understanding how the details of a message's sonic organization reflect, reinforce, or resist the operations of various sound technologies.

In order to elucidate the diverse array of devotional materialities that are assembled in Broadcast Religion, this book draws together an eclectic set of disciplines and discourses. This study draws extensively from historical, theoretical, and theological treatments of African American religion, especially its Pentecostal varieties. The work of such scholars as Anthea Butler, John Giggie, Cheryl Sanders, Estrelda Alexander, and Amos Yong have been of particular benefit.[29] The historical, philosophical, and anthropological treatments of Pentecostal reformations beyond the Black Church—by such researchers as Grant Wacker, James K. A. Smith, David Edwin Harrell Jr., and Nicholas Harkness—have also contributed to this investigation.[30] *An Eternal Pitch* is indebted to scholars of religious broadcasting—American and African American—including Marla Frederick, Tona Hangen, Quentin Schultze, and Jonathan Walton.[31]

Given the sermon's place at the heart of this investigation, the homiletical insights of scholars David Buttrick, Henry Mitchell, and William Turner have been vital, as has scholarship on the sociality and materiality of the singing voice, especially the essays collected in co-editors Martha Feldman and Judith Zeitlin's volume *The Voice as Something More*.[32] This book takes its example from theories of materiality (from Anderson Blanton, Birgit Meyer, Patrick Eisenlohr, Charles Hirschkind, and Matthew Engelke) in relation to a diverse group of religious traditions, including Southern Appalachian Charismatics, Zimbabwean Pentecostals, and Mauritian and Egyptian Muslims.[33] And the work of media studies scholars (especially John Durham Peters and Jonathan Sterne) and scholars of religious media (including Gavin Feller and Pamela Klassen) helps me to historicize many of the social and technical resources that are deployed in Patterson's Broadcast Religion.[34]

RELIGIOUS BROADCASTING

The conceptual and material bases of Patterson's Broadcast Religion are nestled within the broader fields of American and African American religious broadcasting. From Great Awakening–era tracts to viral videos disseminated across contemporary social media platforms, the zealous embrace of communications technologies has been one of the most consistent features of American Christianity. Tucked into this seeming stability are innumerable tales of contingency and flux, including the emergence, evolution, and endurance of religious radio. Since Pittsburgh radio station KDKA first broadcasted the radio choir of that city's Calvary Episcopal Church on January 2, 1921, an ever-expanding set of electronic media has extended the reach of American religious communications.[35]

As the first platform for "electronic church," radio necessarily became the site of significant conflict between denominations of American Christianities, all of which were vying for access to this new realm of technological possibility. The 1920s and 1930s were shaped by high-stakes contests about the place of fundamentalist theology in the public square, especially as evidenced by the 1925 Scopes Trial. During religious radio's first two decades, airtime was not available for purchase. Instead, it was donated to representatives of three of the United States' religious groups: Catholic, Jewish, and Protestant. Within the Protestant category, liberal mainline denominations were treated preferentially due to the influence of the Federal Council of Churches of Christ in America (FCC) on the National Broadcasting Company (NBC) advisory board. Fundamentalist ministers and organizations—many of whom would begin to identify as "evangelical" in the 1940s—were forced to purchase time on smaller networks and local stations. Out of this predicament there emerged an infrastructure of celebrity ministers, funding networks, and technoliturgical templates, which would lead to the eventual dominance of these brands of Christianity on air and in society.

The fact that religious radio in general and Fundamentalist Protestant voices in particular thrived during the early decades of radio broadcasting is remarkable because of the adverse regulatory conditions of the moment. Historian Tona J. Hangen helpfully details the complicating factors, which include "the consolidation of nationwide radio networks; changes in the regulatory structure of broadcast signal allocation; the lean years of the thirties, when donations thinned; and the 'golden age' of American broadcasting, when many radio programs were thinly disguised commercials for cosmetics or automobiles."[36]

The survival of this religious economy depended on the affordances of the medium and the agency of its audiences, both of which were marshalled to great effect. The zeal with which broadcast audiences assembled around the voices of Paul Rader, Charles Fuller, and Aimee McPherson, among many others, highlights the resonances between radio's mechanics and other revivalist convictions about the efficacy of prayer. The rise of fundamentalist radio religion in the early and mid-twentieth century was motivated by the belief that this medium could provide palpable access to divine presence, which was precipitated by a host of spiritualist fascinations with wireless telegraphy.[37] Although a growing literature illumines the role radio and television played in twentieth-century debates about fundamentalism—fomenting a host of social phenomena, including the rise of the Religious Right—relatively little attention has been given to the crucial contributions of a host of African American religious practitioners to this technosocial field.

Although Black Americans' access to radio broadcasting was limited by the forms of white supremacy that reigned between World Wars I and II, a number of notable African American radio ministers still found a way to get their message out over the air. Bishop Samuel M. Crouch, one of the most important ministers in COGIC's "pioneer" generation (its first group of denominational leaders), was also a pioneer in radio broadcasting. He first went on the air in Fort Worth, Texas, in 1924.[38] In the 1930s radio broadcasting figured centrally in the ministries of popular religious figures in Chicago, including Spiritualist leader Rev. Clarence Cobbs and Pentecostal legend Elder Lucy Smith.[39] Elder Lightfoot Solomon Michaux, a Black native of Newport News, Virginia, and one of the foremost exponents of radio religion, began broadcasting on station WJSV in Washington, DC, in 1929.[40] Founder of The Church of God, Michaux, who was referred to as the "Happy Am I Minister," rose to prominence through sustained programming on the Columbia Broadcasting Company (CBS), a network that purportedly reached ten million listeners with an audience that stretched from coast to coast over fifty-two distinct stations and traveled into international airspace through short-wave transmission.[41]

Throughout the 1930s Michaux's radio programming was often in competition with Mother Rose Artimus Horn's "Radio Church of God of the Air."[42] A Georgia-born Pentecostal healing evangelist, referred to as the "Pray for Me Priestess," Horn was the founder and pastor of Mount Calvary Assembly Hall of the Pentecostal Faith Church, located at 400 Lenox Avenue in Harlem, a church that drew thousands, including a teenage James Baldwin, every Sunday. Broadcast along the East Coast from New York station WHN, Horn's radio religion invited her far-flung audiences to experience the ecstatic unfolding of her church's meetings from the comfort of their own homes.

While Michaux and Horn's contributions formed an essential part of the theological, cultural, and technological reservoir that fed Patterson's Broadcast Religion, his relationship to the radio ministry of Rev. Clarence LaVaughn (C. L.) Franklin was shaped by personal interaction.[43] The father of Aretha Franklin, C. L. Franklin was a pioneering Black radio minister in Memphis beginning in World War II, when he served as pastor of New Salem Missionary Baptist Church. While the 1942 premiere of Franklin's *The Shadow of the Cross* radio program did not make him the first Black radio minister in Memphis, historian Nick Salvatore suggests that Franklin "may have been the first pastor to broadcast directly from his church."[44] After a brief stint at Friendship Baptist Church in Buffalo, New York, where Franklin broadcast the weekly *Voice of Friendship* radio program, he settled in Detroit, where he served as pastor of New Bethel Baptist Church. Although it took years for Franklin to secure a Detroit-area radio slot, his persistence eventually bore transformative fruit. At 10 p.m. every Sunday evening, thousands would tune into Franklin's radio service on popular radio station WJLB. He was also an especially successful exponent of "phonograph religion," religious studies scholar Lerone Martin's term for the production, marketing, and consumption of recorded sermons that played a key role in the rise of so-called race records, the music industry's response to the Great Migration–era emergence of a Black mass market.[45]

One of the most celebrated members of phonograph preaching's second generation, Franklin intervened in a field that had been shaped by the contributions of Calvin Dixon, Leora Ross, J. M. Gates, and COGIC Bishop F. W. McGee, among many others, who, in Martin's words, "created the first and enduring model of popular black religious broadcasting."[46] Both the rise of Black religious radio and the recorded sermon are windows into the systems and strategies by which Black Americans incorporated new technological possibilities into their everyday practice of faith. The rise of mass-mediated religion contains many important parallels to the ways social media users would use these platforms to live religion online more than a century later.

Televangelists—Black and white, Pentecostal and Evangelical—presented Patterson with models to emulate and archetypes to avoid. In 1971, Frederick J. Eikerenkoetter II (Rev. Ike) became the first Black minister to broadcast on national TV. While he had grown up in and presided over Baptist and Pentecostal churches in South Carolina, by the time Rev. Ike came to fame, he was an exponent of a new philosophy, the Science of Living, a kind of "self-image psychology" that located divine power in the human mind.[47] Even as he was widely criticized for his curious philosophy and flashy displays of material prosperity, Eikerenkoetter sat atop a media empire of unprecedented size and scope. While he was a guest minister for the dedication of Temple of Deliverance's new sanctuary in 1978, Patterson would, in later years, take great pains to critique Eikerenkoetter's notion of "positive self-image."[48]

If Rev. Ike's controversial beliefs and ostentatious wealth served as a counterexample to Patterson's "old-time religion," the sophistication of Ike's broadcasting infrastructure set a standard of production that Patterson's Bountiful Blessings, Inc. emulated. In a conversation with me, Bishop Patterson's widow, Louise, recalled an instance when staff at a local television station used one of Rev. Ike's broadcasts to point out flaws in one of Patterson's early VHS recordings. As Patterson recalled, "that was the last time anyone would ever describe anything my husband produced as substandard."[49] But as Patterson replicated Rev. Ike's technological sophistication, he bathed himself in layers of convention. His preference for the dark suit, clergy collar, and robe over Eikerenkoetter's brightly colored and finely tailored suits mirrored his commitment to Black Pentecostal dogma.

Patterson and Eikerenkoetter were both powerfully influenced by the broadcasting practices of Oral Roberts, one of the most prominent religious broadcasters and healing evangelists of the twentieth century. As historian Jonathan Walton writes: "Roberts' ministry served as the prototype not only for Rev. Ike but for a whole expanding class of revivalists in the twentieth century."[50] Although Roberts's ministry built on many of the practices that had coalesced into modern healing revivals in the 1920s, the decade following his birth, no single figure brought these elements into a more influential constellation. Roberts's *Healing Waters* television broadcasts created a template for Pentecostal broadcasting. In contrast to the more mainstream broadcasts of evangelists like Billy Graham, the theological and aesthetic imperatives of healing revivalism required the televisual transmission of revivalistic fervor and its attendant healing efficacy. Finding himself unable to convey revival-tent energy from inside a television studio, Roberts pioneered the practice of recording live from the enormous metal tent that scaffolded his national crusades.

This was no mean feat. First, Roberts needed to acquire recording equipment with costs in the hundreds of thousands of dollars. Second, he had to accustom his live audiences to the presence of bulky, mid-century television cameras, convincing them to behave as if no recording was being produced. Third, he had to modify the ritual elements of the crusades to build segments that could be easily formatted into television slots. Fourth, he had to convince viewers and donors that the spiritual power present in revival tents could indeed travel into their homes. Despite these obstacles, thousands of viewers wrote in over the following decades to testify of the healings they received while watching Roberts's broadcasts. *Healing Waters* succeeded, inaugurating a new template for healing revivalism on TV.

Roberts's significance for Black religious broadcasting was mediated by his relationship with Carlton Pearson, a Black preacher-musician who grew up in the Church of God in Christ, attended Oral Roberts University, and gained access to previously all-white venues as Roberts's protégé: a "son in the ministry."[51] Traveling with and preaching for Oral Roberts helped Pearson to overcome the white supremacist forces that excluded most Black ministers from access to an influential religious network like TBN, the Trinity Broadcasting Network. As one of the first Black hosts for the station, Pearson was well-served by the Pentecostal code-switching he had honed as a member of Oral Roberts's traveling ministry team. Knowing when and how to access Pentecostal fervor and Black vocality in spaces that were unaccustomed to Black voices put Pearson in a position to advocate for other Black ministers, even as his affiliation with TBN raised certain suspicions about him.[52]

As late as 1996, despite his growing renown, Bishop Patterson did not have a broadcast on TBN, which was the most prominent network of its kind. This changed soon after Patterson preached one of his staple sermons ("And David Recovered All") at Carlton Pearson's Azusa conference on April 14, 1997. By February 1998, when Patterson served as a featured speaker in TBN's Henderson, Tennessee, studio, his *Bountiful Blessings* broadcasts had begun airing on the network at 12:30 p.m. on Sunday afternoons. The template of the broadcasts that made Patterson a household name was shaped by the intersection of healing televangelism and Black Pentecostalism's musical aesthetics. In the early years of his local television broadcasts, then Apostle G. E. Patterson anticipated the complexities of transmitting spiritual power over the airways.

As Chapter 1 details, soon after installing cameras in the sanctuary of the Temple of Deliverance, Patterson exhorted his congregants to not be distracted by this new technology; he urged them to view it as a means through which to effectively convey the presence of God. Patterson's argument, which lies at center of his technophilic Pentecostalism, testifies to Roberts's influence on his ministry, a mutual appreciation that led to Patterson being invited to preach for Oral Roberts conferences and receiving an honorary doctorate from Oral Roberts University. Even more influential than Roberts's televisual model is a set of Black Pentecostal convictions and practices that concern the instrumentality of the human voice.

ECSTASY AND BLACK PENTECOSTAL INSTRUMENTALITY

Patterson's Broadcast Religion is a distinctive articulation of Black Pentecostalism as it has been practiced since the turn of the twentieth century. Patterson's Broadcast Religion clarifies that more than a creed, holiness code, or group of denominations, Black Pentecostalism is a set of sonic techniques, strategies that use sound to manage the relationship between the spiritual realm and the material world. Positioned at the intersection of Black musicality and Pentecostal speech, Black Pentecostalism responds to the expectation that the human voice can (or should) become an instrument of relatively unmediated divine speech, whose presence is announced through the phenomenon of glossolalia, or speaking in tongues. Religious studies scholar Ashon Crawley clears important ground for this argument in what he terms Blackpentecostal aesthetic practices, including tarrying, whooping, shouting, and tongues.[53]

A study of Patterson's Broadcast Religion has implications that extend past the analysis of Patterson alone: it demonstrates how music offers an invaluable sonic infrastructure for the working out of Black Pentecostalism's theory of religious mediation; even more than ecstatic speech, whether glossolalic or otherwise, music offers a framework for the patterning of sound, especially through reiteration and intensification. The unusual systematicity of the musical techniques through which Bishop Patterson has facilitated (and continues to facilitate) religious experience reveals how the voice anchors a network of devotional materialities in Black Pentecostal instrumentality. Here, too, Crawley is helpful: "to desire to be made instrument, to desire use for meditative, sacred practice as a means of connecting with others," he argues, "illustrates will and volition that emerges from a different epistemology, a Blackpentecostal epistemology."[54] By this, Crawley alludes to the otherworldly knowledges that stream into and are produced within Blackpentecostal vocality and instrumentality, whether of the voice or of the person.

Bishop Patterson's Broadcast Religion is one such epistemology that envisages with particular clarity the potential for sacred instrumentality in a host of devices—from the human voice to the microphone to the iPhone. The religious imagination manifested by Patterson's sonic techniques also fuels his preoccupation with various sound technologies, tools that enable sound reproduction and transmission, incarnating modes of technological possibility that productively reflect and reinforce Black Pentecostal understandings of spiritual power. Patterson's virtuosic practice of Black Pentecostal instrumentality comes into particularly clear relief in a sermon he delivered during Temple of Deliverance's last meeting in their original edifice. During that moment of achievement and transition, Patterson spoke about two days of even greater significance [▶ **Video Example INT2a**].

It was Pentecost Sunday 1999, the annual celebration of the biblical event that is used as the basis for "speaking in tongues," so Patterson preached from Acts 2:1–4, which reads: "And when the day of Pentecost was fully come, they were all with one accord in one place. And suddenly there came a sound from heaven as of a rushing mighty wind, and it filled all the house where they were sitting. And there appeared unto them cloven tongues like as of fire, and it sat upon each of them. And they were all filled with the Holy Ghost, and began to speak with other tongues, as the Spirit gave them utterance." After reading this scripture, Patterson gave no title to the message, instead telling congregants: "It's Pentecost Sunday, so we understand what this day is about." Pentecost Sunday offered Patterson the opportunity to repeat one of his ministry's essential claims: "You need the Holy Ghost." Before arriving at this emphatic contention, Patterson spoke without notes, virtuosically reciting lengthy passages of scripture from the Gospel of Mark and three chapters of 1 Corinthians, outlining a trichotomy of Pentecostal speech: other tongues, unknown tongues, and heavenly tongues.

Many of the points Patterson advances in this sermon and throughout his life are present in a compressed form in the interpolations within the scripture (set in bold in the following excerpt) that acted as the base of his sermon. He repeatedly interrupts himself as he reads his chosen pericope's final verse, as though he were speaking with two voices:

> **And they were all filled . . .** [I wanna say that again: And they were all filled. It wasn't 120 up there in the upper room and 5 of 'em got the Holy Ghost, but they were all filled] **. . . with the Holy Ghost, and began to speak with other tongues . . .** [How many of 'em start speaking? They were all filled and all of 'em began to speak with other tongues, not as their tutors taught them, not as one began to imitate another, but] **. . . as the Spirit gave them utterance.** [All of 'em received the Holy Ghost. All of 'em had the same sign. They began to speak with other tongues, that simply meant they began to speak other languages other than the language of their native tongue.]

The philosophical freight of Patterson's statements is helpfully illuminated by the anthropologist Nicholas Harkness's work on glossolalia in South Korean Protestantism. Harkness views ecstatic speech as both a ubiquitous social fact and a practice that highlights the problems of language.[55] Patterson's interpolations here show that the phenomenon of glossolalia in Black Pentecostalism is also "a widespread but profoundly ambivalent practice."⁵⁶ After describing various genres of ecstatic speech, Patterson makes clear that he is not principally concerned with fine linguistic distinctions—between xenolalia and glossolalia, between "missionary tongues" and heavenly tongues. What most matters is the fact of interworldly conversation itself. "If you have the Holy Ghost," Patterson asserted, "you ought to be speaking something." The difference Patterson draws out between authentic glossolalia—that which the Spirit gives utterance—and others based in pedagogy or imitation affirms Harkness's claims that "glossolalia depends on the nonreplicability of its uttered texts," such that "glossolalic quotation is normally avoided."⁵⁷ In Patterson's reading, his interruptions emphasize the expectation that all those who are filled with the Holy Spirit will engage in this ecstatic speech. His voice is braided together with the voice of Luke, the writer of Acts, producing a heteroglossic commentary on the practice of glossolalia.

Patterson's heteroglossia articulates the doctrine of "initial evidence," whose importance prompts Patterson to recall the moment when he first spoke in tongues [▶ **Video Example INT2b**]. Given the centrality of speaking in tongues to Broadcast Religion, I quote Patterson's testimony at length:

> I'll never forget it. Whew. Never forget it. One day in May of 1951, I claimed Jesus as savior. I was only eleven years old. I didn't have that drive and that determination and that hunger and thirst to be filled then. My family moved on to Detroit that next year, '52, and all of a sudden, as I was coming up on my sixteenth birthday, I started becoming concerned. And while I was sixteen, but before I was seventeen, I decided, "I'm gonna get the Holy Ghost. Something in my spirit. I feel a call on my life, but I'm not gonna be able to do it without the Holy Ghost." And on Sunday night, September the 16th, 1956 (at that time, my uncle, the late Bishop J. O. Patterson, he was my hero, he was my idol, and I had him to come up to Detroit and bring the Pentecostal ensemble for something that I was having on the fifth Sunday in September. Amen. And that was in 1956.) And I had said to the late Reverend [C. L.] Franklin, "I want you to make uh this announcement for me." Rev. Franklin said, "Oh, I'll be happy to make it." And he went on to tell me how well he knew Bishop J. O. And so it was on Sunday night, the third Sunday, between 10:30 and 11:00 on Sunday night September the 16th, 1956, Reverend Franklin's broadcast was on from 10 to 11, so I started out the door about 10:25 because I wanted to turn on the car radio. (Didn't have a radio in the office. I wanted to make sure he was making the

announcement.) My father had finished preaching and the saints were dancing and praising God. I'd never danced in church but something was burning in my spirit. And I walked down the step to go out the side door to the car, but instead of turning to the left to go out the door, I turned to the right and started dancing and praising God. Got out there around the communion table and after 'while all of my steps were disrupted and all I was doing was jumping up and down and saying yes to the Lord. And, after 'while, I jumped up and it was as though I jumped up and didn't come down: I got enveloped in a cloud. Church jam-packed, but after 'while I couldn't hear nobody. I could hear the echo of my own voice saying yes to the lord. And after 'while that "Yes, Lord" turned to three or four words in another tongue. And as soon as I spoke those words, the devil entered into my cloud: "Now, don't you believe that you got the Holy Ghost. Didn't nothing happen to you! You just got your tongue twisted." And while the devil was saying that, I kept saying, "Yes, Lord." And after 'while the Holy Ghost just began to flow. And it wasn't two or three words, but paragraph after paragraph, just flowing through me. It wasn't coming through my mind, but I could hear it coming out of my mouth. And my teaching told me that when you speak in tongues like that it means you have the Holy Ghost.

Although the event Patterson recalled took place nearly forty-three years before this 1999 sermon, he repeatedly refers to the date in question, marshalling its specificity as proof of that day's singular importance to his life and ministry.

Patterson's testimony yields three observations about Black Pentecostalism's vocal instrumentality. First, language does not function as a system of signs. Rather, as an idea and audible phenomenon, language is itself the sign of spirit baptism.[58] Second, the speech that unfolded that evening was not transmitted through Patterson's mind but out of his mouth. While Patterson had been saying "Yes, Lord" before his registral leap, he could not know the meaning of what he was saying after he began to speak in another tongue. This ambiguity makes it hard to discern the path of ecstatic speech, for as Harkness notes, "in glossolalia, it is not always clear in which direction the communicative channel is flowing: from God to human (as in command or prophecy) or from human to God (as in confession or praise)."[59] The relocation from mind to mouth highlights glossolalia's relative disregard of denotational language, or an utterance's ability to reliably refer to another class of things, to link a usual signifier to something usually signified. Third, Patterson's spirit baptism was a thoroughly choreosonic affair. It was both the first time he danced in church and the first time he spoke in tongues. That the holy dancing carried him into "a cloud" wherein he began to speak in other tongues affirms Crawley's contention that "glossolalia not only enacts a disruption of grammar and lingual form but also enacts spatiotemporal incoherence, produces a 'floating nowhere' for celebratory speaking, for ecstatic praise."[60]

Even if "Yes, Lord" was not what Patterson first spoke in the other tongue, these English words were what brought him to the threshold of another language. But they were not just words. Uttered in the context of post-sermonic praise by a Black Pentecostal preacher and musician, "Yes, Lord" could not avoid musicality. Instead, Patterson intensively exclaimed "Yes, Lord" over and over until repetition produced modulation, converting his English speech into glossolalia. While Patterson's "Holy Ghost baptism" interrupted his desire to tune into Rev. C. L. Franklin's radio broadcast, these recursive musical techniques allowed him to tap into another kind of transmission. While in his testimony Patterson said that there was not a radio in the church office, this event proved that there was another kind of receiver in the sanctuary: the voice of a teenage G. E. Patterson. Patterson's "Holy Ghost baptism" hinged on an enduring formulation of Black sacred speech: the "Yes, Lord" praise. This song (often attributed to COGIC founder Bishop C. H. Mason) is comprised of seven iterations of its title lyric, "Yes, Lord."[61]

Thus the transcript of Patterson's spirit baptism would be indistinguishable from an extended performance of this chant. This song's presence in Patterson's recollection of this life-altering event points to its canonicity and to the choreography it contains. As Crawley writes, the chant's constitutive "repetition elucidates the catechismal nature and meditative quality of Blackpentecostal choreosonic performance."[62] In another worship service Patterson led his congregation in a song that is even more emphatic about the claim that language-changing spiritual power can be accessed through the intensive reiteration of short fragments of sacred speech:

> Just keep on praising God.
> Just keep on praising God.
> If you wanna be filled with the Holy Ghost,
> just keep on praising God.

> Just keep on saying yes.
> Just keep on saying yes.
> If you wanna be filled with the Holy Ghost,
> just keep on praising God.
>
> Keep telling him "thank you, Lord."
> Keep telling him "thank you, Lord."
> If you wanna be filled with the Holy Ghost,
> just keep on praising God.

As it conjoins intensity, iteration, and pithy phrases of praise, this song lays bare Black Pentecostal sound techniques, the musical aesthetics with which believers pursue the defining experience of spirit baptism, gaining the evidence of speaking in tongues.

The musical techniques through which Patterson's voice conveys spiritual power—during his life and after his death—are on display in the moments that frame Patterson's aforementioned testimony. His recollection is paradoxically marked: he deescalates, leaving the chanted discourse of the preceding sermonic section for unmarked speech, even while recalling a moment of high spiritual intensity. But before and after he tells his congregation about what happened on September 16, 1956, Patterson utters a set of musical fragments that stretch across decades of his preaching life, a group of musical phrases that epitomizes Black Pentecostal instrumentality. In the seconds before his testimony, Patterson thunders, "you need the Holy Ghost," oscillating between the tenor G♭ and A♭, G♭4 and A♭4. Just then, he drops an octave to A♭ in a lower register, intoning on an ambiguous word that might be roughly translated as "uh." After lingering on this pitch, Patterson converts this one note into the incipit of a five-note run, an ascending melisma that moves from A♭-C-E♭-F before ending on A♭ in the higher octave. This passage, which transduces one A♭ into another, more potent A♭, unlocks Patterson's memory, leading him directly into the lengthy testimony that is printed earlier. And this is fitting. This five-note ascending gesture is one of the defining features of Patterson's musical toolkit—it shows up in scores of sermons and in every key, across decades of his life. I call it the eternal riff.

Immediately after his testimony, when he returns to chanted song, abandoning the testimony's spoken phonation, Patterson finds his way to a note that is of even greater significance for Broadcast Religion

[▶ **Video Example INT2c**]. Hovering about the tenor A♭ as a reciting tone, Patterson exclaims:

> You need//You need the Holy Ghost!
> It's God's power//coming on earth//to energize the believer.
> You need the Holy Ghost!//He gives you power to step on serpents and scorpions.
> You need the Holy Ghost!//To build you up when you're torn down.
> You need!

Instead of finishing this last phrase, Bishop Patterson pitches it. This final "need" is the only word in this sermonic segment that stretches across more than one note. On "You," Patterson reaches down from the A♭ to E♭, only to leap up to the tenor B-natural, B4, on "need." There, as the final "need" becomes "neeeeeed," Patterson accesses this sermon's highest note, just before falling back down to earth. This arresting gesture is far from a unique moment in his preaching. Across decades of his ministry, in countless sermons, delivered in countless keys, Patterson finds his way to this one note in moments of final emphasis. As such, this climactic pitch links each sermonic moment to countless other homiletic events, connecting this catalog of musical fragments to a force that lies beyond it. This ecstatic sound is Patterson's eternal pitch.

Like the eternal song, the recurring musical rendering of 2 Chronicles 20 with which this introduction began, the eternal riff and the eternal pitch are defining features of Patterson's Broadcast Religion. The recurrence of these musical devices in countless sermonic contexts lends an unusual systematicity to his articulation of what has been called "the musicality of Black preaching."[63] Beneath these three arresting gestures are many more strategies for using musical sound to turn spiritual power into a physical reality, each of which is discussed in this book.[64] Patterson's theory of religious mediation takes musical form from a set of repeated musical devices that show up across decades, linking each sermon to the eternal transmission of spiritual power. Musical gesture instrumentalizes the human voice such that it becomes a channel of divine speech. As these musical devices stand apart from the rest of a message's sonic infrastructure, they embody "various indexes of otherness," thereby accessing a defining and desirable feature of glossolalia.[65] The glossolalic effect of these musical structures is strengthened by the fact that Patterson's eternal riff and eternal pitch are often uttered on words that are difficult to discern. When Patterson's voice conveys words and music that seem to belong to some other place, he offers evidence that the sermon has become a bridge between the material world and the spiritual realm. These ecstatic moments are larger than life.

Patterson's sonic techniques are distilled into enduring musical fragments. These enact a longitudinal kind of repetition—a spatiotemporally transcendent form of antiphony. What relationship emerges at these musical intersections of time and eternity, sermon and scripture, sounding event and technological reproduction? As the conviction that the human voice should become an agent of divine communication is foundational to the efficacy of Broadcast Religion's sound techniques, this belief also feeds a very down-to-earth preoccupation with a variety of sound technologies. As I have argued, Patterson's Broadcast Religion is the sense that spiritual power can travel from the spiritual realm, out of a human voice, through microphones, cameras, and recordings, and into the homes of various believers. Black Pentecostal instrumentality is the musicotechnical practice that flows out of Broadcast Religion. Like the devices that enable various modes of religious broadcasting, the musical recursion at the heart of Patterson's eternal pitch is also technological, for, as media theorist Alexander Weheliye argues: "Any sound re/production is technological, whether it emanates from the horn of a phonograph, a musical score, or a human body."[66]

The overt technicity of Patterson's homiletic musicality makes this claim all the more applicable. Both the musical mechanics that convert the human voice into a holy instrument and the created tools that enable sound reproduction and transmission productively reflect and reinforce Black Pentecostal understandings of spiritual power. As such, Patterson's Black Pentecostal instrumentality—its understanding of the means through which believers can gain access to interworldly power—affirms religious studies scholar Anthony Pinn's claim that religion itself is a technology, "a method of interrogation and exposure."[67] The spiritual power, enduring affect, and improbable immediacy that results from these ecstatic moments is what I call Afterliveness.

ANALYZING AFTERLIVENESS

Beneath a YouTube video of the Pentecost Sunday sermon mentioned earlier, one YouTube user made a striking but pervasive assertion, writing: "His spirit lives on! And his message live on with the same anointing power that they had back then, thank God for video recording."[68] As it gives praise for the modes of technical mediation that enable her ongoing experience of Patterson's "anointing," this user's comment distills the convictions and mechanics that fuel Bishop Patterson's afterlife. Afterliveness—the ongoing efficacy produced by the posthumous circulation of Patterson's recorded messages—is a resonant force that travels freely between the phases of Patterson's existence. Afterliveness is a polysemous social force. As an experience, Afterliveness connotes a peculiar sense of immediacy, both to scenes recorded in scripture and to the moments when Patterson preached about them. As a rhetorical tool, Afterliveness frames tens of thousands of individual assertions about the distinct potency of Patterson's messages—in person and online, unveiling a network of practice and remediation that we have come to know as Broadcast Religion. As a homiletic aim, Afterliveness is expressed in Patterson's customary pre-sermonic prayer, the repeated appeal for power with which "to speak as an oracle of Christ." As a mode of existence, Afterliveness hovers across the entire catalogue of Patterson's sermons, inhabiting an "otherwise temporality" that is manifested by the set of recurring gestures that collectively constitute eternal pitch.

Like numerous theories of "liveness," the notion of Afterliveness grows out of technological possibility.[69] If liveness arises as a vocabulary for describing relationships between events and the mediations that emerge from technical modes of sound reproduction, then Afterliveness is what surfaces when liveness meets Black Pentecostal instrumentality. Black Pentecostalism is a set of sound techniques that respond to the expectation that the human voice should and must become a vehicle of divine speech—a body of sonic tools that manage the relationship between the material world and the spiritual realm. In this way glossolalia is also an argument about technological possibility. As such, Bishop Patterson's eternal pitch is a duet of Black music and sound technology, a suite that is installed in a centuries-long genealogy of self-conscious encounters between Black musicians and sound reproduction.

In its rising concern with the enactment of Black life, even and especially in the face of anti-Blackness, Black Study has much to contribute to this book's investigation of Patterson's afterlife. For one, the notion of *afterlife* that animates this study comes out of literary theorist Saidiya Hartman's conceptualization of the persisting power of slavery in the modern world, which makes its way into music studies through Shana Redmond's trenchant theorization of Paul Robeson's musical afterlife. While the forms of social death this world so ably produces have justly been placed at the center of much Black critical thought, cultural theorist Kevin Quashie's contention that "an aesthetic of aliveness" emanates from a host of Black aesthetic forms helps us get at the phenomenon that provokes this book. Quashie's Black aliveness "is an argument for blackness oriented toward towardness," a case that "can only be made through a discourse of relation and in the terms of material habitat enacted within the poetic."[70]

Following Quashie, I argue that Afterliveness does not to belong to Patterson as an individual; rather, it flows through him as the instrument positioned at the center of a Black Pentecostal assemblage. As literary scholar Maurice Wallace writes of Martin Luther King Jr. in his theory of King's sonic life, Patterson is "not so much a *biographical* figure in this work as *a figure for the aural exorbitance of black cultural history itself*."[71] While memory and honor are actions that might be invoked by those who live religion in relation to Patterson's many digital artifacts, life, as the above YouTube user's comment illustrates, is the category that most interests these social media users. As they affirm sociologist Alondra Nelson's important problematization of the so-called digital divide, which bears an "underlying assumption . . . that people of color, and African Americans in particular, cannot keep pace with our high-tech society," the members of Patterson's virtual congregation offer an online extension to his technophilic Pentecostalism.[72]

This book includes Facebook, Instagram, and TikTok posts, YouTube comments, and (even) obituary (Legacy.com) messages that are shot through with the claim that Patterson's message remains alive more than fifteen years after the messenger passed away. These assertions, like the decision to view traces of Patterson in life or after death, are enunciations of preference, which are central to the intercalation of religion and consumption in contemporary American popular culture, for, as scholar of religion Kathryn Lofton argues: "These small decisions are where we organize ourselves, consciously or unconsciously, as political and economic actors, in alignment with certain demographics and social wholes and implicitly or explicitly in dissent from others."[73] Some evangelists of Afterliveness go so far as to claim that Patterson's sermons are more powerful now than when they were first proclaimed. Whatever kind of life this is, it must be a Black religious social life that is not vulnerable to ordinary death. Nor did this life result from death. Whatever is alive about Patterson's message was never just alive only in the sense of physical animation grounded by logics of spatiotemporal coherence. During those ecstatic moments when Patterson's eternal pitch surfaces, the members of a local or broadcast congregation felt carried into earshot of eternity such that another kind of archetypically Black life broke through: Afterliveness.

If Black Study is to account for this form of life, then much more attention must be paid to the practical and theoretical innovations of Black religious practitioners. This book provokes a conversation between Black studies, religious studies, and music studies. Alongside the recent contributions of Vaughn Booker, Ashon Crawley, and Alisha Jones to the study of Black religious musicalities, *An Eternal Pitch* is especially drawn to the convergence of race and technology, a conjunction that has predominately been worked out through music.[74] The writings of Louis Chude-Sokei, Anthony Reed, Tsitsi Jaji, and Alexander Weheliye are particularly important to this study. While Weheliye theorizes "the singularity of black sounds as they ricochet between 'humans' and modern informational technologies," Chude-Sokei historicizes the coeval construction of race and technology that underpins these "black technopoetics."[75] Moreover, Jaji's "stereomodernism" and Reed's "black media concept" helpfully characterize the combined force of Broadcast Religion's infrastructural, confessional, and aesthetic elements.[76] Yet despite this growing attention to the interaction of Black sound and sound technologies, Black Pentecostal practices remain untouched, even as their defining instrumentality make them a prime site for such investigation.

Both Chude-Sokei and Reed agree that musicological analysis has little to offer studies of Black sound's intercalation with sound technologies. While

Reed claims that musicological analysis "obscures more than it reveals," Chude-Sokei describes cases in which musical materials "function less as music per se and more as signs of technological reproduction in which Blacks function with some degree of primacy."[77] As is evident in this book's title and throughout its pages, this examination is animated by a different persuasion, one that learns from the musicality of Patterson's preaching. Just as Patterson places bluesy Black musicality at the center of his religious broadcasting network, this book finds great benefit in directing close attention to the details of particular homiletic events. To turn away from music toward something that might be called "sound" would be to deny Patterson, the musicians with whom he worked, and the audiences to whom he preached a quality of musicianship—a devotional acoustemology—that was obviously quite important to their own self-understandings. There is a formalism to Black religion: a grammar.[78] And that grammar is musical.

The overt technicity of Patterson's homiletic musicality suggests that close analysis, musical analysis, is best positioned to demonstrate the nature of Patterson's direct participation with sound technologies and to uncover the logics that fuel his digital remediation. Indeed, Patterson's oeuvre is so thoroughly musical that close attention to it provokes a reexamination of fundamental musicological concepts like the system of key. For example, it would be hard indeed to describe the significance of the single pitch (B4) that appears again and again in Patterson's catalog without being able to show how it transcends the gravitational force of the musical key. Patterson's oeuvre and this project exemplify the benefits of one of music studies' venerable traditions: inviting the phenomenon to produce its own analytic. In conjunction with the book's overall aim to understand how Patterson's vocal and technological forms of religious mediation conditioned his message's uncommon endurance, each chapter returns to Patterson's recurring gestures, pursuing an ever-sharpening sense of his art—the sermons convey an eternal transmission through each homiletic event.

BOOK OVERVIEW

Chapter 1 defines Bishop Patterson's Broadcast Religion, the nexus of faith, media, and music that lifted him to the heights of ecclesial power during his lifetime while laying the groundwork for such a pervasive posthumous presence. Both Patterson's persistent preoccupation with various forms of technological mediation and the extraordinary musicality of his sermons are shaped by a technophilic Pentecostalism that views instruments like microphones, radios, televisions, cameras, and the human voice as channels through which spiritual power can flow. As Patterson's voice and media infrastructure produce intimacy with countless scriptural scenes, they enact a "black media concept," Reed's term for the fusion of "aesthetic practice, communication, and its intended publics" central to Black sound's intervention.[79] Through a dialectic of mediation and immediacy, Patterson's Broadcast Religion practices Afterliveness. An argument about the relationship between homiletic events, Afterliveness accounts for the palpable presence Patterson's sermons gives to various biblical events, the reception of Patterson's broadcasts during his period of physical animation, and the posthumous efficacy that many social media users locate in his recorded messages. Transcending any single sermon's moment of proclamation, Afterliveness depends on embodied sound reproduction, effected by Patterson through both the practice of recording and ecstatic acts of musical repetition.

Chapter 2 focuses on Bishop Patterson's voice, the most essential instrument of his Broadcast Religion. This chapter attends to the five enunciative modes that give Patterson's voice interworldly efficacy: modulating voice, choral voice, tired voice, dying voice, and eternal voice. The vocal syntax of Patterson's sermons is formed by a "modulating voice," which appears in the self-conscious movements between speech, chant, and song. These perceptible alterations often broadcast the presence of another biblical character or human author, sounding the sociality referenced by the term "choral voice." The material affordances that enable one instrument to personify so many become both audible and visible on occasions when Patterson is in "tired voice," a condition that discloses the multiple abilities that comprise his vocality, while displaying the cumulative exertion of his homiletic medium. The conjunction of Patterson's media ministry and his years-long physical decline make it possible to attend to the transformations that populated the last years of his life, his "dying voice," revealing much about his unmarked vocal ability. Finally, the chapter attends to "eternal voice," which emerges when the act of repeating asserts the transcendence of the voice over any single event of proclamation. The sonic materials characterized by these five vocal categories work together to produce Afterliveness, organizing the relationship between Patterson's various congregations and a host of scenes from scripture.

Chapter 3 outlines the interworldly design of Patterson's sermons, a formal logic that operates on two hierarchically distinct levels. First, Patterson's sermonic forms yoke the conventional practice of "tuning up" to a distinctive broadcasting practice of "tuning in." Instead of marshalling homiletic musicality as "ecstatic reinforcement" for a given sermon's content, Patterson does not arrive at his sermonic argument until the end of a message, in the ecstatic frame whose heightened musicality confirms the centrality of a given word or phrase to the unfolding message. As such, the crux of Patterson's messages is always delivered in a musical "other space," the apotheosis of a homiletic trajectory that inculcates intimacy with various scriptural locales. What is true on the broadest level of the sermon is true on the most local level as well: Patterson's overarching ecstatic design is driven forward by his penchant for *amplification*.

With this word, I mean to summon both the general rhetorical category and the electrical intensification of sound, both of which are key to Patterson's musicality and media theory. Throughout his catalog, amplification appears as the method by which brief ideas—textual and musical—are spun out into emphatically musical phrases, marshalling repetition and rhetorical devices like anaphora and epistrophe to foment an experience of power. Amid a thoroughly musical unfolding, these points of inflection create a further sense of elevation, permitting an emergent congregation to go from tuning up to tuning in to a higher plane. This sermonic modulation enables the message to garner a most prized possession: homiletic fidelity.

Chapter 4 explores the tonal phenomenology of Bishop Patterson's sermons, examining the interrelated and interworldly politics of key and pitch in his messages. These sonic relationships organize Patterson, band, and congregation into an ensemble, choreographing collective transit between the material world and the divine realm whose presence the sermons broadcast. Located at the literal center of this system, keys form an emergent sonic infrastructure that produces an immersive, antiphonal musical environment. While the preacher's reciting tone dictates the emerging tonal center, each key activates specific affordances of his vocal instrument, structuring his improvisational performance. Across decades of Patterson's preaching and in a host of tonal contexts, one note, B4, recurs over and over again. This reverberant pitch functions as a resonant frequency, a definable musical telos that Patterson understands as essential to his capacity to produce immediacy. Given its frequent place as the highest note in, and the very last note of, Patterson's sermons, this single sonority transcends both space and time. As the last note uttered in Patterson's last sermon, it serves as a symbol of—and direct bridge into—his practice of Afterliveness. Serving as an antenna that connects a specific sermon to an eternal transmission, this pitch is a piercing sonorous channel through which Patterson brings his congregations into the presence of God.

Chapter 5 uncovers the links between the musical dimensions of Broadcast Religion and the material regimes that scaffold the experience of Patterson's "anointing" on both sides of the grave. Two phrases elucidate the mechanics of Patterson's religious imagination: "the logic of the prayer cloth" and the idea of Broadcast Ensemble. The logic of the prayer cloth—the production and dissemination of spiritual power through the practice of fragmentation—holds together the diverse media of Bishop Patterson's Broadcast Ensemble, enabling the sermon, the song, and the human voice to stand on similar footing with microphones, cameras, oil, cloth, television, radio, and the internet as potential conduits of divine power. Through a Eucharistic transformation, garments and recordings are converted into highly transmissible fragments, linking up with the audible fragments that fuel Patterson's eternal pitch.

The transcendent function of these tangible and audible devotional materials arises from their minute scale and the resulting sense that they belong to some other moment. Bishop Patterson's Broadcast Ensemble is a Black Pentecostal assemblage whose particularly salient configuration of Pentecostal materiality, sound reproduction, and musical preaching make a distinctive contribution to religious broadcasting in the United States. The unusual systematicity of Patterson's homiletic musicality makes his ministry an ideal representative bridge between the practices of first-century Christians, twentieth-century Healing and Charismatic Revivalists, and twenty-first-century social media users.

Taken together, these chapters demonstrate how concepts and processes—resonance and amplification, frequency and modulation—are equally at home both within the aesthetic and technological realms of Patterson's Broadcast Religion. Through their recurrence, these areas of focus reveal the structural similarities between the musical infrastructures that sustain Patterson's sermons and the broadcasting systems that deliver these messages to their audiences. As a suite of technological assemblages lend Patterson's voice some of the transcendent quality that inheres in divine speech, each of his proclamations becomes an eternal pitch.

1 Broadcast Religion

In the last two years of his life and ministry, Bishop Patterson's record label, Podium Records, released two recording projects: *Bishop G. E. Patterson and Congregation Singing the Old Time Way, Volume 1* (2005) and *Volume 2* (2006). While both of these nostalgic and self-consciously archival recordings showcase Patterson's preoccupation with tradition, an event captured on the 2006 album casts a particularly clarifying light on the centrality of sound reproduction to Patterson's religious imagination [▶ **Video Example BR1**]. Near the end of that live recording, Patterson calls his congregants to the altar, signaling his intention to move into a different phase of this worship service: "I feel the time has come, now, for prayer. Somebody, tonight, needs a touch of God's hand. This recording project, we expect it to go into tens of thousands of homes, behind the prison bars, hospital rooms, and so many different places. And on this particular CD, cassette, DVD, VHS, whatever format our different contributors will desire to receive it in, the Lord spoke to my spirit and said, 'this time make sure that a prayer of deliverance goes everywhere that this project goes.'"

As he invited his congregants to approach the area nearest the pulpit to partake of this communal prayer, Bishop Patterson expressed his conviction that the material traces of that evening's live recording would be disseminated, in many formats, across space and time, spreading a sonic power whose efficacy would extend far beyond the original context of its invocation. While the assembled hundreds approach the altar of Temple of Deliverance's four-thousand-seat sanctuary, Patterson launches into thanksgiving:

> God, I wanna thank ya. I wanna thank ya for the hundreds who are present here in Temple of Deliverance. I wanna thank you for the hundreds of thousands that will receive this project, *Singing the Old Time Way*. But, God, I want you to anoint the songs, but I want you to anoint this prayer. Somebody tonight is behind the prison bars. They are incarcerated in the city, the county, the state, or the federal institution, but I know that you can send your word. You can break the shackles. You can rebuke the hand of the enemy.

In this prayer Patterson implies that while his voice could only reach its distant audiences after being recorded, the divine's sent word could instantly travel to any site of need. Even more, he implies that sound technologies would give to his human utterances some of the transcendent quality that inheres to divine speech. While pleading for a spiritual force to affix itself to every reproduction of that day's recording, Patterson modulates his voice, finding his way to the mode of expression that characterizes the heightened, musical frame of his sermons. At that very moment the team of musicians, who had been playing the hymn "I Surrender All" softly below Patterson's prayer, shift into the rumbling musical accompaniment that is used to sustain a sermon's incantatory conclusion. The concomitance of Patterson's vocal inflection and his discussion of holy power's diffusion in recorded form suggests a fundamental connection between the form of Patterson's ritual utterances and the infrastructures designed to transmit these messages to their intended audiences. What is the nature of this theological, technological, and cultural conjunction?

Patterson's enduring and evolving concern with devices that can be used to capture and disseminate sound cannot be understood apart from his homiletic style. His Afro-modernist Pentecostalism—one that conceives of machines like microphones, radios, televisions, cameras, oil, and cloth as conduits through which divine power can work—has its basis in the Pentecostal doctrine that the human voice should become a channel of divine speech. As a system for the patterning of sound, music offers Black Pentecostal instrumentality a set of sound techniques, organizing an assemblage of sound technologies that enfleshes Black Pentecostal understandings of spiritual power.

Patterson's Broadcast Religion incarnates Afterliveness, grounding his voice within a dialectic of mediation and immediacy—calling attention to faith's technological scaffolding while proclaiming the transcendent efficacy of these regimes.[1] Unlike rhetorics of "liveness" and "virtual liveness," Afterliveness clarifies what Patterson's voice does for his congregants on both sides of the grave: bringing near a host of ancient scenes, palpably reaching audiences that cannot assemble in a single physical space, and effectively refusing the silencing sting of death.[2] Hovering above any single sermon's enactment, waiting to be pulled down, Afterliveness arises from the embodied reproduction of sound, in person or on tape, which Patterson carried out through the practice of recording and interworldly acts of musical repetition.

RELIGIOUS BROADCASTING

From beginning to end, Bishop Patterson's media ministry was motivated by the pursuit of vocal omnipresence. In one of his earliest appearances in his denomination's archives, a greeting published in the souvenir journal for COGIC's 1966 International Youth Congress informs delegates that then Elder Gilbert E. Patterson, "one of Memphis's youngest and most progressive leaders," could be heard each Sunday on WLOK (1340 AM) during two hour-long radio broadcasts.[3] The advertisement continues by noting that Patterson's "familiar voice" could also be heard twenty-four hours a day via his church's dial-a-prayer line. Using the mechanism of an answering machine, believers could call 901-946-9963 at any time of the day, accessing a taped supplication whose interworldly efficacy is indicated by its this-worldly availability. As the dial-a-prayer system makes Patterson's prayer audible well beyond the context of its articulation, two systems of communication are brought into alignment in this early instance of technological mediation. If, as philosopher Avital Ronell argues, "the telephone is a synecdoche for technology," this snapshot from a lifetime of religious broadcasting shines a light on the ever-expanding architecture that conveyed Patterson's songs, sermons, and prayers on the phone, radio, television, and the internet during his life—an architecture that extended to social media platforms like Facebook, Instagram, and TikTok after Patterson's death.[4] This ongoing pursuit of vocal transcendence—a desire to give the message he preached a form whose endurance evidences the permeance and power of the eternal word—lies behind the technosocial assemblage of Broadcast Religion (Figure 1).

During the first decade of Elder G. E. Patterson's pastoral ministry, he began a decades-long practice of religious broadcasting, which religious historian Jonathan Walton defines as "the broad-based use of electronic media as a primary tool of proselytization."[5] Between the aforementioned 1966 publication and the greeting disseminated in the souvenir journal for the Church of God in Christ's 1969 Holy Convocation, Elder Patterson's radio ministry expanded from two one-hour broadcasts each Sunday to six weekly shows, airing on two radio stations (Figure 2).[6] Every Sunday, Patterson appeared on WLOK at 10:30 a.m., 4:00 p.m., and 9:00 p.m. Patterson was on air at KWAM (990 AM) from 4:00 p.m. to 4:30 p.m. every Monday through Friday. As a radio minister, he used his broadcasts to share the gospel and advocate for social justice. In addition to serving as one member of a nine-person strategy committee for the 1968 Sanitation Workers' Strike—the Memphis movement that brought Dr. Martin Luther King Jr. to town twice, the last visit being interrupted by an assassin's bullet—Patterson used his religious radio slot to distribute information and encourage participation in this collective effort.[7]

Religious broadcasting was an even more permeant feature of Patterson's ministry than his formal affiliation with the Church of God in Christ. Following a years-long denominational and familial—struggle between Patterson's father, Bishop W. A. Patterson, and his uncle, Bishop J. O. Patterson, G. E. Patterson resigned from the pastorate of Memphis's Holy Temple Church of God in Christ, left the denomination, and founded an independent ministry he called Bountiful Blessings Deliverance Church, Inc. In the absence of denominational affiliation, Patterson's emerging media infrastructure organized the dissemination of his Holiness-Pentecostal message, much as COGIC's denominational

Figure 1. Greeting published in International Youth Congress of the COGIC, Souvenir Book and Official Program, 1966. Pentecostal and Charismatic Research Archive, University of Southern California Digital Library.

O MAGNIFY THE LORD WITH ME AND LET US EXALT HIS NAME TOGETHER—Psalm 34:3

Greetings from New Jerusalem Church of God in Christ, 7361 Linwood Avenue, Detroit, Michigan. The church where no stranger feels strange and all are welcome.

WORSHIP SCHEDULE

Bible Study each Sunday 10:00 to 11:45 A. M. — Worship 12:00 noon and 8:00 P. M. — each Tuesday and Friday 8:00 P. M. — Prayer services each Monday and Wednesday 12:00 noon and Sunday Morning 9:30 A.M. The Bible is our Text Book and Jesus—the center of attraction.

BISHOP W. A. PATTERSON
Member Board of Directors

ELDER GILBERT E. PATTERSON
Co-Pastor, Holy Temple C.O.G.I.C., 1254 Wilson Street, Memphis, Tennessee — Pastor and Founder Holy Temple C.O.G.I.C., Walker Homes and Humboldt, Tennessee.

RADIO BROADCASTS

Sunday: WLOK (1340) 10:30 A. M.
4:00 P. M.
9:00 P. M.

Monday through Friday: KWAM (990)
4:00 – 4:30 P. M.

ELDER GILBERT E. PATTERSON

Figure 2. Greeting published in Sixty-second Annual Holy Convocation of COGIC, Souvenir Book and Official Program, November 4–14, 1969. Pentecostal and Charismatic Research Archive, University of Southern California Digital Library.

infrastructure would make visible Patterson's rising media celebrity in the 1990s.

During his thirteen-year hiatus from the Church of God in Christ, Patterson made the crucial transition from his solely audible platforms—telephone and radio—to television. While the sermon catalog his ministry released after his death begins on March 6, 1983, that day's message, "A Time To Remember," is labeled "Tape no. 199," inviting readers to wonder how far the archive stretches. When Willie Douglas, Bountiful Blessings's chief media engineer, predicted the perpetuation of Patterson's television broadcasts on the day of Patterson's death, he noted that the ministry's vault contained messages that reached back to the 1970s. And Patterson's TV broadcasts are mentioned in local publications like the *Tri-State Defender* as early as March 1979.[8] Yet, in messages from 1983, Patterson often makes mention of prospective television audiences and of the new devices that would capture worship services for later transmission. Along with an archive that shows that Patterson had a slot on Memphis station WMKW-TV30 as early as Sunday, February 5, 1984, this concurrence suggests that his catalog's start date represents a meaningful nodal point in then Apostle Patterson's broadcasting career.

An ad in a 1980 issue of *TV Guide* illustrates television's emerging place in Patterson's Broadcast Religion, offering a glimpse of the way this religious system grappled with technological change (Figure 3). First, the ad clarifies that Patterson had only recently arrived on television. Second, the image asserts that these telecasts were "spirit-filled," implying that the change in medium did not indicate a diminution of the spiritual power believed to operate in Patterson's long-standing radio ministry. Third, the invitation to mail prayer requests to Patterson after viewing the broadcast shows how this new arm of Bountiful Blessings's media ecology was woven into the rest of the fabric that, in Chapter 5, I term Patterson's Broadcast Ensemble.

In 1988, when Patterson returned to the Church of God in Christ as a Jurisdictional Bishop, his broadcast schedule included appearances Monday through Saturday on local station WPTY TV24, alongside five weekday slots on radio stations WLOK (1340 AM) and KWAM (990 AM). By 1989, Patterson had returned to WMKW TV30, broadcasting at 9:00 a.m. every Sunday through Friday, while appearing on radio station WDIA on Sunday at 10:00 a.m. and WLOK at 12:15 p.m. from Monday

Figure 3. TV Guide advertisement demonstrating Bishop Patterson's appearance on WMKW-TV30, 1980.

through Saturday. Finally, in 1989, Patterson's voice could be heard every day of the week on a Memphis-area radio station. That same year, his ministry filed with the Federal Communications Commission (FCC) for the 1480 AM radio band in Memphis, fulfilling a vision that he described "early in his ministry for a 24-hour, authentic gospel-formatted radio station."[9] Finally, WBBP AM 1480 added online streaming to its reach in 1999, setting the stage for the intermedial reverberation that lies at the heart of this book.

The path Patterson traveled—his thirteen-year denomination hiatus from 1975 to 1988; his return as a COGIC Jurisdictional Bishop in 1988; his election to the church's twelve-member General Board in 1992; his narrow loss in the 1996 Presiding Bishop election; and two overwhelming victories for the church's highest post in 2000 and 2004—would all have been inconceivable were it not for the remarkable expansion of Patterson's media ministry in the last two decades of the twentieth century. These developments comprised a move to local television at the end of the 1970s, the launch of radio station WBBP AM 1480 in 1991, and the foundation of his record label in 1998. Yet none of these was a more effective means to "garner spiritual authority" than Patterson's expansion to national and international television in the 1990s.[10]

While other prominent COGIC leaders such as Detroit-based Bishop P. A. Brooks boasted robust local television ministries, reaching hundreds of thousands in their respective metropolitan areas, in 1990, Bishop Patterson became the first minister from COGIC—the largest African American Pentecostal denomination since the early twentieth century—to present a weekly national television broadcast. Patterson continued to be COGIC's lone national televisual representative until 1999, when Bishop Charles Blake's West Angeles Church of God in Christ arrived on national television. Throughout the 1990s, Bishop Patterson's messages were disseminated to far-flung audiences via national networks including Black Entertainment Television (BET) and Trinity Broadcasting Network (TBN) as well as a rotating set of local stations in Chicago and Decatur, Illinois; Los Angeles and San Francisco; New York; Orlando; Philadelphia; and Shawnee, Kansas.[11]

After its founding in 2000, Patterson was a staple on the WORD Network, a cable station devoted to African American religious broadcasting. Thanks to this unprecedented reach, virtually every discussion of Bishop Patterson's life in the immediate aftermath of his 2007 death hailed his media infrastructure, prominently featuring phrases like "media savvy" and "television ministry." Bishop Charles Blake, Patterson's First Assistant Presiding Bishop, lauded Patterson as a "media ministry pioneer," using the language often associated with the denomination's founding generation to highlight Patterson's success at carrying the gospel and the COGIC banner into millions of homes. But aside from lifting Patterson to the heights of ecclesial authority and shining a brighter light on the Church of God in Christ in particular, Patterson's religious imagination provided a commentary on the very relationship between broadcasting and religious experience. His Pentecostalism therefore should be understood as a Broadcast Religion.

BROADCAST RELIGION

At COGIC's Annual Holy Convocation in 1995, instead of a more typical sermonic presentation, Bishop Patterson delivered a lecture titled "Communication and the Media." The mere existence of this lecture indicates that, as much as he was any other thing, Patterson was a media theorist. His lifelong preoccupation with the devices, networks, and practices that could be used to disseminate the gospel shared a formal logic with the messages themselves. Broadcasting was as central to Patterson's ministry as was the divinity of Jesus to his faith. In his last sermon (preached on Monday, December 25, 2006), Patterson used broadcasting and the incarnation to explain each other. Preaching from a chair because of the physical weakness made evident by the thinness of his frame, facing the end of his preaching ministry, Patterson tied together the eternal existence of the word he had long preached and the infrastructure that would transmit his messages long after his death [▶ **Video Example BR2**].

Near the end of "The Gospel According to John," the sermon Patterson delivered that day, he returned to the gospel's opening verses: "John, in writing his gospel, said, 'I want you to know that this is where he came from: the word, and the word was made flesh, came and dwelt among us.' That's the only thing that happened in Bethlehem. Only thing that happened in Bethlehem is that the word (hallelujah) became personified." As Patterson sought to help his congregation grasp what it might mean for the word to be made flesh, he described the sonic materiality of the words he spoke to them. "You know, I'm talking, and words are all out here. You can't see it, but the word is all out here." Not only were they unable to see the words he spoke, words reverberating in the air they shared, but, in Patterson's words, "you don't even know it, but all kind of things are going on here now. All of the stuff you're gonna watch when you get home on ESPN. Yeah, you brothers that love football, you know football game is going on right now. Right now, they're playing football. They're playing basketball all over this place here now, but you can't see it."

Although the congregants cannot see these things, Patterson implies, their invisibility does nothing to reduce their availability—that is, their reality. Crucially, he clarifies what must happen in order for them to see it: "You know what you got to do to see it? You got to get the right kind of receiver and turn it on the right dial. You don't hear me! It's going on, but you gotta have something that is capable of picking it up." Like an antenna, translating a transmission into an audible and visible form, the incarnation of Jesus translated divinity into a discernible form. Although "Jesus, the son of the living God, the word, was always here," the incarnation was an event of mediation: "God said, 'I've gotta fix the word in such way where you can touch it. I've gotta fix the word in such way that you can know it's for real.'" The twin assertions that "the word was always here" and that "you got to get the right kind of receiver and turn it on the right dial" show how the convictions Patterson proclaimed were bound up with the infrastructure through which they traveled. As such, his final sermon offers valuable insight into his Broadcast Religion.

But the media-centricity of this all-important sermon was far from unique in Patterson's catalog. In a 2003 sermon, "The Importance of the Holy Ghost," Patterson used broadcasting to explain the New Testament's assertion that "the Holy Ghost will teach you." In the face of many "passages of scripture [which are] difficult to understand," Patterson told his listeners that "if you allow him, if you have the Holy Ghost, he will teach you." Teaching, Patterson contended, is a process with "two sides":

> I'm standing at the microphone sending out a word, but you've got ears and you are receiving. It's just like the satellite communications. (Some of you see our telecast on BET and TBN and Word Network.) But from the central location, a signal is shot out into space, it bounces off of the satellite, and it comes back down. And somebody has a big receiver dish. And if you don't have the receiver dish, if you are hooked up with the dish by cable, you can still receive what comes off the satellite. But, if you don't have cable and you don't have a dish, it's going out but you can't get it! I'm trying tell you the word is going out, but if you don't have the Holy Ghost you don't have the receiver unit!

That this Pentecostal minister repeatedly turns to televisual broadcasting to explain both the incarnation and the functions of the Holy Spirit shows the intercalation of theology and technology in Patterson's religious imagination. While so much of Patterson's life's work was bound up with finding increasingly powerful ways to transmit religious messages to current and potential believers, he, like the Apostle Paul, could only disseminate what he had received from another source.

In this way, Bishop Patterson's Broadcast Religion exemplifies literary critic Anthony Reed's "black media concept" in its combination of "aesthetic practice, communication, and its intended publics."[12] Patterson's theology, his various convergent congregations, and the incantatory form of his messages are mutually defining and mutually reinforcing elements of a Black Pentecostal ensemble. Thus, attending to any one side of this religious imagination brings the others into clearer relief. Patterson's media theory forcefully comes into view in the comments and sermon he delivered at COGIC's 1998 Presiding Bishop's leadership conference. Before beginning his message, Patterson—then a member of the church's twelve-member general board but not yet Presiding Bishop—described his television ministry as a vehicle for his denomination's message: "I'm looking to see what God is going to do with us once we break into the twenty-first century. Things are happening for us now. I was saying to the Presiding Bishop today that I've carried this ball of being the church's representative on national television, but, on the first Sunday in February, on TBN, Bishop Charles Blake and West Angeles will make their debut. And you'll have two churches on national television."

Patterson continued by looking forward to the denomination having its own broadcast, viewing it as an ideal way to convey the gospel: "We have the opportunity now as never before to win the whole world. There are still areas of this world where the gospel of Jesus Christ has not been preached, but through satellite communications and new satellites . . . we can reach the world for Jesus." Soon, Patterson marked a transition into an even more direct line of conversation. After urging the audience against "misunderstanding" him, he insisted that "in those areas where previously they have only had the European American's voice, the world now wants to hear African Americans." To be sure that these denominational leaders did not miss his racialized assertion, Patterson dramatically uttered "hello."

Patterson's commingling of race, voice, and technology exemplifies his ministry's contribution to what anthropologist Marla Frederick calls "colored television," the way that alongside "the predominantly white male voices of traditional religious broadcasting . . . black Christian faith is made and unmade both in front of and behind the camera."[13] As the first COGIC minister on national television, Patterson sought to convey "oldtime Pentecostal power," contending that its highest expression could be located in his historically Black denomination. But the Blackness of COGIC was not inevitable. Although COGIC was founded and has always been led by Black ministers, its membership had an Azusa-inspired interracial stream for the first seven years of its Pentecostal phase. Between 1907 and 1914, COGIC stood as the first incorporated Pentecostal denomination in North America, until a Jim Crow–era mass exodus of white Pentecostals into denominations including the Assemblies of God. "The saints," as the members of COGIC refer to themselves, were therefore shaped by the intercalation of Black music and Pentecostal conviction. This Pentecostalism is so Black that it affirms literary theorist Ashon Crawley's refusal of lexical separation in his work, his preference for the portmanteau "Blackpentecostalism" as a way of denoting ecstatic form and interworldly function.[14]

A tradition defined by the pursuit and achievement of spiritual power's sonic transmission, Black Pentecostalism is an ideal aesthetic framework for the emergence of Broadcast Religion. Thus, when Patterson celebrates the arrival of Black Pentecostal voice in various televised venues, he vents a concern with what cultural theorist Alexander Weheliye terms "sonic Afro-modernity . . . the singularity of black sounds as they ricochet between 'humans' and modern informational technologies."[15] Pentecostalism's defining understandings of the instrumentality of the human voice make Black Pentecostalism an especially instructive formation from which to investigate this intersection. Throughout *An Eternal Pitch* I show that Bishop Patterson's Broadcast Religion, built around bluesy Black vocality, epitomizes the centrality of Black musical aesthetics to Black Pentecostalism's sonic techniques. As otherworldly force travels into the material world through the medium of scripture, the musical modulation of Patterson's voice conveys a homiletic signal into the arms of his media ecosystem, transmitting spiritual power across space and time.

These musical mechanics of Broadcast Religion are on display in "Hold On! Help Is on the Way," the sermon Bishop Patterson preached after making the aforementioned comments. Drawn from 1 Samuel 11:1–11, this message recounts the improbable victory of an ancient hamlet named Jabesh-Gilead against the military might of Nahash, the king of the Ammonites. Faced with the probability of disgrace and destruction, the Jabesh-Gileadites were given the encouraging news that is paraphrased in the title of Patterson's message. The triumphant course of this narrative's unfolding can be gleaned by comparing the first two utterances of his message's title [▶ **Video Example BR3a**]. First, Patterson reads his focal scripture, 1 Samuel 11:9, before announcing the title of his message in a mode of address that is indistinct from his preliminary remarks. Although the phrase "Hold on! Help is on the way!" is the title Patterson gives to this sermon, these words would not be heard again for nearly twenty minutes. In their place Patterson crafts an expansive narrative, unfolding the stories that lie behind the story he seeks to tell this day.

As Patterson reconstructs the setting of a village besieged by a seemingly invincible enemy, he clarifies the problem to which his sermonic contention is the answer. When, after the intervening minutes, his theme reemerges, it has acquired a new urgency and immediacy [▶ **Video Example BR3b**]. Chanting in D♭, Patterson thunders: "And, over night, he raised an army of three hundred thousand Israeli soldiers and thirty thousand men of Judah. And they sent word to the men of Jabesh Gilead, saying don't worry about your eyes being put out. Hold on! Help is on the way. 330,000 soldiers are on their way to defend your cause. And all I want you to do is just get ready because by tomorrow, by the time the sun gets hot, in other words, by noon tomorrow, you shall have help." An audible and palpable intensity separate these two statements of the sermonic theme. And their distance is the key. Their distance proves that the message's unfolding has brought its hearers into a different relationship with the contents of scripture. Patterson has made the customary homiletic movement from speech toward song, settling on and in D♭, enacting the escalating practice that is referred to by names such as "tuning up." For Patterson, *tuning up* is a musical precursor to *tuning in*: throughout his decades-long ministry, Patterson modulated his voice to produce intimacy between an ancient story and a listening audience, broadcasting its contents to generate immediacy.

Patterson's Broadcast Religion is fueled by sermons in which both the pervasive practice of tuning up and the distinctive, broadcast homiletic of tuning in depend on tuning itself. As Patterson settles on a reciting tone, he directs the band to the tonal environment that will sustain the musical frame of his sermon, creating a heightened, liminal space whose outsideness foments the congregation's intimacy with a biblical scene. The palpable sense of being grounded in the musical system known as key is vital to the experience of being taken *inside* the scripture. When all of the interpersonal and interworldly effects of an emerging tonal center are considered together, these phenomena collectively disclose a "politics of key," which is theorized in Chapter 4. Religious ecstasy is one name for what the musical inflections of Patterson's messages produce, not simply in the sense of getting beyond or outside oneself but in something like literary historian Lindsay V. Reckson's notion of "being beside" that is "necessarily constituted by what lies outside or beside it."[16]

What does it mean to constituted by an outside? What is the exterior that gives form to both Black Pentecostalism and Broadcast Religion? For the audiences whose support sustained Patterson's media empire during his life (and sustain his presence after his death), religious experience is defined by the access it provides to this otherworldly space. Black Pentecostal believers are marked by their preoccupation with what lies beyond the reach of their senses. As Patterson's sermons invoke immediacy—a sense of deep, embodied closeness—with events, individuals, and groups defined in scripture, these messages are taken up by devices that are designed to carry them across boundaries of space and time. As this outside is brought in through the medium of sound,

Patterson's Broadcast Religion reveals its participation in "the Gospel Imagination," the performative and interpretive moves through which gospel congregants use musical sound to convert spiritual power into a physical reality. In Patterson's Broadcast Religion, the Gospel Imagination is tied to a media theory, two reinforcing systems of thought and practice that are inextricable from Patterson's virtuosic bluesy vocality.

The transformation of the phrase "Hold on, help is on the Way" from a line of speech into a chanted refrain evidences the indispensable role voice plays in Broadcast Religion, a transcendent function that is more fully elaborated in Chapter 2. These vocal qualities arise in a 1997 article in the *Memphis Commercial Appeal*, in which journalist David Waters dissected Patterson's voice, describing it as "deep, resonant and flexible," writing: "His voice has many modes, from talk to preach, from whisper to quiver to sing." Crucially, Waters contends that Patterson "doesn't read scripture, he transmits it. He doesn't carry a tune, he transports it."[17] Although it is possible to dismiss Waters's words as a display of journalistic hyperbole, I take them seriously. I want to tarry with the claim that Bishop Patterson's voice itself was a technology of transmission, for to do so would be to contend that Patterson understood his sermons and the media through which they gained wide dissemination to be animated by the same force [▶ **Video Example BR4**]. In an early VHS, Patterson urged his congregants:

> Don't let the video cameras hinder us from worshiping the Lord, for the cameras are here to capture this spirit-filled service as we worship the Lord. That as people across this nation and even around the world will sit in on these services by videotape, that the same presence of God that we feel tonight will beam out of their television screen. Whether it's in penal institutions or in hospital rooms, wherever men and women are seeking an answer to the vexing problems of life, we need to tell them that Jesus is the answer.

Here, then Apostle G. E. Patterson contends that the broadcasting technologies that powered his communication with audiences spread across space and time also communicate power to these far-flung believers. Although it precedes the second live recording of *Singing the Old Time Way* (the scene with which this chapter begins) by more than twenty years, its shared argument about what can be captured and transmitted through broadcasting technologies is quite instructive.

The belief is summarized in one line from the prayer with which this chapter opens: the moment when Bishop Patterson exclaims: "I know that you can send your word." This image of divine power traveling across space is grounded both in the New Testament's gospel of Matthew and in the psalter. In both instances healing is accomplished not through a physical interaction but through the power of the transmitted word. These scriptural traditions ground one of Patterson's best-known phrases, an audacious utterance distilled in his television broadcasts' opening scene: "I command you be healed, be delivered, and be set free." These words clarify the late Bishop's conviction about the power that faithful utterances can unleash. Moreover, the scriptures pertaining to the sending of the divine word help us understand the phrase Patterson often prayed before beginning any one of his sermons.

TO SPEAK AS AN ORACLE OF CHRIST

When Bishop Patterson stood to preach, as his musicians repeated the refrain of the pre-sermon selection, he offered a prayer of consecration, a supplication that frequently contained the following words: "Now, Lord, we ask that you would anoint these lips of clay, allowing us to speak as an oracle of Christ, and not just as a man." Although the request for divine assistance is customary, the content of Patterson's prayer is distinctive. Patterson's prayer begs the question: What if his radio and television broadcasts weren't the only Patterson broadcasts? If Waters is right, if Patterson's voice "transmits scripture," then these weekly and daily instances of one-to-many communication must be broadcasts of broadcasts.[18] Patterson's sermons themselves would then constitute the first step in a broadcasting sequence, marshalling his remarkable vocal instrument as a vehicle of an eternal transmission. Is this what it must mean to speak as an oracle of Christ?

In likening Patterson's voice to a radio transmitter, I too am arguing that the various arms of his media ministry function as radio relays, amplifying and redirecting the homiletic signal. Even if this suggestion seems audacious, it is buttressed by the analogy that the pioneering media theorist Marshall McLuhan draws between the voice and radio: "If the human ear can be compared to a radio receiver that is able to decode electromagnetic waves and recode them as sound, the human voice may be compared to the radio transmitter in being able to translate sound into electromagnetic waves."[19] McLuhan calls attention to the dialogic nature of broadcasting, to the listeners who must actively grapple with these recorded utterances, a responsibility that persists as Patterson moves between media, new and old, for, as media theorist John Durham Peters notes, "the advent of digital media returns us to fundamental and perennial problems of communication and civilization."[20] In Broadcast Religion this intermedial movement, which anthropologist Patrick Eisenlohr glosses as "the paradox of a search for immediacy through ever more complex forms of media technology," finds anchor in the one instrument that transcends the phases of Patterson's ministry: his voice.[21]

Adding another dimension to his vocal instrumentality, Patterson's television broadcasts invite viewers to see and hear him "as an oracle of Christ." Many sermon broadcasts would amplify the resonances between his words and various scriptural sources by emblazoning a text box full of scripture onto the screen at the very moment Patterson recited them, showing that his extemporized utterances were indeed transmissions of the "word of God" [▶ Video Example BR5a]. In a broadcast of a 2000 sermon, "The Hope of Our City," as Patterson tells the story of a recalcitrant prophet named Jonah, the scriptural passage unfolds on screen (Figure 4). This confirms how well Patterson is able to transmit its contents [▶ Video Example BR5b]. A few minutes later, when Patterson describes the role contemporary believers play in bringing hope to their cities, on-screen text amplifies his recitation of 2 Chronicles 7:14: "I heard him when he said, 'If my people who are called by my name, if they will humble themselves and pray, seek my face, *turn* from their wicked ways, I'll forgive the sin and I'll heal the land.'"

Not content to chant the words, Patterson uses his body to make a complete circle, illustrating the key word: "turn." These convergences of sound and image problematize any hard-and-fast distinction between philosopher Walter Ong's famous formulation of "orality and literacy."[22] At the same time, they point to the virtuosic recall and other qualities of mind that fuel Bishop Patterson's ability to speak as an Oracle of Christ, to serve as a vehicle through which venerable text achieves contemporary reality.

Figure 4. Screenshot of Jonah 2:10 from Bishop G. E. Patterson's sermon "The Hope of Our City," New York, Sunday, May 14, 2000.

Although it is not unusual to project a sermonic text during a service of worship or television broadcast, the degree to which these broadcasts used imposed text to confirm Patterson's extemporaneous movement between various scriptures is remarkable. As they visualize Patterson's audible transmission of sacred writ, the broadcasts materialize the divine's answer to the Bishop's prayer, the petition for power through which to speak as an oracle of Christ.

In this way the oracular design of Bishop Patterson's television broadcasts reveals the motivations and relays the structure of his sermons' Broadcast Grammar. But this influence worked in both directions. As we have seen, Patterson often showed a deep awareness of and fascination with the technologies that would convey his messages to their future publics [▶ **Video Example BR6**]. Before beginning a 1983 sermon, "All We Need Is at Home," then Apostle Patterson turned a communal celebration of the purchase of new church property into an opportunity to encourage prospective viewers. First, he asks the choir and ministers to stand up and point to camera number 1, the device installed in the back of the sanctuary, and to repeat an inspirational message:

> I want to encourage that young man and that woman that the Lord has called into his ministry. And the devil is telling you, you're never going to get out of your living room. I want every choir member and every preacher to

stand up and look at that camera in the balcony. And I want you to point your finger into that camera, and I want you to tell the folk that's watching what God has done for us! [What God has done for us!] By faith! [By faith!] He'll do it for you! [He'll do it for you!] Amen somebody!

Second, he asks for "camera number 2 to turn around and face the congregation," who then stood, facing this camera, and echoing a similar inspirational message.

I want . . . I want camera number 2 to turn around to the audience, and I want the audience to stand up, and I want you to tell people that are discouraged and disgusted because it looks like that church isn't moving anywhere. I want you to point in that camera and tell them, it is no secret! [It is no secret!] What God can do! [What God can do!] What he has done for us! [What he has done for us!] If you trust him! [If you trust him!] He'll do it for you! [He'll do it for you!]

The facility with which Patterson choreographs this improvised part of a worship service, breaking a metaphorical "fourth wall," indicates something of his deep facility with devices such as these and with their capacity to turn a sanctuary into a broadcasting studio.

Decades later, on Sunday, August 7, 2005, Patterson had a private conversation with his media engineer in that pulpit's public venue. After explaining to the congregation that the photographers moving around the sanctuary were there in preparation for a piece in *Newsweek* magazine, he noted that "my chief media engineer, Bro. Willie Douglass, is up there having a fit every time they get in the line of the camera."[23] Patterson then muses: "That's why the cameras should be isolated so that you can always have another angle." Crucially, he clarifies, "I'm talking to them, I'm not talking to you all." These remarks reveal the ambidexterity with which Patterson fomented his congregation's communion with the divine while directing his media team's management of the ministry's broadcasting instruments. All this suggests that he understood his evangelical zeal and his technophilia to be mutually sustaining intellectual commitments. His lifelong preoccupation with tools capable of transmitting the gospel, a confessional articulation of what Black Studies scholar Louis Chude-Sokei calls "black technopoetics," relies on his beliefs about what could be transmitted through his broadcasts: not just sound and image but holy power too.[24]

For Bishop Patterson the way broadcast technologies funnel information and affect across space and time bears some deep relationship to the way spiritual power travels from one world to another. In addition to exemplifying McLuhan's famous contention that "the medium is the message," the Patterson phenomenon affirms communications theorist Jonathan Sterne's proposal that sometimes "the medium can be the metaphysics."[25] There is a disciplinary question to be addressed here regarding the best way to characterize this phenomenon: Is it a theology, a philosophy, an aesthetic, or something like the sum of these three? I tend to agree with Crawley's resistance to these categorical distinctions.[26] Patterson's musicality, media celebrity, and Holiness-Pentecostal theology are multiple sides of a single object, such that we might understand them as a "black media concept."

Understood in this light, it becomes clear that Bishop Patterson's technophilic Pentecostalism, his lifelong preoccupation with religious broadcasting, vents a theory of preaching too—a view that the sermon is an opportunity to transmit the word the of God. And his preaching vents a Broadcast Grammar: like frequency and amplitude modulation, preaching's signal is conveyed through musical modulation. These facets of Patterson's ministry disclose a Broadcast Religion, a phrase inspired by religious historian Lerone Martin's notion of phonograph religion.[27] More than denoting the inextricable ties between religious practice and its co-constitutive materialities, Broadcast Religion suggests that there is an uninterrupted epistemology connecting Patterson's preoccupation with religious broadcasting, his fascination with its enabling technologies, his homiletic imagination, and his vocal instrumentality.

A CATHEDRAL FOR BROADCASTING

After spending more than three decades building a media infrastructure that would deliver Patterson's messages to millions of homes each week, Temple of Deliverance Church erected a new sanctuary to meet the needs of his ever-growing congregation.²⁸ While not even the four-thousand-seat sanctuary that was dedicated on May 31, 1999, could contain the audiences who tuned into Patterson's message on radio, television, and the internet, the needs of this virtual congregation were etched into the very architecture of the space: Temple of Deliverance's new worship center was built to be a cathedral for broadcasting—and in many ways a cathedral *to* broadcasting. Mance Aytchan, Bishop Patterson's long-serving minister of music, recalled that during the construction project "Sony [Corporation] moved here for a while because Sony built the studio in the church." Affirming the aforementioned indications of Patterson's technophilia, Aytchan asserted that Patterson "knew every facet of it, he knew how he wanted to sound, he knew how he wanted the cameras to be, he studied that kind of thing." Patterson was ever in search of "a better way to do ministry" [▶ Video Example BR7].

While Patterson foreshadowed the new sanctuary's "theatrical lights package" during a 1998 sermon, "The Departed Glory Shall Return," he did not put that medium to its most memorable homiletic use until Palm Sunday in 2005, delivering a message that raises the following question: If, as Patterson contended, spiritual power can be captured by microphones and beamed out of television sets, might the blood of Jesus be transmitted by light? That day, at the end of a sermon titled "A Vicarious Victory," Patterson proclaimed that Christ's passion is the ultimate vicarious victory. As he sought to "fix the word" for his congregants, Patterson tuned up in A, settling on A3 as a reciting tone, a sonic location from which he began, using one of his recurring set pieces to narrate this most macabre scene:

> They took a crown of thorns, pressed it upon his head, blood began to run from his head.
>
> They, they, they had already whipped his back and bloody streams were running from his back.
>
> They put an ol' rugged cross on his shoulder that pricked his flesh and blood was running from his shoulder.
>
> They got him to calvary, and then they nailed his right hand and nailed his left hand and nailed his feet.
>
> And then they lifted the cross (um-um hallelujah) blood was flowing from everywhere!

But there was as solider that said, "I can't believe he's died this quick. Give me a spear." And he drove the spear through the lower right side, and it went through his abdomen and went up and pierced his sacred heart.

Blood began to flow from his side.

After narrating the gruesome details of the crucifixion, Patterson places himself in conversation with one of the writers of scripture: "I'm asking the prophet Isaiah, 'Why would they do him in such a manner?'" Answering for Isaiah, Patterson continues: "But Isaiah said, 'I want you to know: surely he's born our grief, carried our sorrow. Yet we did esteem him stricken, smitten of God, and afflicted.'"

Leaping for the first time up to A4, the transcendent version of his reciting tone, Patterson exclaims: "But he was wounded for our transgressions." Repeatedly reaching up to this triumphant sonority (arrivals announced by the underlined text), Patterson proclaims a paradoxical connection between the numerous physical violations of Jesus's body and the solution to the common maladies of his parishioners' bodies. In so doing, Patterson makes a convincing case for the somatic relevance of Christ's passion:

> But when they nailed his hand, it was to take care of the healing in your hand and in your arms!
>
> When they nailed his feet, it was to take care of your swollen feet and falling arches. And all of the trouble in your ankles, and anything that happens in your leg!
>
> When they put a crown on his head, it was to take care of your migraine headaches and to take care of anything that happen in the region of your head!
>
> When they speared him in the side, it was to take care of your appendix problem and your stomach problem and anything that would happen in the torso area. And it was to take care of your wounded and your broken heart!

Exhorting his parishioners to imagine a deep, corporeal connection to these ancient events, Bishop Patterson uses the force of his elevated musical speech and the evocative amplification to foment a deep intimacy with this scene that is most fundamental to their faith. For many congregants the return to this illumination of the passion must have also recalled its place in Patterson's most-often preached sermon, "The Dawn of a New Day," the Easter message he preached almost every year.

But on that Sunday, Bishop Patterson had conceived an even more effective way to materialize the moment that lies at the very center of his religion. As he finished the recurring narration, Patterson turns his proclamation to "the blood of Jesus," the macabre motif that serves as a gripping synecdoche for Jesus's physical suffering. Reciting on A4, the transcendent version of that sermon's tonal center, Patterson says: "And I wish//I could take this whole house//and bathe it in the blood of Jesus." As he says these words, Patterson points above him, presumably to the media and production staff, signaling them to switch the light. Suddenly the lights turned, filling the sanctuary with what Mance Aytchan vividly recalled as "a red haze." Bathed in red, Patterson kept on preaching, asking, "is anybody in here who can say I've been redeemed? I've been washed! I've been washed! I've been washed in the blood of the lamb!" The irruptive grammar and escalating arrangement of this phrase, whose third declaration, "I've been washed," reaches above the transcendent tonic to B4—a pitch with singular importance in Patterson's ministry—marks it as the rhetorical climax of the sermon, the place he was always trying to go. Patterson's apparel clarified that this moment was the message's telos. Rather than preaching in a suit, or his Presiding Bishop robe, that day Patterson chose to preach in a crimson cassock overlaid with a white surplice, an outermost garment that turned red when the lights were triggered (Figure 5).

Congregants immersed in the sermon's red glare erupted in an extended period of holy dancing, responding to a moment of arrival, fed by the mutually reinforcing elements of sermonic design, apparel, musicality, and lighting—all designed to mediate "the blood of Jesus," the ultimate mediating force for these Black Pentecostals. As such, the period of holy dancing evoked by this message's ending affirms anthropologists Birgit Meyer and Jeremy Stolow's contention that "light-bearing techniques and technologies for directing, projecting, intensifying, or even extinguishing light have indeed been deployed in the service of various 'spectacular' religious ends, endowing the users of such instruments with the power to attract, to instruct, to excite, to subdue, or even to overpower viewers through the generation and manipulation of colors, projected figures and

Figure 5. Screenshot of Bishop G. E. Patterson, robe bathed in red lights, from his sermon "Vicarious Victory," Memphis, Tennessee, Palm Sunday, March 20, 2005.

forms, and other effects."[29] On that Palm Sunday, through the combined force of the media of sound and light, Patterson gave his congregation a way to experience being "washed in the blood of Jesus."

More than fifteen years after this sermon, the scene rushed into the mind of Mance Aytchan during our interview, a moment that is inscribed in a YouTube video, which has been viewed more than four hundred thousand times. This memorable and viral sermonic scene displays what Meyer and Stolow call a "theological aesthetics of light, in which conceptualizations of the Christian God as the ultimate light merge seamlessly with the use of specific devices that activate and direct beholders' gaze toward the divine."[30] This fusion is key, for when Patterson says he wants to "bathe the whole house in the blood of Jesus," no qualification is given, no minimizing comment about the relationship between the lights and the blood. Speaking in this manner, is he suggesting that the lights do indeed bathe his congregants in the blood of Jesus? Do these lights materialize the blood? If spiritual power can be captured by microphones and beam out of television sets, might blood be transmitted by lighting?

On the basis of this message and the balance of Patterson's catalog, the answer to these questions would seem to be a resounding yes. More than just a sermonic illustration, the incarnational force of these media practices epitomized the conjunction of belief and technological possibility that is Broadcast Religion. For Patterson and his Black Pentecostal parishioners, being washed in the blood is an immediate reality: this is what it means to be redeemed. This is what it means to be a COGIC "saint." Enabling congregants to sense this conviction is among ministry's highest goals. Using lighting to mediate the blood of Jesus enables congregants to feel the salvific immersion around which many of them have constructed their identities. As such, the conclusion of "A Vicarious Victory" offers these time-bound "saints" a fleeting opportunity to experience the eternal through equally striking audible and visible inflections. In point of fact, the power of this moment derives from remediation: the arresting shift in the church's lighting by which the house was bathed in Jesus's blood relays Patterson's movement from speech into that sermon's concluding key, A. As it extends the escalating grammar of Patterson's sermons, light illuminates the immersive contribution sound routinely makes to Broadcast Religion.

PENTECOSTAL PLAYBACK: A PHONOGRAPHIC CONCEPTION OF SCRIPTURE

What if Bishop Patterson's conflation of broadcasting and the incarnation of Jesus Christ in the final segment of his last message revealed the conception of scripture that animated his entire ministerial career? As Patterson describes the divine's desire to "fix the word . . . that was always here" in a form that allows humans to "know [that] it's for real," he points to one of the chief assumptions of Broadcast Religion: a phonographic conception of scripture that imagines sacred writ as an eternal transmission whose contents can be "picked up" by "the right kind of receiver." Sermons, then, are instances of "Pentecostal playback," homiletic events that translate a portion of the eternal word into an audible form. More than an analogy for preaching, Pentecostal playback flows out of Broadcast Religion; it is Patterson's technopoetics, an aesthetic practice grounded in the material realities of his broadcasting infrastructure.

As the medium through which Bishop Patterson immersed his audiences in an innumerable set of scenes from scripture, the sermon forms the crucial first step in the trajectory of each Patterson broadcast. Turning scripture into sound and speech into song, Patterson's serial movement from tuning up to tuning in constitutes a broadcasting format, a self-consciously transcendent "set of decisions that affect the look, feel, experience, and workings of a medium."[31] His homiletic format is exemplified through the striking sonic and irradiating shifts that converted the contents of scripture into "Hold on! Help is on the Way" and "A Vicarious Victory," the two immersive homiletic events discussed earlier in this chapter. "A set of rules according to which a technology can operate," Patterson's sermonic format comprises a Broadcast Grammar (the focus of Chapter 3).[32]

Holding together form and content, meaning and substance, Broadcast Grammar is what Meyer terms a sensational form, a "relatively fixed mode for invoking and organizing access to the transcendental, offering structures of repetition to create and sustain links between believers in the context of particular religious regimes."[33] If Patterson's sermons are understood as a ritual technology and tuning up is grasped as a vocal technique, their intersections with his media system occur within the matrix of "links and relays between twentieth-century black cultural production and sound technologies" that Weheliye terms "sonic Afro-modernity."[34] If we think of Black Pentecostalism as a technophilic enterprise, this conjunction of race, belief, and technology pushes back against derogations of both Blackness and Pentecostalism, buttressing Meyer's claim that "Pentecostals have shown to be very successful in seizing the newly available media technologies and incorporating them into particular sensational forms that bring about immediate encounters with the Holy Spirit."[35]

While the technological mediation of religion is anything but restricted to the Black experience, Black Pentecostal instrumentality makes this context particularly distinctive. Musicality itself proves indispensable in this regard, given its centrality to "black technopoetics," Chude-Sokei's term for "the self-conscious interaction of black thinkers, writers, and sound producers with technology."[36] As seen through engagements with cameras, microphones, lights, and voice, the technopoetics at work in Patterson's Broadcast Religion, which we have come to know as Black Pentecostal instrumentality, understand there to be an uninterrupted link between the sermon's musical remediation of scripture and various technological mediations of Patterson's messages.

Example 3. Eternal song in A♭ major, Temple of Deliverance Church, Memphis, Tennessee, December 15, 2002.

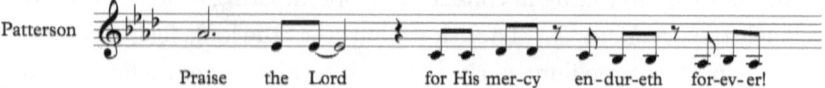

Reflecting and reinforcing the affordances of its allied sound technologies, "Pentecostal playback" is a sonic technique that enacts sermonic sound reproduction. Pentecostal playback, the brand of repetition that is epitomized by Bishop Patterson's trademark musical gestures, is the sonic product of his Black Pentecostal instrumentality. As Patterson does to his voice what his sermons do to scripture, he argues for the sanctified voice's fitness for divine communication. When brief bits of music are pulled from a set of "pre-existent elements" into a message's sonic unfolding, Patterson affirms that a given sermon is "necessarily constituted by what lies outside it," shaped by its desire to conduct an eternal transmission of scripture [▶ Video Example BR8].[37]

This phenomenon is especially evident in a sermon Bishop Patterson preached from Psalm 18 on Sunday: "It's Time for You to Sing Your Song," a message about King David rejoicing over divine protection. As he shifted into the sermon's ecstatic frame, a characteristic sermonic sound reproduction came into view. Turning away from his message's focal text, Patterson tapped into the moment of martial musicking with which this book began. Moving from the psalter to the scene of battle described in 2 Chronicles 20, Patterson returned to his recurring musical exegesis of that biblical event, telling of three nations gathered in enmity against Jehoshaphat's Southern Kingdom, an overwhelming wall of opposition that was to be undone by a wall of sound. Then it was time for Bishop Patterson to sing his song. As he repeated the prophetic instruction to "hide the army behind the choir," he implicitly called his congregation to action just before leading them in singing that scripture's most musical phrase: "Praise the lord for his mercy endureth forever."

Alongside the falling melody depicted in Musical Example 3, much about this phase of the sermon is identical to the analogous section of his 2001 sermon, "Dealing with Life's Battles," and to many other iterations of this set piece. In each of these messages Patterson broadcasts another of the text's key phrases, "it's not your battle," with the aid of a three-note descending passage, which is answered by an octave leap. In many ways this passage—a paraphrase of Jahaziel's prophetic utterance—inverts the melodic shape of Patterson's eternal song. But both of these melodic fragments appear in each sermonic context; they are repeated, they are reiterated, and they are voiced during each homiletic event. When in the context of the media infrastructure he spent his life building, Patterson chooses to repeat himself, he puts an in-progress sermon in conversation with those that precede and follow them, lending an ecstatic existence to these homiletic entities. Like the eternal riff and eternal pitch that will be theorized in the following chapters, the enmeshment of Patterson's eternal song in his broadcasting ecology affirms Weheliye's argument that "any sound re/production is technological, whether it emanates from the horn of a phonograph, a musical score, or a human body."[38]

As these brief musical instants lend phenomenal weight to an eternal transmission, they enact an ongoing affront to the alleged ephemerality of sound, rearticulating the "central, nonsublatable tension at the core of sonic Afro-modernity."[39] The question these events raises is: What kind of relationship emerges between the events in which this eternal song is uttered and what is produced by these instances of Pentecostal playback? While I have argued that the heightened utterance distilled in this musical example steps outside the already musical context of a sermonic conclusion, I now want to emphasize that its potency—that is, its capacity to evoke a sense of relationship to both scripture and the events described therein—depends, in part, on the relationships Patterson calls into being between a single homiletic event, previous and forthcoming proclamations, the biblical text from which it is extracted, and the recordings that enable these improvisational performances to endure. I call this "Afterliveness."

AFTERLIVENESS

Although Bishop Patterson's sermons were robustly antiphonal—linking preacher, band, and congregation in an intensive musical collective—it would be inaccurate to claim that his Broadcast Religion was shaped by a "traditional performance paradigm," using a rhetoric of "liveness" to elevate specific performances over their reproductions.[40] The notion of liveness arose in the 1930s to help audiences and producers distinguish between recorded broadcasts and their less-mediated alternatives, growing into the discourse used to market early television and to strengthen the economic prospects of "live" musicians. With its emphasis on spatial and temporal co-presence, liveness became a way to reckon with performance in an increasingly mediatized society, a cultural ferment whose origins lay in the late-nineteenth-century emergence of sound reproduction technologies.

When read against liveness's concern with spatiotemporal concomitance, Bishop Patterson's repeated assertion that spiritual power, experienced and recorded during a worship event, could "beam out of televisions" and presumably leap out of radios too, shows that the well-established emphasis on in-person sociality in Patterson's Black Pentecostal contexts is exceeded by an even greater preoccupation with accessing an invisible force—the Holy Spirit. Both Patterson's musical life and the particular intensity of his afterlife are animated by cycles of mediation, wherein voice, sermon, and broadcast technologies work together to convey a presence that cannot be seen. Thus Patterson's Broadcast Religion expresses a media concept I refer to as Afterliveness.[41]

As Patterson's messages simultaneously enact mediation and invoke immediacy with a host of scenes from scripture, they initiate a broadcasting trajectory that is shaped by Afterliveness: the pursuit of an audible intimacy with events, places, and persons whose eternal lack of physical presence is overcome by religious mediation. Afterliveness names the phenomenal reality Patterson's eternal song gives to the singing that occurred on Jehoshaphat's ancient battlefield. Afterliveness describes the multisensorial immersion that enabled Patterson's congregants to experience being "bathed in the blood of Jesus." Afterliveness is the palpable proximity a sermon provides to the arrival of divine "help," an improbable synchrony with the characters recorded in a biblical text. Moving past theories of "liveness" and "virtual liveness," Afterliveness is an assertion about the relationship between divergent sonic events.[42] Afterliveness, this multivalent concept, describes the intimate presence Patterson's sermons gave to various biblical scenes during his period of physical animation, whether in-person or when broadcast. Afterliveness also names the ongoing efficacy that viewers continue to locate in Patterson's recorded messages. Transcending any single sermon's enactment, Afterliveness is a Black Pentecostal form of life, which transcends ordinary death and spatiotemporal limits, deploying a distinctive voice's familiar pitch as a hotline to eternity. These enduring realities are defined by their access to an energy that both anticipates and outlasts any single spatiotemporal instant—the persisting power of an eternal transmission.

For Bishop Patterson, Afterliveness is both a pursuit, a practice, and a possession. Building from Saidiya Hartman's theorization of the persisting power of "afterlives of slavery" and Shana Redmond's investigation of Paul Robeson's musical afterlife, Afterliveness uncovers the resonant forces that travel between the phases of Patterson's existence.[43] Redmond's notion of "antiphonal life," which occurs when and where "the repetition of a call is met by his response in and beyond the time of [Robeson's] physical animation," resonates with the rhetoric of posthumous power that pervades social media posts of and about Patterson's message.[44] In an audacious extension of the theme of Patterson's still-airing television broadcasts—"the messenger sleeps; the message lives on"—an unnamed user's March 17, 2017, post on Patterson's Legacy.com obituary reads: "Bishop G. E. Patterson, I still listen to your sermons and they are more powerful than before. Thanks for being a great leader and example of the gospel."[45] This comment shows that although "social networking sites enable expansion—temporally, spatially, and socially—of public mourning," remembrance and mourning are not the principal topics in Patterson's posthumous circulation.[46]

Rather, there is a recurring preoccupation with making the late Bishop's messages the centerpiece of contemporary lived religion, asserting that they still convey spiritual power. On March 23, 2020, one Facebook user shared a viral excerpt of a sermon recorded in April of 1983, "Delivered from Fear." The caption is telling: "BISHOP G. E. PATTERSON SHARES A MESSAGE ON THE CORONAVIRUS PANDEMIC. . . . 35 years before it happened! And, we are now marking 13 years since he passed away. #prophetic #mylatepastor Tape #204—Deliverance from Fear."[47] This user's description details their deep awareness of the Bishop's date of death and his sense that the Bishop's words speak to the present moment

Figure 6. Screenshot from the *Bountiful Blessings* broadcast, July 12, 2020.

with an uncommon, "prophetic," and *eternal* kind of relevance. The user's sense of this viral object's power is grounded in the characteristically musical conclusion of this two-minute sermonic excerpt.

As Patterson commingles concern about volatile stocks and international pathogens with paraphrases of scripture and quotations from two hymns, he initiates a transcendent dialogue that stretches from 1983, back to the time of scripture, and forward to the year 2020. For the tens of thousands of users who shared this video and the hundreds of thousands who viewed it in March 2020, this old clip seemed to provide some eternal assurance in the midst of contemporary uncertainty. As they viewed, reacted to, and shared this digital artifact, these netizens asserted that there is something peculiarly resonant about Bishop Patterson's voice. But the mere availability of this video for viral circulation is a direct consequence of Patterson's Broadcast Religion, an antiphonal call that generates manifold responses, turning numerous social media users into a new kind of religious broadcaster (Figure 6).

The enduring and pervasive presence of Bishop Patterson's message on television, radio, and a host of social media platforms is fueled by an assemblage of technologies, agents, and beliefs that we have come to know as Broadcast Religion. The key to Patterson's rise to ecclesial power and the source of his posthumous resonance, Broadcast Religion gives spiritual significance to his media infrastructure. More potent than other media, Patterson's voice uses its serial inflections to connect his sermons with a host of biblical events and with diverse set of audiences—past, present, and future. As Patterson's Pentecostal playback uses both the practice of recording and ecstatic acts of musical repetition to tap into an eternal transmission, with each homiletic event yielding an experience of Afterliveness, a palpable sense of a sermon's place into a transcendent conversation. As Patterson's articulation of Black Pentecostalism holds together faith, aesthetic practice, and sound reproduction, Broadcast Religion intervenes in the co-constitutive histories of race and technology.

2 Broadcast Medium

"I did not know he was dead." So wrote one Floridian in an October 27, 2020, post on Bishop Patterson's Legacy.com obituary.[1] This arresting confession—made nearly fourteen years after Patterson's 2007 death—invites readers to imagine the familiar scene that precipitated it: a social media user belatedly stumbles across the news of a popular figure's much publicized passing, stunned to find that an individual with so broad a virtual footprint had long since departed this life. At the same time, her sincere shock highlights the even more noteworthy set of conditions that made it possible for her—and any number of others—to overlook the fact of Bishop Patterson's death. After noting that even "in 2020," she still listens to "this awesome man of God," she extends "thanks to the family of Bishop Patterson [for ensuring] that his voice is still here teaching."

Although this description of Patterson's iconic voice as a source of enduring instruction was made possible by the decades-long dissemination of his message on radio, television, and the internet, this persistence was conditioned by certain audible attributes of Patterson's instrument. These commingled communicative media not only played a defining role in Patterson's Broadcast Religion during his period of physical animation, they also enabled a new form of animation in his afterlife. Then and now, these instruments and infrastructures worked together to funnel Patterson's messages across boundaries of space and time, conveying his Pentecostal convictions far beyond the location of his mortal body. The intimacy virtual audiences feel with Patterson's posthumous voice, in other words, is fed by the intense proximity his live sermons cultivate with distant scenes of scripture. Even as these systems translate Patterson's message, they mirror the expressive intentions that animate his sermons. What aspects of Patterson's vocality make physically distant phenomena seem at hand? How does the voice of this "oracle of Christ" fulfill its function as a broadcast medium?

This chapter listens to the knotted textures of Bishop Patterson's voice, the resonant vehicle whose sonic materiality is the most essential element of his Broadcast Religion. Practicing a critical vocal organology, this chapter attends to the five enunciative modes that collectively constitute Patterson's interworldly instrument: modulating voice, choral voice, tired voice, dying voice, and eternal voice. "Modulating voice" appears in the self-conscious movements between speech, chant, and song that form the vocal syntax of Patterson's sermons. Often these moments of re-registration—obvious inflections in the mode of phonation—announce the presence of another biblical character or human author, sounding the sociality referenced by the term "choral voice." The material affordances that enable one instrument to embody so many come into particularly clear relief on occasions when Patterson is in "tired voice," a condition that helps parse the multiple abilities that comprise his vocality, while displaying the cumulative exertion of his homiletic medium.

The conjunction of Patterson's media ministry and his yearslong physical decline make it possible to attend to the transformations that populated the last years of his life, his "dying voice," clarifying much about the abilities of the voice that had not been touched by illness. Finally, the chapter attends to "eternal voice," which resounds in moments of musicking when the act of repeating asserts the transcendence of the voice over any single event of proclamation. The material facts that are illuminated by these five heuristics work together to produce Afterliveness, organizing the relationship between Patterson's various congregations and a host of scenes from scripture, using the musical modulation of the voice to relay an eternal transmission.

MODULATING VOICE

What is in a voice? Or, to put a finer point on it, what is a voice? What arises from the interaction of breath and vocal folds, resonators and articulators? Given the voice's "unique location . . . both inside and outside our bodies," what connects these aspects of physiology with the realms of sociology and theology, the planes where vocal sound works to enflesh religious belief?[2] Between nearly mumbled responses to an interviewer's questions and an eternal pitch exclaimed in homiletic ecstasy, a wide range of phenomena are held together by the instrument known as Bishop Patterson's voice. When one speaks of Patterson's voice, do they refer to the content of his sermons, the sound of their delivery, the techniques of their production, the embodied source of their emission, the scriptural characters reanimated during their unfolding, or the worlds built around these expressions? And which voice? The youthful energy of the 1960s through the 1980s, the gravity and power of the 1990s and early 2000s, or the lighter, sweeter voice that paradoxically characterized Patterson's last and sickest days? Above and beneath this refractory web of sounding phenomena there is a recurring thread through which Patterson becomes the answer to the prayer "to speak as an oracle of Christ": that is, modulation—movement, itself [▶ **Video Example BM1**].

One example of such modulation occurs at the end of a December 2000 sermon titled "Discouraged?," which conveys a message about what believers ought to do in disconcerting times. Just as Patterson finished the characteristically musical phase of his message, he signaled his intent to move further into song. Gesturing as if holding a pen, Patterson observes: "The songwriter asked a question one day: why should I feel discouraged? And why should the shadow come? And why should my heart feel lonely, and long . . ." This ellipse points to the particularity of Patterson's rendering of Charles Gabriel and Civillia Martin's hymn "His Eye Is on the Sparrow." While Patterson typically weaves song lyrics into the ecstatic conclusions of his sermons, using the same pitch material characteristic of his preaching, this time Patterson yields to the song's conventional melody, moving from the quasi-sung sermon's parlando to sustained expression of full-throated song. Delivered in A♭ major, oscillating between speech and song, each fragment of this hymn's well-known opening phrase is punctuated by a kind of pregnant pause, the last of which gives way to this performance's most distinctive feature.

The aforementioned ellipses depict the interruption of the song by an explanatory aside. After singing "and long," Patterson comes out of song, returning to speech in order to muse: "See, the devil will make you wanna leave here. Look at somebody and tell them, 'it ain't time for you to die.'" With these words Patterson disrupts the unfolding of a phrase to clarify its meaning, emphasizing what it might mean to "long for heaven at home." Only after interrupting the line in question does Patterson complete it, repeating the operative word "long" in an intensive nod to the passion it conveys. Patterson's next disturbance of the hymn anticipates the forthcoming words, this time through negation: before singing of Jesus "a constant friend is he," Patterson exclaims that "he's not sometimey." Both disruptions of this hymn's verse draw attention to the manner in which he sings the song—not as a part of his sermon but as a freestanding composition. Attention is drawn to sonic form because Patterson's overarching movement toward song is punctuated by speech, a relatively plain mode of address that would be equally at home in at the beginning of his sermon or during a television interview.

In this case, the spoken style of Patterson's personalizing interruptions reinforces the message of the song, instead of the more typical reverse, in which musicality reinforces the argument of his sermons. His message shows a reversal of what music theorist Steven Rings calls a "contextual asymmetry," a conventional arrangement of speech and song that determines which functions as figure and which as ground. In this message speech "emerges as a marked figure against the unmarked ground of more conventionally coded musical sound."[3] Moreover, all of this takes sound within earshot of the conventional tuning-up conclusion to his sermon "Discouraged?" This message's chanted conclusion adds a third vocal presentation to the scene in question, highlighting the subtle modal shifts through which Patterson enfleshes his religious message.

The agile movement along a speech-song continuum that characterizes the ending and aftermath of "Discouraged?" is the central feature of Bishop Patterson's vocality. As such, this performance is an opportune site from which to more precisely describe what is referenced in appeals to Patterson's voice. My understanding of the resonance that holds together Patterson's innumerable performances is informed by musicologist Brian Kane's model of the voice. Patterson's case is elucidated by Kane's contention that "voice . . . is distinct from three other terms with which it is often identified . . . echos (ἦχος), logos (λόγος), and topos (τόπος)—roughly, sound, meaning, and site."[4] In this sense voice "involves the movement, or displacement" of the three terms—a process reflected in Patterson's shifts between speech, chant, and song in the concluding moments of "Discouraged?" Following Kane, if we understand voice as emerging through the interaction of "its purely sonorous aspect" (echos), "the content of its utterances" (logos), and "the site of its emission"(topos), the three relatively distinct modes of vocal production in the concluding moments of this sermon's message prove essential to the recognition of its preacher's voice.[5] This is to say, descriptions of Patterson's vocality seem to extol this very capacity for movement, this very desire to shift in so little temporal space between distinct modes of expression. It is through this movement that voice calls attention to its presence as the instrument that connects message and messenger.

Modulation is the first and most important of Patterson's vocal strategies. It is named explicitly in journalist David Waters's 1997 *Memphis Commercial Appeal* article, "He's One of the Greatest Preachers in the World." There, Waters observes that each of Patterson's sermons "starts slowly, steadily, like a steam locomotive lumbering out of the station. The tone and pace of his voice are measured so carefully the words seem merely able to crawl out of mouth. Don't be deceived. He's warming up—clearing his windpipe, stretching his vocal cords, preparing his voice box to receive and deliver the plain truth, the raw gospel, the inspired, infallible, indestructible word of God."[6] Waters's locomotive metaphor grasps at the crux of the way Patterson's nimble manipulation of his instrument fuels his congregation's transit between their material confines and the biblical scenes summoned in his messages. This capacity is the reason Waters declares that "Patterson's voice is his signature. It's [a] deep, resonant and flexible voice, capable of expressing a wide range of emotions from solemn to sanctified. His voice has many modes, from talk to preach, from whisper to quiver to sing." It is precisely the voice's "deep, resonant flexibility" that calls attention to its presence, its instrumentality.[7]

More than the familiar trajectory from speech to song, what I call "Modulating Voice" is a kind of technique that, as Kane suggests, creates "gradients and differentials," disturbing "the circulation of phoné by rearranging and redistributing topos, logos, and echos."[8] Creating difference: this is the central effect of vocal modulation, and its efficacy is striking. In the scene from "Discouraged?" the affective interpenetration of speech and song demands notice. That speech becomes the domain of Patterson's personalized discourse is noteworthy because, as ethnomusicologist Aaron Fox argues, singing usually "heightens the aural and visceral presence of the vocalizing body in language, calling attention to the physical medium of the voice, the normally taken-for-granted channel of 'ordinary' speech."[9] That day, speech and song competed for markedness in a space where their admixture would be more common. In this movement between registers the medium reveals itself, calling attention to its conveyance of another energy [▶ **Video Example BM2**].

Bishop Patterson's modulatory technique comes into particularly clear relief near the end of the live recording of the second volume of his congregational music album, *Singing the Old Time Way*, a scene referenced in Chapter 1. Just as he finished singing the unmetered congregation song, "Jesus Breaks Every Fetter," Patterson freed himself from the evening's plan: "While there are really two more songs left on this agenda, tonight, I feel that the time has come, now, for prayer." Inviting his audience to join him at the altar, Patterson expressed his certainty that "somebody, tonight, needs a touch of God's hand." The touch elicited by this prayer, Patterson clarified, would not be limited to that evening's participants. After enumerating the many forms in which that evening's service would be reproduced, and describing the various audiences to which that "project" would travel, Patterson informed the congregation that "the Lord spoke to my spirit and said, 'This time make sure that a prayer of deliverance goes everywhere that this project goes.'"

Although Patterson's preface implied that the recording would transmit a sonorous power to all its far-flung auditors, he would soon use the serial inflections of his voice to press that claim. After signaling his intention to move into this time of prayer, Patterson began to sing the familiar hymn "I Surrender All." While the band sustained a D♭ major sonority, the subdominant of this preceding song's A♭ major tonality, Patterson looked in the direction of these musicians, intoning "all to Jesus," the first three words of the forthcoming hymn. Although he would sing this song in the same key, its initial melodic oscillation between C4 and D♭4 produced a fleeting dissonance with the harmony his musicians had been sustaining, pulling them back to the tonic in a subtle display of vocal power and religious authority—two inextricable forms of symbolic capital. As Patterson sang one verse and one refrain of this canonical selection, hundreds of attendees approached the altar, hoping to be the first recipients of the promised "touch."

Accompanied by a soft, instrumental refrain of "I Surrender All," Patterson launches into an initially spoken prayer, a set of requests that were shrouded in expressions of gratitude. After giving thanks for the audience gathered in the sanctuary, and for "the hundreds of thousands" who would receive copies of that evening's recording project, Patterson prayed that God would anoint the songs and "this prayer." Immediately turning to those who might most need access to the energy captured that evening, he prayed for institutionalized individuals, contending that their location "in the hospital room, or behind the prison bars . . . in the city, the county, the state, or the federal institution," did not place them out of the reach of a God who could touch them just by sending the Word. Just as he describes the transmission of the divine Word, both Patterson and his band made rather noticeable musical shifts. Simultaneously, the Bishop moves from speech into the kind of chanted vocal expression that characterized his sermons and the musicians stop playing "I Surrender All."

Abandoning their measured groove, the band switched to the kind of antiphonal accompaniment that characterizes the concluding moments of Patterson's sermons. As Patterson took vocal residence in A♭, repeatedly rising to A♭4 as a transcendent reciting tone, his prayer shifted from supplication to renunciation. No longer simply speaking to God, Patterson uses this new sonic space to assert spiritual authority over Satan on behalf of his present and future auditors, using a sharpening sense of musical orientation to materialize the power of which he spoke. Just as his prayer ends, he tells the audience that their "total deliverance depends on whether you have followed the instruction" in the gospelized version of the Elisha Hoffman hymn "Is Your All on the Altar?" Still in A♭, Patterson voiced the first line of this hymn: "You have longed for sweet peace and for faith to increase." After a few seconds of singing this song, the band finds Patterson's new tempo and begins to iterate another bluesy rhythmic framework, lending a sense of metrical organization that is analogous to the A♭ tonal environment that has governed this entire segment of the live recording. That Patterson tarried in A♭ while swinging in and out of regular meter, and moving between sung, spoken, and chanted modes of voice, imparts authority to the various shifts of stance and address, yielding a set of compound modulations that draw preacher, band, and congregation into an increasingly immersive experience of another world's presence—a touch of God's hand.

If modulation is Bishop Patterson's project and the crux of his vocal techne, if it is the means through which he ritually secures a spiritual touch, then what exactly is the deep theoretical understanding revealed by this practice? For Patterson and his many audiences these movements reveal the connection between his vocal instrumentality and the media infrastructure that was his life's other preoccupation. As a broadcast medium, the voice's capacity for re-registration and manipulation lends an audible spiritual conductivity to Patterson's sermons, songs, and prayers. I want to emphasize that his celebrated articulation of one of the most pervasive characteristics of ritual speech—interworldly communication—gleans its particularity from the other dimensions of Broadcast Religion. One way to characterize the inextricable ties between voice and Patterson's other technologies would be to claim that their assemblage constitutes something more than metaphor. Such an assertion, however, would drastically understate the role metaphor plays in human sociality. As linguists George Lakoff and Mark Johnson famously argued, "the concepts that govern our thought are not just matters of the intellect. They also govern our everyday functioning down to the most mundane details . . . structuring what we perceive, how we get around in the world, and how we relate to other people."[10]

For Bishop Patterson, broadcasting was a "metaphor to live by." Thus it should come as no surprise that his vocality would be animated by a view that instruments—like the human voice—can link contemporary audiences with eternal transmissions. In *Healing for the Soul*, I show that the practice of "tuning up," the routine shift from speech toward song at the end of the sermon, evidences a dialectical understanding of the relationship between the material and spiritual world; in Patterson's performances, however, this motion is not just a matter of oscillating between speech and song, nor is it simply binary at all.[11] As the preceding performances show, in Patterson's ministry these different registers enjoy a more ductile interrelation. In this way their interpenetration makes for an exceptionally effective mechanism for signaling and producing the kind of interworldly conversation that is the purpose of gospel's sacred rhetoric. It is in the movement between these characteristic modes of expression that Patterson's instrument shines through. Modulation, then, is the primary characteristic of Bishop Patterson's voice.

CHORAL VOICE

What does the modulatory character of Bishop Patterson's voice produce? What—or whom—do these inflections make present? There is an emphatic sociality to Patterson's utterances, a heteroglossic predilection that I term "choral voice." The shifts that prove so essential to his various utterances enable his individual instrument to give vent to a host of speakers, spread widely across both space and time. Chorality connotes the emergent, sonic, and collectivizing qualities of Patterson's homiletic polyphony [▶ **Video Example BM3**].

At the end of his 2001 sermon "There's Power in the Blood," for example, Patterson interrupts a period of ecstatic dance—the collective performance that usually punctuates other ritual actions—with an equally urgent memory:

> I'll never forget when I was just a youngster growing up in the church, I heard my father, the late Bishop W. A. Patterson say, "You know the blood of Jesus is a mystery. Said I don't understand how a brown cow can eat green grass and then you can get from him white milk. That's a mystery. But another mystery is how God could can take my black heart and dip it in his red blood and wash me white as snow." Oh, it's a mystery but I know I've been washed! Can you say "I've been washed?" I've been washed in the Blood of the Lamb.

Preaching in the key of D, buttressed by an antiphonal conversation with his band and congregation, Patterson commingles his instrument with the voice of his deceased father, another prominent COGIC minister, Bishop

W. A. Patterson. Although the elder Patterson is given credit for this agricultural illustration of the mystery of salvation, it is the younger Patterson who can be seen and heard uttering these words in their new context. While Patterson could have used this metaphor without crediting it to his late father, he called his parishioners' attention to the enduring nature of this formulation. That these words punctuated the climactic expression of religious ecstasy suggests that something about this kinetic space made the elder Patterson's voice more accessible, more available for a polyvocal reanimation, a statement whose overt basis in the past imputed authority to its contemporary reincarnation.

More striking than Patterson's conveyance of one of his father's expressions in a single message is the immediacy he consistently sought to give to the voices of speakers and writers recorded in the pages of Christian scripture [▶ **Video Example BM4**]. In the climactic moments of a 1989 sermon "The God of All Supply," Patterson uses the familiar story of Paul and Silas, two imprisoned preachers, singing at midnight to exhort his congregants to think about navigating the dark moments of their lives, an exegesis whose spiritual force is strengthened by this Black congregation's material knowledge of unjust policing practices. As he settles on A3 as a reciting tone, Patterson instructs his congregants to "look over and ask somebody, How do you handle your midnights?" After moving through a series of midnight scenarios as an apophatic litany, a list of ways believers ought not "handle their midnights," Patterson proclaims, "but I hear Paul and Silas in the middle of the night. Paul and Silas said, 'Well, I think the best way to handle my midnight is to have a prayer meeting.'" Translating their ancient carceral scene into contemporary discourse, Patterson reminded his congregation that Paul and Silas "sung their way into an attitude of praise."

This ancient scene of musicking is the space-time Patterson's sermonic conclusion seeks to bring near. His pursuit of an audible intimacy leads him to make an audacious assertion about what these biblical characters sang in their prison, a contention that has much in common with the recurring exegesis of 2 Chronicles 20, which I refer to as Patterson's eternal song. As he renders Acts 16, he interpolates a contemporary song into a scriptural story to connect his congregation to this eternal transmission. When Patterson gets ready to share his hearing of Paul and Silas's carceral prayer meeting, he exclaims "over in the middle of the night" a prepositional precursor to an interrupted sentence, whose disruption is prompted by the affective state of the preacher's body. After uttering this half-sentence, Patterson paradoxically makes an intensifying turn away from the congregation, facing instead the preachers who were seated behind him. Repositioned in this way, Patterson rocked up and down on his feet, shaking his entire body in religious ecstasy. When he turns back to the microphone, facing his congregation, Patterson finishes the incomplete formulation, intoning in the key of A: "I hear Paul say, 'I once was lost in sin, but Jesus took me in, and then a little light from heaven filled my soul. It filled my heart in love and wrote my name above. And just a little talk with Jesus will make it alright.'"

Undulating between A3 and E4, Patterson notes that Paul did not speak alone: after Paul sang the verse, Silas sings the chorus: "Let's have a little talk with Jesus. We can tell him all about our struggle. He'll hear our faintest cry. He'll answer by and by. Feel a little prayer wheel turning. I know fire is burning, Just a little talk with Jesus, oh, he'll make it alright." Although these words are not recorded in the scripture—in fact, the words Patterson puts into Paul's and Silas's mouths were not composed until nearly nineteen centuries after they occurred—this is precisely what Patterson claims to hear. This is "Pentecostal playback"—sermonic sound reproduction of an eternal transmission.

Throughout his decades of preaching, over and over again, Bishop Patterson says "I heard" or "I hear" when reanimating passages of scripture during the heightened musical frames of sermons. These assertions are portals into the experience of Afterliveness. Literary scholar Anthony Reed's thinking is helpful here, when he contends that "sound is always (also) a re-sounding; it resounds in the presence of prior hearing and ways of hearing; it resonates within history's mutable chambers."[12] In Broadcast Religion the voices of Patterson's father, Paul and Silas, Jehoshaphat's hastily assembled choirs, and so many others are "hearded," literary theorist Nathaniel Mackey's term for "*hear*'s past tense's past tense . . . multiply removed from the present, someone else's having heard presumed to be one's own."[13] Patterson's frequent repetition of these phrases, and their location within the ecstatic phase of his messages, suggests that we take them seriously as rhetorical markers, indicators of movement into a recitation or quotation of a scriptural passage, but also as evidence of the kind of relationship Patterson imagines to the texts in question.

What is Bishop Patterson reiterating when he repeatedly claims to *hear* scripture's unfolding? Is this a method, an approach, a technique, or is Patterson expressing a theory of preaching? The way Patterson moves his body and modulates his voice as he testifies of this hearing suggests that he is actually *hearing something*, that his preaching is fed by a phonographic imagination of scripture: suggesting that, as expansive sections of scripture were etched in Patterson's memory, these scenes took on a sonic form, such that when he recalls verses from the Bible, he really does hear a coterie of voices, an aural resonance that I refer to as an "eternal transmission."

Patterson's Black Pentecostal instrumentality hinges on movement between vocal registers, modulations that materialize the presence of multiple speakers. In the 1989 iteration of "The God of All Supply," Patterson's rising vocal trajectory takes an antiphonal form, illustrating the texture of the carceral performance. While the refrain Patterson gives to Silas is transcribed earlier in this chapter, its actual sounding event was much more dialogic (with four bolded interjections): "Let's have a little talk with Jesus. **Oh!** We can tell him all about our struggle. He'll hear our faintest cry. **Oh!** He'll answer by an' by. Feel a little prayer wheel turning. **Oh!** I know fire is burning, Just a little talk with Jesus . . . **Oh!** He'll make it alright." On each of the interjections, Patterson leapt up to A4, an intensified version of his reciting tone, an ecstatic sonority whose intensive quality is clarified by its irruptive location. Patterson's approach here is not like actors fabricating characters "through the adroit manipulation of their voices and their bodies," yet instead his vocal modulation is a technique of presencing.[14]

The piercing, "jagged grain" of this expression is the highest note of Patterson's sermon.[15] This indicates that the congregation has indeed been granted access to this ancient scene, easing the distance between what the jailed disciples might have sung and what Patterson suggests that they did sing, thus permitting congregants to claim to hear these events too. The efficacy of this sermonic conclusion—and many others— relies on the audience's familiarity both with the much-discussed scene recorded in Acts 16 and the gospel hymn Patterson chooses to engraft into that setting. These twin experiential templates activate the audience's collective memory, deepening their connection to the sermon, an intensifying immersion through the medium of Patterson's voice that is evident from the congregation members' escalating embodied engagement in this message's final moments.

Beyond this individual scene, the conjunction of Patterson's homiletic intertextuality and his vocal instrumentality endow his broadcast medium with a distinctive chorality. While his vocality is the central focus of this chapter—and in many ways, this book—a question might be asked about the grammatical number I attribute to Patterson's voice. While he is described as an unusual *individual*, his messages, by contrast, sound rather *plural*. Patterson's preaching is an exercise in "chorality," literary scholar Steven Connor's term for "the sonorous actualizing of the otherwise abstract or merely attributive idea of a collectivity."[16] There is nothing abstract about the sheer power of Patterson's voice, the interworldly aggregation of speakers it pulls together, or the robustly embodied congregations the messages draw into religious ecstasy. Notwithstanding Patterson's undeniable place in a tradition and a genealogy of Black preacher-musicians, the renown he achieved during his life and the peculiar intensity of his mediated afterlife is animated by concerns with his singularity—from YouTube users to Legacy.com commenters to the historian of Pentecostalism Vinson Synan's proposal that Patterson was "one of the greatest preachers in the world."[17]

Yet if Patterson's preaching must be called singular, it can only be a plural singularity—or a singular plurality. Like cultural theorist Fred Moten, I am interested in "a kind of *radicalization of singularity*." While Moten discussed such a radicalization with reference to Bessie Smith, his formulation is equally at home in the present discussion. If, as Moten contends, such figures are "sent to give us some message" regarding singularity itself, we might call Bishop Patterson "an effect of sociality . . . sent by sociality to sociality," evidence of a "deep and fundamental entanglement . . . to and by way of and as a function of this intense, radical, constant differentiation."[18] This movement, this oscillation, this radicalization of singularity names one of the key mechanisms of Patterson's instrumentality. Bishop Patterson was singular because of his plurality—his distinct capacity to draw together a transcendent host of voices and characters. Reminding "the saints" of their most treasured convictions made Patterson's voice an instrument of sociality, in turn transforming him into a conductor of an interworldly chorality, an oracle of Christ.

TIRED VOICE

While Bishop Patterson's appearance at the California Northwest Jurisdiction's Forty-seventh Holy Convocation (2004) began in a customary fashion, with a prayer and a song designed to prepare the assembled congregation to hear "a word from the Lord," there was a crucial sonic difference at work in that scene [▶ **Video Example BM5a**]. As he launched into a verse of "Sweet Jesus," a canonical congregational praise song, it soon became apparent that this well-known preacher sounded a bit unlike himself. While a markedly relaxed mode of delivery might have signaled an intention to conserve energy for the forthcoming message, Patterson's vocal delivery sounded much more effortful than what his audiences had come to expect. The normal hardness that characterized his bluesy vocality had been coupled with an unfamiliar roughness. Bereft of a certain richness of timbre, sounding the lack of certain characteristic partials, the Bishop was clearly not in good voice. Before launching into the sermon titled "The Healing of King Hezekiah," Patterson commented on the curious comportment of his voice:

> You can see my voice is a bit impaired on tonight. We had, um, in Memphis, this week, um, the National Baptist Convention Congress of Education. And we had so many hundreds of delegates that attended our church all day Sunday and Tuesday night. And this is the first time in a long time that I'm here tonight after having preached three times Sunday, Tuesday night, and then last night in Dallas. Uh, what is this, my sixth message for the week? [I] Haven't done that in a while! And, so, if my voice is a bit, uh, husky, then you can understand.

The self-styled "huskiness" of Patterson's voice, its audibility from the very beginning of his set, and his assumption that his audience would attend to these sonic realities all affirm musicologist Martha Feldman's contention that "the vulnerable voice exceeds language and sense to reveal voice in its very voiceness."[19] As it trains focus on the instrument for and by which he was known, Patterson's vocal predicament—evidence of both fatigue and exertion—raises a set of urgent questions. What does it mean to hear fleeting impairment? How does this temporary limitation accent the instrumentality of the voice? Is fatigability essential to human vocality?

Does Patterson's unimpaired voice hover as a kind of contrafact alternative to this sounding event? Or is impairment a surplus added to a typical timbre? What, in other words, does the event of "bad-voicedness" clarify about the form and function of Patterson's broadcast medium?

Though prefaced by the acknowledgment of vocal limitation, "The Healing of King Hezekiah" unfolds according to Patterson's typical sermonic form. The body of the sermon was spent outlining the history of Hezekiah's reign, focusing on the military victory that was undercut by the sudden onset of illness. In this story, recounted in 2 Kings 20 and Isaiah 38, Hezekiah develops a terminal skin condition. When he consults the prophet Isaiah, the prophet tells the king that death is imminent. Then the king "turns his face to the wall," asking to be healed, after which the prophet turns around, returning to tell King Hezekiah that he had been granted fifteen more years to live. In keeping with his homiletic narratology, Patterson finds his way to a reciting tone, G3, just as he begins to preach about Hezekiah's illness. This moment, located roughly twenty minutes into Patterson's sermon, brings his vocal fatigue into clear relief. As he hovers about G3, the normal focus and clarity of his homiletic expression is masked by a noisy exterior. The cracks, gaps, and breaks that attend to his utterances evidence exertion. Patterson's characteristically effortless melismas seem strained and belabored.

Comparing two riffs from this sermon with another message delivered that same summer helps put this strain into relief. Both vocalizations—the bluesy riff that connects his reciting tone, G3, to its transcendent version [▶ **Video Example BM5b**] and the descending run that functions as a reflective intensifier [▶ **Video Example BM5c**]—resist phonation on the evening in question. In contrast, at the end of "The Power of the Word," a message Patterson delivered to another California jurisdiction that summer, these figures are precisely intoned a half-step higher [▶ **Video Examples BM6a and BM6b**]. As he galloped toward the end of "The Healing of King Hezekiah," Patterson did not reach for the high end of his instrument, the A4's and B♭4's that one would expect to hear at the end of a message in this key. The fact that he did not go for these notes reflects his deep knowledge of his broadcast medium, his awareness of his vocal limitation. Yes, a certain effortfulness is the chief sign of vocal impairment. Even so, this very impairment, this very weakness, the "drastic knowledge" laid bare through this event, clarifies what audiences have come to expect of Patterson's voice.[20] Good voice, then, is defined by the possibility of its opposite [▶ **Video Example BM7**].

On another occasion—in an August 2001 sermon, "The Password"—Patterson lamented the limitation of his voice, even though he *seemed* to be in great voice. "I wish I had my voice," he declared near the end of a message he concluded in the key of D♭. Yet after hearing him repeatedly traverse the space between D♭4 to A♭4, one wonders, what more might Patterson have wanted? The only vocal phenomena missing from this sermon's conclusion were the ecstatic shouts normally made from the very top of his range. In D♭, Patterson often found his way to B♭4 or B4 in the very final moments of message, a sonorous summit through which the presence of power from another world would become unmistakable. That the strength or weakness of his body was most evident at the moment of the most intense spiritual ecstasy acts as a statement on materiality and mediation, a comment on the process through which Patterson became an oracle of Christ. These notes vent an interworldly form of what musicologist James Q. Davies calls the voice's "mysterious and magnificent belonging."[21]

These ecstatic notes, often uttered in a movement from ordinary language to something else, are extraordinary demonstrations of an otherworldly power. Given the Pentecostal intention that underlay Patterson's vocality, it is understandable that he might miss this upper extension, understanding their absence as tantamount to not having his voice. Even so, the inability to access this transcendent register, especially in relationship to bodily fatigue, accents the instrumentality of Patterson's voice, for, as musicologist Emily Wilbourne notes, "the disruption of regular vocal production brings the body of the singer into sharp focus."[22] Drawing focus to a body that was so routinely implicated in interworldly performance, this vocal nostalgia foreshadows the posthumous endurance of an instrument that would far outlive the body by which it was contained, giving afterlife to Patterson far past the day of his death.

DYING VOICE

After the event of bad voice (discussed earlier), Patterson would go on to deliver many more sermons and songs in ways that indexed vocal strength and agility. Besides this fleeting moment of vocal impairment, the mid-2000s would mark a period of vocal change, running parallel to Patterson's public struggle with metastatic prostate cancer. His physical decline is evident in his dramatic weight loss, evident even when wearing finely tailored suits and clerical apparel. Alongside the changes in his body size, Patterson's physical performances became less animated. He was more likely to walk across the pulpit than to run across it, more likely to move arms in synchrony with his band's shouting music than to engage his full body in the holy dance. Through it all, Patterson continued to preach, using his changing instrument to deliver an enduring message. How to describe his instrument's transformation? What can we learn from the voice of a dying man?

To answer these questions, we might compare two sermons preached from the same text: "Dealing with Life's Battles" from August of 2001 [▶ Video Example BM8] and "Focusing Our Eyes upon the Lord" from October of 2006 [▶ Video Example BM9]. Besides being based in an ancient scene of battle described in 2 Chronicles 20, both performances share a specific rendering of the musical performance said to have attended that biblical event. At the end of both sermons, Patterson makes mention of one of the most surprising features of this text. The army, Patterson notes, was not to march into battle alone, but they were to be accompanied by a group of musicians. Instead of "hiding the choir behind the army," Jehoshaphat was instructed to "hide the army behind the choir." The choir would represent a kind of vanguard whose expression of praise possessed a spiritual fortitude that would prove more effective than any display of traditional military force. Alongside the instructions to gather musicians and send them into battle, the young prophet Jehaziel instructed the king to have the singers chant eight words: "Praise the lord for his mercy endureth forever."

These words, which can be found in the psalter, are a common part of the ancient Hebrew devotional lexicon. Rather than simply recalling the words recorded in scripture, Patterson recuperates this recitational practice, rendering these words in the form we have come to know as the eternal song. In both sermons Patterson sings this phrase once by himself and then invites the congregants to repeat it at least two times, so that his display of homiletical musicality produces a moment of congregational song.

Example 4. Eternal song in A♭ major, Temple of Deliverance Church, Memphis, Tennessee, August 26, 2001.

As discussed earlier with regard to Patterson's interpolation of the hymn "Just a Little Talk with Jesus" into Paul and Silas's jail cell, I am most interested in the argument being made here and in what music is being used to do here. Although Patterson does not imply that the bit of song described in 2 Chronicles was identical to his own musical setting, his utterance of this material suggests that there is some profitable resemblance, some productive similarity between what he intones and what these ancient musicians sang.

In this repeated refrain, Patterson discloses something fundamental about what he is up to every time he stands to preach: his audacious intimacy with any number of distant events, his refusal of distance, has everything to do with broadcasting. With a melody that spans an octave, Patterson's choral vocality transmits the soundscape of an ancient battle. And when considered alongside his phonographic conception of scripture, it becomes even more apparent that, through the eternal song, the preacher aims to tell his congregants what he hears when he recalls this text. As it mediates between numerous messages from Patterson, the sermonic reproduction of this ecstatic gesture lends Afterliveness to the events recorded in scripture, functioning as a synecdoche for the sacred and the place of the human within it. How does the recurrence of the eternal song over the last five years of Bishop Patterson's preaching contribute to the endurance of his message after his passing? In the 2001 sermon "Dealing with Life's Battles," Patterson both looks and sounds hearty. He closes his sermon in A♭, lighting on A♭4 as a reciting tone. Therefore, when it comes time to play the eternal song, Patterson belts this melody in A♭ (Musical Example 4).

That day, his voice possesses the weight, range, and malleability that had characterized it throughout his life. As he intones the final part of that message, Patterson traveled across the pulpit with speed, strength, and

Example 5. Eternal song in E major, Temple of Deliverance Church, Memphis, Tennessee, November 5, 2006.

flexibility. From the looks of it, Patterson's voice and body were easy collaborators that day. But in the November 2006 sermon "Focusing Your Eyes upon the Lord," much had changed. Patterson has clearly lost a considerable amount of weight. His steps are shorter, his movements more deliberate—his struggle with serious illness is obvious. His voice is also different. The voice feels much lighter and accrues a more songlike quality; as it loses some of its weight and husk, in turn it seems to become more melodic, moving further toward the song axis of the speech-song continuum. Here sounds what philosopher Roland Barthes famously called "the grain of the voice," "the materiality of the body speaking its mother tongue."[23] Yet at the end of this message, which like "Dealing with Life's Battles" is drawn from 2 Chronicles 20, Patterson returns to the eternal song, singing it in E major, the tonal center for that day's sermon (Musical Example 5).

His concluding reanimation of this brief bit of musical material suggests that this refrain is inscribed in his understanding of the scripture. This act of repeating, like the fact of these sermons' videographic reproduction, allows audiences to observe the transformation of Patterson's voice and body during his yearslong decline. Even as these two devices enable such comparison, they convey the presence of his voice far beyond the limits of his physical body. Documented in its multiple performances, Patterson's eternal song calls attention to the fundamental instrumentality of his voice, a paradoxical situation that makes the voice a reflection of the health and strength of his physical body and the source of transcendence over the travail of one's frame.

In search of "dying voice," one might ask, between these two performances, what is consistent? What persists despite such obvious bodily transformation? One of the remarkable characteristics of Patterson's voice is the weight that he carried at the very top of his vocal range, the chestiness with which Patterson belted out tenor A♭, B♭, B-natural, and C's. In his dying voice, the weight of Patterson's voice changes. If speech and song are placed on a continuum, his late voice seems to move in the direction of song as a result of this newfound lightness. Now, I do not seek to draw a one-to-one correlation between Patterson's body weight and vocal weight; in her discussion of the contradictory concerns of soprano Maria Callas's weight loss and vocal decline, musicologist Nina Eidsheim clarifies that no simple connection can be drawn between body weight and vocal quality.[24]

In Patterson's case, however, dramatic physical changes resulted from an ongoing battle with metastatic prostate cancer. And the strength required to undertake vocal feats from the 1960s through the early 2000s seemingly could not be summoned in the last months of his life. But even through these final months, Patterson's voice, though with diminished heft, was still characterized by its wide range and agile motion. The audible difference in vocal weight is not the same as the event of bad-voicedness discussed earlier. Runs and melismas remain ready at hand for Patterson. He is still able to sing his eternal song, comfortably unfolding an octave in a few seconds, demonstrating the range and motion that obtained even in his dying voice. Something of the irreducibility of Patterson's instrument is evidenced by the peculiar interval of the octave, a musical relationship that (as the forthcoming chapters will show) remains ubiquitous even amid the deterioration of Bishop Patterson's health.

ETERNAL VOICE

At the end of Bishop Patterson's last message to the Church of God in Christ's Ninety-ninth Annual Holy Convocation, "Jehoshaphat's Prayer and God's Answer," he made his way to the recurring musical exegesis of 2 Chronicles 20 that I have called the "eternal song" [▶ **Video Example BM10**]. After inviting his audience to join him in singing "praise the Lord for his mercy endureth forever," Patterson elaborated on the virtues of praise. Preaching in F, he thundered:

Tell somebody, "While everybody else is fighting, learn the secret of praise!
Because as you praise the lord, enemies will fall in your way!
As you praise the lord, demons are casted out!
As you praise the lord, sick bodies are healed!
Miracles are performed, *uh-as you praise!*"

Here, Patterson ends this stretch with an unanswered anaphoric call "as you praise," an incomplete phrase that derives a sense of closure from its melodic presentation on the same octaval melisma—running from F3-A3-C4-F4—with which this idea began. Like this sermonic text and Patterson's eternal song, this brief bit of music serves as a resonant thread that connects this message to Patterson's catalog and the eternal transmission his ministry sought to convey.

This riff—an ascending motif that moves from scale degree 1 to 3 to 5 to 6 to 1 in the higher octave—recurs across decades of Patterson's sermons, from his preaching prime in the early 1990s to his last sermons in 2006. Patterson repurposes this collection to striking effect in scores of sermons, preached from a wide range of scriptures and in an assorted array of keys over many years. Here, I want to think about this motif, the "eternal riff," as the sound of Patterson's eternal voice, a self-conscious instrumentalization that places each individual utterance in relationship with many antecedent and consequent statements. This motif reveals the voice behind, beside, and above Patterson's broadcast medium, the secret, eternal, prophetic register whose fleeting emergence highlights the transcendence of his instrument over any single sonic event, casting a broad transmission that stretches across both space and time, linking Patterson's life and afterlife.

At the end of a 1993 sermon, "Neither Were They Thankful," Patterson repeatedly exhorted his congregation to give God the glory, building intensity for his final instruction: "turn to somebody beside you and say, I don't know about you, but I'm gonna be thankful" [▶ **Video Example BM11**]. The last word of the sermon is hard to define in purely lexical terms. It is something like "yeah" or "yeeeeh," a heightened vocable whose meaning is clarified by its musicality, an articulation of Patterson's eternal riff (Musical Example 6).

The last word that appears in G♭ in the 1993 sermon reappears as the final utterance of both "Lord, Let Your Glory Fill This House" and "The

Example 6. Eternal riff in G♭ major, Temple of Deliverance Church, Memphis, Tennessee, November 25, 1993.

Faith of Strangers," two of the messages Patterson preached in 1999 during Temple of Deliverance's first year in their new sanctuary [▶ **Video Example BM12**]. In both of these messages Patterson's riff appears in F, connecting F3 to F4, using a discursive expression whose enunciation is as ambiguous as its intensifying effect is obvious. In both cases this motif functions as a double bar line for a thirty- or forty-minute sermon, enacting a linguistic turn toward an "otherwise" grammar.[25] Traversing an octave in just a few seconds, this motif highlights Patterson's expansive range and the agility with which he navigates melismas. Indeed, before taking his seat at the 1993 worship service, Patterson led his congregation in singing the traditional praise song "I Thank You Jesus, I Thank You Lord." In this endeavor Bishop Patterson repeatedly found his way up to a chesty, belted D♭5, moving adroitly across two octaves from the time his sermon began to the time the service ended. Vertiginous movements such as these characterized Patterson's ministry, and its capacity is distilled in the eternal riff.

In the last decade of Patterson's life, this same motif showed up in various guises at moments of particular homiletic emphasis. Often this phrase is used to amplify a scriptural passage that Patterson quotes from memory. Consider, for example, a 2004 sermon, "The Power of the Word," delivered at the West Angeles Church of God in Christ in Los Angeles [▶ **Video Example BM13**]. Patterson used this riff to exclaim "for there's no other name" as a part of quotation of Acts 4:12, which reads "for there's no other name under the heavens given among men, whereby we must be saved." In a 2005 sermon, "A Compassionate Father," Patterson used this motif to accent "turn," the operative word of Psalm 119:59 [▶ **Video Example BM14**]. And in a 2005 sermon, "Will You Dare to Be Different?," the phrase accompanied a passage from Isaiah 41, "when you're walking through the water" [▶ **Video Example BM15**].

The motif serves a similar framing function in a September 2006 sermon, Philippians 2:5–11, as Patterson uses it to begin a quotation of a canonical song lyric: "my heart is fixed, my mind is made up" [▶ **Video Example BM16**]. Although the riff typically appeared only once in a sermon, there are exceptions, like another 2006 message, "After the Dust Settles," where the riff appeared twice, connecting C3 and C4, allowing its salient combination of repetition and difference across Patterson's catalog to be experienced in a single message [▶ **Video Examples BM17a and BM17b**]. Even in Patterson's last sermon, preached on Christmas Day 2006, this motif began the final minute of this message, linking B2 and B3 [▶ **Video Example BM18**]. This "final" articulation, during this most significant event, asserted the eternal riff's importance to Patterson's Black Pentecostal instrumentality as a recurring signal of Patterson's concern with endurance—both of the eternal word and the reverberation of his preached word.

Bishop Patterson's eternal riff has much in common with one of the most enduring fragments of Black sacred music—the "Yes, Lord" praise: "Yes! Yes! Ye-es! Ye-ee-es! Ye-ee-es! Yes, Lord!" Attributed to and made popular by Bishop Charles H. Mason, the founder of the COGIC denomination into which Patterson was born and over which he would one day preside, this brief musical affirmation functions as an improvisational response to a host of liturgical phenomena.[26] As musician Pearl Williams-Jones notes, periods of holy dancing often "give way to a chant in slow tempo such as, 'Yes, Lord' which is an unmetered chant [that] originated in the early days of the Church of God in Christ"[27] A fitting answer to virtually any ritual event, this brief bit of music, an expression of what literary theorist Ashon Crawley calls "Blackpentecostal Breath," brings any individual worship service into contact with more than a century's worth of Black sacred musicking, functioning as "a kernel that has within it the whole and hull of the testimony song and tarry praise noise in its intensity and repetition."[28]

Often its original lyrics are replaced with other phrases including "I love you, Lord" and "Have Your Way," as in one of Bishop Patterson's moments of communal song at the Church of God in Christ's Ninety-fourth Annual Holy Convocation (2001). Just as often, Patterson appended this COGIC chant to the end of another song, allowing the song and the affirmation to remake each other. In so doing, he enacted a kind of "COGIC contrafacta" [▶ **Video Example BM19**]. Consider, for example, the way Patterson concludes the hymn "He'll Understand, He'll Say Well Done" at the first live recording of *Singing the Old Time Way*. Just as he finishes singing that song's chorus, he looks up and says: "He'll say well done. He'll say well done. He'll say well done. He'll say well done. He'll say well done. He'll say well done." Singing this to the tune of the "Yes, Lord" chant, Patterson instructs the congregation to "come on and ring it out," venting his certainty that, armed with this most familiar harmonic, melodic, and affective framework, they could find their place in this declaration. Patterson did the same thing during the final moments of "Jesus Breaks Every Fetter," at the end of the second live recording of *Singing the Old Time Way*.

In both cases the effect of this sudden turn away from an unfolding song into the refrain that transcends every other melody in the COGIC church invites his audience to hold these two expressions together, oscillating between "Yes, Lord" and whichever song is being undone. Every time Patterson makes a move such as this, it produces an unmistakable intensification in the audience's engagement with an unfolding service. This is COGIC contrafacta, which affirms ethnomusicologist Kay Kaufman Shelemay's assertion that the "contrafact procedures [that] both characterize and serve to habituate religious practice . . . are of signal importance in inculcating philosophical ideas concerning the manner in which transformation of sound can be equated with transformation of belief."[29] The articulations of the eternal riff in and across Patterson's sermons are compressed instances of COGIC contrafacta, self-conscious acts of repetition through which Patterson engrafts the sonic emblem of endurance into a fleeting homiletic event. As he riffs, Patterson positions himself in relationship to Bishop Mason, the denominational founder whose frequent invocation and memorialization, even to the moment of this writing, is one of the preconditions for Patterson's own posthumous resonance. Indeed, during an appearance at a 1998 COGIC Leadership Conference, Patterson used the fact that his television broadcasts begin with the sound of him singing "Yes, Lord" as proof that, even after the controversial 1996

Presiding Bishop election, he remained firmly planted in the Church of God in Christ.

Even in 2023, more than sixteen years after Patterson's death, the sound of his voice singing "Yes, Lord" in E♭ still marks the beginning of his broadcast every Sunday on The Word Network, the Bountiful Blessings website, and YouTube.[30] By the end of these telecasts, this same voice often finds its way to one or more articulations of the eternal riff, this Pattersonian leitmotif. These two enduring refrains link Bishops Patterson and Mason. On the day of Patterson's death, Bishop Charles E. Blake, then the denomination's First Assistant Presiding Bishop, described Patterson as "a pioneer of media ministries." In this gesture Blake conjoined the language used to describe the denomination's first generation of leadership with the domain in which Patterson made his most distinctive contribution, reinforcing the connection between Patterson and Mason.[31] Perhaps this is why, during a 2014 interview, commemorating the seventh anniversary of Bishop Patterson's passing, COGIC pastor Antonio Buckley, one of Patterson's chief adjutants, declared: "Bishop Patterson was my Bishop Mason."[32]

Hovering outside each sermon, like a transmission awaiting contact with a vocal antenna, the eternal riff radicalizes the singularity of each sermon, drawing preacher, band, and congregation into a more intimate connection with the enduring substance of Patterson's message, lending an Afterliveness to sermons and scripture. In so doing, this motif functions as an "isolated and rare gesture" whose articulation affirms that there are "different kinds or modes of music that inhabit a single work," even a characteristically musical sermon in which audible difference becomes the mechanism of homiletic chorality.[33] Going from one dimension of musicality to an even more emphatic one, the eternal riff becomes a moment of revelation, the unveiling of Patterson's eternal voice, using its sensuous force to claim a purpose and awareness that sits above its musical surroundings. As it calls attention away from the individual sermon, away from any single word or phrase, it directs focus to the voice itself, highlighting its interworldly instrumentality.

By attending to Bishop Patterson's voice as a modulating, choral, fatigable, dying, and eternal phenomenon, this chapter has elucidated the techniques through which Patterson's instrument became a broadcast medium. Through its arresting shifts between registers of speech, chant, and song, Patterson's instrument presenced an interworldly assembly of voices. As it experienced impairment and endured grave illness, it clarified the specific capacities that made it so effective. As various forms of repetition enabled it to transcend any single event of its sounding, Patterson's voice gave scripture's distant scenes a particular immediacy for innumerable audiences. Moreover, working as a broadcast medium and with other broadcast media, voice also conditioned the possibility of Patterson's posthumous resonance. The undoing of distance—spatial and temporal—during the period of Patterson's active ministry set the stage for his musical and homiletic afterlife.

3 Broadcast Grammar

On Sunday, March 4, 1990, during the celebration of Temple of Deliverance's fifteenth church anniversary, Bishop Patterson preached a message titled "The Next Fifteen Years." Drawn from a passage in which the ancient Israelite King Hezekiah's life was extended by fifteen years, Patterson's sermon self-consciously stood between the past and future of the church he served as founder and pastor. Before reading his sermonic text, Isaiah 38:1-6, Patterson told his congregation: "There is a phrase that I want to get to and, if the Lord permits, we may get back to it. But I make no promises." As he informed them that the given theme's recurrence was a mere possibility, Patterson engaged in a rare bit of meta-homiletic discourse, calling attention to sermonic design, while promising submission to divine direction. Continuing in this vein, Patterson stated: "Once I tell you what my theme is, after a while, I'm gonna start talking about just the opposite."

And he did just that: in fact, it would be more than thirty minutes before Patterson began discussing "the next fifteen years." In between the title's initial statement and its fuller elaboration, he delivered a message that was "somewhat reminiscent," talking in great detail "about the last fifteen years." By the time he returned to the stated theme, and the scripture by which it was inspired, Patterson was nearing his emotive, musical, and rhetorical climax. By the time he turned to the future, Patterson was almost ready to sit down. Thus, in contrast to his claim, the title assigned to this sermon served as a rhetorical promissory note, a homiletic landmark that clarified the destination that stood at the end of the message's affective trajectory. While the specific focus of Patterson's anniversary sermon seemed to require him to move backward and forward in time, the "opposites" that structured that day's message reveal far more consistent features of his aesthetic practice. Expressing, abandoning, and then belatedly returning to a message's title is one of the central elements of Patterson's preaching. But why? How does the form of Patterson's sermons manifest his Broadcast Religion? In what ways can Patterson's pursuit of Afterliveness be discerned from the structure of his messages? And what aspects of Patterson's sermonic design contribute to his congregations' routine experience of religious ecstasy?

This chapter attends to the ecstatic design of Patterson's sermons, a formal logic that operates on two hierarchically distinct levels. First, I show how Patterson's sermonic forms yoke the conventional practice of "tuning up" to a distinctive broadcasting practice of "tuning in." Instead of marshalling homiletical musicality as "ecstatic reinforcement" for a given sermon's content, Patterson does not arrive at his sermonic argument until the end of a message, in the ecstatic frame whose heightened musicality confirms the centrality of a given word or phrase to the unfolding message. As such, the crux of his message is always delivered in a musical "other space," the apotheosis of a homiletic trajectory that inculcates intimacy with various scriptural scenes. What is true on the broadest level of the sermon is true on the most local: Bishop Patterson's overarching ecstatic design is driven forward by his penchant for amplification.

With this word, I mean to summon both the general rhetorical category and the processual intensification of sound, both of which are key to Bishop Patterson's musicality. Throughout Patterson's catalog, amplification appears as the method by which brief ideas—textual and musical—are spun out into emphatically musical phrases, marshalling repetition and rhetorical devices like anaphora and epistrophe to foment an experience of power. Amid a thoroughly musical unfolding, these points of inflection create a further sense of elevation, permitting an emergent congregation to go from tuning up to tuning in. The sermonic movement from tuning up to tuning in enables it to garner a most prized possession: homiletic fidelity.

THE THEME AS DESTINATION

On Sunday, June 3, 2006, just after reading his message's focal scripture, Galatians 3:26–29, Bishop Patterson asked his congregation to participate in the announcement of his sermon's theme: "Can you just say it? 'I'm an heir to the promise.'" As these words reverberated across the sanctuary, Patterson clarified their significance, stating: "That's where we're going today." This phrase, uttered after stating his title and before beginning his message, affirms that the moment in which a sermon's title is announced is of singular homiletic importance. When given, the title orients the audience's engagement with the forthcoming message, inviting them to expect the recurrence of the phrase and the presentation of a general set of "moves" that develop the idea. In Patterson's preaching, as in many other contexts, African American and otherwise, the given title accents the most important idea or concept of the sermon. But for Patterson, the given title is not a thesis or argument that is stated, developed, and complicated during the sermon's unfolding. While each of his messages is clearly *about* the stated theme, only gradually does its *aboutness* become apparent. Bishop Patterson's sermon titles are destinations, end points of a sermon's trajectory. Even as they delimit the course in which Patterson's sermon will unfold on a given day, they inject a new level of uncertainty, inviting audiences to wonder, "How will he get back to this theme?"

The homiletic trajectory outlined by Bishop Patterson's sermonic broadcasts is helpfully elucidated by a 2005 sermon titled "I Can't Keep It to Myself" [▶ **Video Example BG1**]. That day, Patterson recounted a story that is recorded in both Luke 5:12–15 and Mark 1:40–45, a narrative of a leprous man who, when healed by Jesus, disregards Jesus's instruction to keep his miraculous encounter to himself. Calling their attention to "an instance of healing during the earthly ministry of our Lord and savior Jesus Christ," Patterson invites his congregation to focus on an event rather than a text. In so doing, he implies that his message will in fact engage with more than one passage of scripture, using their differences to get a sharper image of the ancient scene. After noting the story's presence in the gospels according to Luke and Mark, Patterson says that despite Mark's more detailed explication of the story's crucial last move, he prefers to preach from Luke's account. Something about the structure of Luke's narrative makes it a more inviting record for Patterson's Broadcast Religion.

After proclaiming the theme of this message, Bishop Patterson spent the first quarter of his roughly thirty-minute message discussing the importance of testimony, recalling the prevalence and intensity of testimony services in the churches of his youth, the eventual decline of the liturgical practice, and the way testimony's ecclesial decline has been met by its emergence as a commercial marketing strategy. But testimony is at its best, Patterson argues, when a recognizable human voice uses their experience to authenticate the expression of divine power. While the testimony of his text's central character is distilled in the title of Patterson's message, it would be more than twenty minutes before the message's theme reemerged. Returning to Luke's account, roughly eight minutes into this message, Patterson gives a set of clues about why he is so fond of this version of the story, a pericope that begins with the following phrase: "And it came to pass, when he was in a certain city, behold a man full of leprosy: who seeing Jesus, fell on his face, and went to him, saying, Lord, if thou wilt, thou canst make me clean." Regarding this opening, Patterson confessed: "I like that because the namelessness of the city has something to say to you and me." After noting the Bible's many references to specific locations—Jerusalem, Bethlehem, Jericho, Bethany, Nazareth, and Capernaum, among others— Patterson asserts that "the city is nameless because this morning that city can very well be Memphis, Tennessee." Memphis could become a site of transformative encounter because "the Lord Jesus Christ, right now, even though I cannot see him standing in a flowing robe, but he's here, my hand cannot reach out and physically touch him, but I do know that he is here."

Reinforcing his interest in the text's generative ambiguity, he then notes its description of "a man," observing: "Here again this leaves the door open." Then he claims that the text's description of "a man," not Bartimaeus, Simon Delotis, nor "any of the men or women named in the Bible," invites each gathered believer to turn to those beside whom they are seated and assert: "I am the man or the woman." Although it is often the case that

Patterson uses a text's abundant details to make its contents immediate for his congregants, here he uses the absence of detail in the same way, showing that immediacy itself is his message's highest aim. The desire for "experiential encounter" motivates the organization of his sermons.[1] As Patterson's expository oscillation between a bit of Lukan text and an assertion of its meaning and contemporary relevance continues, he notes that the scripture's interest in the ambiguous one "who was full of leprosy" also makes any current malady an opportunity for a similar healing.

Alongside Patterson's patient, oscillating unfolding of this narrative, there are two other teleological arcs at work: (1) the confidence that he will at some point make the customary movement from speech to song, and (2) the sense of expectation engendered by both the title of this message and routine structure of Patterson's sermons. The first of these arcs articulates a centuries-long tradition of musical Black preaching, which was reanimated during the Great Migration, yielding a "mixed-type preaching," shaped by a moment of transformation that is indexed by numerous emic formulations, including "tuning up."[2] Between the twenty-minute mark and twenty-minute-thirty seconds of this message, G♭ emerges as a discernible reciting tone, prompting the band, led by Derrick Jackson, to ground him in this tonal context by the end of this half-minute-long segment of Patterson's sermon. This shift into the sermon's heightened, musical frame, following shortly on Patterson's homiletic turn to the story at hand, suggests that the message would soon arrive at the theme announced at its beginning. After discussing the leprous man's encounter with Jesus, at twenty-six minutes and fifty-one seconds, Patterson makes a sudden shift in persona; no longer is he a distant observer, but now he gives voice to the healed man:

> But as soon as the man left Jesus, "I can't keep it to myself!
> I got to go home: got to tell my wife; got to tell the children.
> I got to go to my job: I got to tell my coworkers.
> I gotta go to school: gotta tell my classmates.
> I gotta go through the neighborhood and tell all of my neighbors what the Lord has done for me."

Bishop Patterson's enunciation of this crucial character's testimony is accented in three ways: (1) this declaration is animated by a new, reiterative grammar; (2) this statement begins with the long-awaited restatement of the sermon's given theme; (3) the reemergence of the message's title is marked by the eternal riff, a recurring musical figure that calls attention to particularly important moments in Patterson's sermons. In this case, the eternal riff—an instance of repetition across Patterson's catalog—combines with the testimony's constitutive recursion to clarify the message's arrival at its single most important moment: the end point of Patterson's "homiletical plot," the sermon's final "movement in consciousness."[3]

The musical context in which the sermon arrives at its organizing point further clarifies its centrality, using the pervasive practice of tuning up in service of a related yet distinct organizing principle. In scholarship on Black sacred musicking, including my own, this moment in the sermon is regarded as a celebrative conclusion, an "ecstatic reinforcement of the sermon's content."[4] But that is an insufficient description for a message that only arrives at its point in the context of heightened musical expression. "I Can't Keep It to Myself" shows that rather than functioning as a thesis or argument, in Patterson's preaching, the theme is a destination, a kairotic moment that serves as the central landmark on a homiletic journey. The entire message's unfolding is guided by interlocking narrative magnetisms: the recorded ending of a given event, the expected shift into homiletical musicality, and the arrival at the moment designated by the sermon's theme.

If, as Patterson preaches and his congregation seems to believe, the healing recorded in this text could also be experienced in their lives, what role does this sermon's form play in the assertion of that possibility? What are the mechanics of this drawing-near? Building on Chapter 1's discussion of Afterliveness, I contend that the sermon, for Bishop Patterson, was an interworldly broadcast in which the voice functioned as a receiver, using musicality to sensitize the assembly to the frequency at which resounds an eternal transmission. Patterson's recurring request for anointing with which "to speak as an oracle of Christ" reveals this intention, pointing to the theory of preaching that lies at the center of Broadcast Religion. Patterson's sermons mediate, standing between his congregation, the biblical events they reanimate, and his many prospective audiences. Patterson's theory of preaching and his technophilic Pentecostalism are both evident in the Broadcast Grammar that shapes his messages.

Broadcast Grammar is both the product and process that combines (1) the plot of a given scripture, (2) the thematic trajectory of a given sermon, (3) the ritual shape of a given service, and (4) the modulatory profile of Patterson's voice—the eventual turn toward musicality: tuning up. These four ineluctably linked courses collectively produce the brand of sonic intimacy that we have come to know as tuning in. Tuning in enables Patterson's vocal instrument to do the work of radio receivers, which, though "often figured as technologies for listening to sound," actually hear "inaudible frequencies: wireless transmissions of electromagnetic radiation, which they make acoustically perceivable for human ears."[5]

Thus listening to what Patterson says is the best way to discern what he hears. To enact this homiletic reception, the sermonic sound reproduction that I have termed "Pentecostal playback," Patterson's broadcast medium—that is, his voice—becomes responsible for the concomitant transformations of scripture into sound and speech into song, two audible conversions that give a modern audience convincing access to remote incidents. These interlocking modulations are the means through which Patterson "turns the dial," "de-severing" distant space-times for the broadcast of religion.[6] Stated at least twice in at least two contrasting registers, the theme of a given message plays a crucial role in this communicative system. The affective trajectory that separates these two articulations engenders the central paradox of Patterson's preaching: the phenomenal difference between the form of the title's first utterance and the shape of its reemergence is what draws the sermon near to its ancient scene. When, in the context of heightened musical expression, the title of the message reemerges, preacher, band, and congregation have gone from tuning up to tuning in.

TRANSDUCTION

"The Arrows of the Lord's Deliverance," a message Bishop Patterson routinely preached from 2 Kings 13, brings the aesthetic, theological, and philosophical contours of his Broadcast Grammar into particularly clear relief. Recalling a scene when a dying prophet named Elisha instructed the king of ancient Israel to shoot arrows out of a window, in the direction of enemy nations, to secure a divine guarantee of military victory, Patterson argues that his congregants can secure assurance of similar triumph if they would learn how to faithfully propel the Word of God. Every time he delivered this message, Patterson read his text, stated the theme, and departed to begin a long winding path, connecting current events with the ministry of the prophets who are recorded in the books of Kings. Thus by the time he arrived at the immediate context of his chosen scripture, Patterson had painted a striking portrait of the spiritual enmity he believed his congregants were facing. To defeat these foes, they would need to reach in their bag of arrows—the Bible—and place it on their bow of faith and shoot it in the direction of the devil.

In the heightened phase of the sermon delivered on Sunday, September 2, 1990, Bishop Patterson landed in G♭ as a tonal context, as he reminded the congregation about a few of "the arrows that are in their arsenal": "When sickness, disease, and infirmity is in your body, or in the family member's body, what am I gon' do? I'm gon' take my bow of faith, and I'm gon' shoot [*shoot*] in the direction of the enemy. I'm gon' shoot Exodus 15:26. And I'm gon' shoot the name that the Lord gave Moses when they came to Marah, where the waters were bitter: I'm gona shoot at the enemy, [*shoot*] 'Jehovah-Rophe—I'm the Lord that healteth thee'" [▶ **Video Example BG2**].

Preaching in G♭, locked in to antiphony with his band and congregation, Patterson continues to name well-known passages of scripture, asserting that each is an ideal response to a host of personal and collective problems. Each time he released a verbal arrow, he gestured with his hand and arm, pulling back and releasing, showing how it would look if he was to actually launch such a weapon. At the same time, he juxtaposes two iterations of a single word: "shoot" and the onomatopoetic *shoot* that resembles the sound of such a martial release. As he uses words to presence the actions he describes, he shows how they might indeed acquire a penetrating force, wounding the spiritual enemy of his assembled audiences.

In a 1999 presentation of this sermon, Bishop Patterson developed an extended discourse on the distinctions between differently potent forms of the Word [▶ **Video Example BG3**]. Lifting up his Bible, he asserted that "the arrows are right here, but the only way to get the arrow from here to your situation, you've gotta to put it on your bow string of faith. In other words, you've gotta take the logos and turn it into a rhema." Leaning into this dichotomy, Patterson elects to "take a minute to explain": "John 1:1 says, 'In the beginning was the logos.' In the Greek that's what he said: 'In the beginning was the logos.' And the logos is the word of God. That God, the father, Jehovah, Yahweh, emptied himself into his Word. And he only took the Word and deposited it into the womb of Mary, and the Word came out in flesh and blood and we called him Jesus. So the whole of God is capsulized in the logos of his Word."

Hovering between speech and song, while being accompanied by the band in his previously defined key of G♭, Patterson talks about the transformation of the logos into something more powerful. Lifting his Bible again, he emphasizes that "the Word is here; you've got the logos, but there are times [when] you can read it and its just reading." Then comes the crucial contravention: "But when something in the Word jumps out of the pages into your situation, that's when the word speaks to you. And when the Word speaks to you, that's called a rhema." Even as Patterson uses an ancient story about a quiver, a bow, and an arrow to describe the mechanism by which the sacred Word achieves a host of miraculous effects, he gives his audiences an immanent sense of the differing sonic forms the Word can take.

When Bishop Patterson delivered this same message on Sunday, November 19, 2006, in what would be one of his five final messages, he explicitly referred to the interaction of bow, arrow, and quiver as "a system" [▶ Video Example BG4]. Reaching behind him, effortfully pulling something out of an invisible quiver, and affixing it to an invisible bow, he shoots this invisible arrow out in the midst of his congregation. Although they can't see it, it is there in the air, reverberating like the words he is speaking. At the same time, Patterson demonstrates the tonal system that he uses to activate the power of sacred words. Preaching that day in A♭, one of his most frequent sermonic keys, Patterson repeatedly juxtaposes A♭3 and A♭4, converting the lower reciting tone into its transcendent form. After an early, excited shout on A♭4, he descends to A♭3, gradually climbing back to the sonic summit over the course of the message's broadcast frame. But this same transmutation is also achieved within the span of a few seconds.

During two slightly varied articulations of the eternal riff, the bluesy passage that links the two forms of any key's tonic, Patterson highlights the expressive and transductive function of the octave for his preaching. In this way this most central element of a tonal system, produced by doubling the frequency, performs the transformation of "the logos" into "the rhema." In one seven-second segment of this sermon's conclusion, Patterson riffs his way from A♭2 to A♭3, before leaping up to A♭4. Uttering three versions of this key's tonal center, Patterson contrasts difference and repetition to enact transformation. Indeed, one would be hard-pressed to find a more effective way to sonify the transduction of the Word into its more powerful form—to covert logos into rhema—than through these arresting octaval motions.

Transduction is an essential element of Bishop Patterson's Broadcast Religion. This stands to reason, for, as communications scholar Jonathan Sterne notes, "all sound-reproduction technologies work through the use of transducers," devices "which turn sound into something else and that something else back into sound."[7] Over and over again, throughout Patterson's career, as "the right kind of receiver," his voice turns logos into rhema.[8] This defining conversion motivates the form of his sermons. When understood as a word "jumping out of the pages, into [a believer's] situation," rhema becomes an event. The Broadcast Grammar of Bishop Patterson's sermons organizes the entire message around the production of this event, not simply in the customary movement from speech to song, but through the moment when the message's given theme reemerges in this ecstatic context. When the assembly arrives at this musico-homiletic destination, the sermon's central contention has been transduced into something else: the sounding substance of an eternal transmission.

AMPLIFICATION

Another expression of Patterson's ecstatic design takes place on a far more granular scale. In fact, it is the method by which brief ideas—textual and musical—are spun out into emphatically musical phrases: amplification. One instructive example of Patterson's amplifying practice comes from a 2005 sermon, "A Compassionate Father," which reanimates the story of the prodigal son recorded in the fifteenth chapter of the Gospel according to Luke [▶ **Video Example BG5**]. In the heightened phase of the sermon, as he worked to render ancient events immediate to his congregation, Patterson exclaimed: "The father looked and saw him coming and said, 'I know that's my boy.'" As he preached in B♭, the last six words of the aforementioned sentence moved up from B♭ to F, before coming right down. In so doing, they established a pattern with which Patterson would linger. "That's my boy," three words that make palpable a father's newfound delight, form a descending riff that falls from D♭ to a twice-stated B♭. An ideal way to end each in a string of sentences, this line punctuates a string of five epistrophic utterances:

> His hair is disheveled, but that's my boy!
> His fingers are bare, but that's my boy!
> He's gotten on ragged clothes, but that's my boy!
> He seems to be walking with a limp, but that's my boy!
> He's lost some weight from hunger, but that's my boy!

Painting an increasingly vivid picture of how this wayward-but-returning man must have looked, Patterson invites his congregation into a deeper engagement with his sermonic text, inculcating intimacy through amplification.

Two excerpts from a 2000 sermon, "Call His Name," further exemplify the way Patterson uses repetition to amplify a statement, musicalizing it in the process [▶ **Video Example BG6a**]. Preaching in E♭, Patterson sought to convey what it means to call Jesus "the prince of peace," he intones: "I know that the United Nations is there in New York." Then, after interpolating a hybrid vowel, an iteration of the eternal riff that starts on "uh" and ends on "oh," he continues: "I know that they periodically have peace conferences in Geneva, Switzerland." Then he asserts that there can be no peace without Jesus. Amplifying this claim, Patterson proclaims:

> There'll be no peace
> On your job
> There'll be no peace
> In your home
> There'll be no peace
> In the church
> There'll be no peace
> In your heart and mind

In this anaphoric sequence Patterson repeatedly climbs up from G♭4 to B♭4 before falling to his reciting tone E♭4. The recurrence of text, rhythm, and pitch, climbing into the farthest reaches of his voice, make urgent his claim. Roughly one minute later, Patterson turns his message's title into another riff, recursively exclaiming, "call him," from B♭4 before falling to the reciting tone:

> Call him
> When the bills are due
> Call him
> When pain is in your body
> Call him
> When trouble is on your job
> Call!
> [▶ Video Example BG6b]

Quite often, Patterson concatenates the ending of such a string of words, a reduction that allows him to lean into the final word, turning what had been the first words of a reiterative episode into a fitting punctuation. Such a potent vocalization makes a claim that Patterson's words were really being heard on high by an auditor whose presence could be felt below.

In a 1998 sermon, "The Saint's Remedy in Times of Trouble," a succession of amplifying passages draws Patterson and congregation into a period of holy dancing. Closing his message in A♭, first he repeats a divine promise: "I will deliver thee" [▶ Video Example BG7a]. Then he gives this transcendent guarantee a contemporary relevance:

> I'll deliver ya
> Out of your financial dilemma
> I'll deliver ya
> Out of your health crisis
> I'll deliver ya
> Out of your family trouble
> I'll deliver ya
> Out of the trouble on the school campus

In this first line of each anaphoric segment, Patterson delivers two syllables on C♭3 and three syllables on E♭4. Returning to C♭3 for the first word of each segment's second line, he falls to his reciting tone A♭3 on the last word of each strophe. As in the eternal song and the eternal riff, these passage's repeated words, rhythms, and contour make these moments stand out even amid a thoroughly musical unfolding. Amplification does within a single sermon what these repeated gestures do across years of Patterson's life and afterlife, linking each individual utterance to a transcendent chorus. That day, Patterson was just beginning to carve out a communal path to embodied ecstasy. Roughly one minute later, he turns from the promise of deliverance to the expected response of gratitude:

> But when I been in trouble
> And when everything else has failed
> And when I call on Jesus
> And when he gives me the victory
> Get out of my way:
> [▶ Video Example BG7b]

Here, all but the last line ends on the transcendent version of his tonal center, A♭4. The fifth line's falling character sonifies the shift that is visualized by the underlined colon. This accumulative passage leads to this sermon's climactic segment. Repeatedly climbing from E♭4 to A♭4, Bishop Patterson thunders:

> I got to praise him
> I got to praise him by lifting my hands
> I got to praise him in the dance
> I got to praise him with everything in me
>
> Because I been delivered
> Satan thought he had me
> But I slipped through one more time
>
> I got to praise him because God brought me out
> I got to praise him because he worked a miracle for me
> I got to praise

As in the final movement of "Call His Name," this section's clipped conclusion provides an occasion for Bishop Patterson to elongate a previously unmarked word, interrupting the expectations he had engendered, only to announce a collective arrival at an even more exalted affective state. Over the course of this last minute, within this heightened homiletic frame,

Patterson's utterances become increasingly regularized. Moving from the hilly, recitational contour of the first five lines to the five-word ascending riff "I got to praise him," he trained an ever-sharpening focus on a plural telos, one manifestation of which is the period of holy dancing that breaks out at the end of the phrase, the climactic expression of religious ecstasy in Patterson's Pentecostal context. The musicalizing effects of repetition in this example—and throughout Patterson's practice—summon a shift what music theorist Elizabeth Margulis calls "a musical way of listening."[9]

But when this audile technique is activated within an already-musical context, what change is left to be made? While this is not a bit of speech (as in psychologist Diana Deutsch's famous example) being transformed by repetition, still something transformative—or might we say, transductive—is taking place.[10] These are moments when the instrumental syntax of Patterson's voice—the plea to speak as "an oracle of Christ and not just a man"—shifts from the latter to the former, performing on a local level what the combination of sermonic form and tuning up do on the global level: "tuning in," which is the ultimate aim of Broadcast Grammar. Elsewhere, I have written about the way in which the unfolding of a gospel song turns lyrics into something much more potent, enacting what I call "the revelation of power."[11] Patterson's preaching achieves a similar effect, both through the Broadcast Grammar that governs an entire sermon's form and through the amplifying practice that animates the delimited sections of these messages. In both cases, an idea becomes something more, sometimes over the course of thirty minutes, or within the span of twenty seconds. This intensifying reiteration seems to allow Patterson to tap into something else, to tune into something more, bringing his various audiences into contact with an eternal transmission. Amplification is central to function of both the voice as a broadcast medium and tuning in as a Broadcast Grammar.

"OLD TESTAMENT PREACHING" AND HOMILETIC FIDELITY

What roles do Patterson's audiences play in the practice of tuning in? If the Broadcast Grammar of Patterson's messages produces a palpable intimacy with the eternal Word, how might congregants name this experience? In the eulogy he delivered at the first of Bishop Patterson's three funerals, then Elder Frank O. White mentioned common descriptions of Patterson as an "Old Testament Preacher." Two of this project's interlocutors also referred to Bishop Patterson in this manner. While discussing Patterson's broadcasts, activist and Pentecostal minister Eugene Rivers claimed that for many believers, "before they go to church on Sunday morning, they were gonna hear G. E. Patterson preach about something out of the Old Testament."[12]

Unprompted, Mance Aytchan, Patterson's long-serving minister of music, also referred to the deceased cleric as an "Old Testament Preacher."[13] After noting that Patterson "seldom used a lot of manuscript ... [but] would write down two or three lines and make you think he had fifteen pieces of paper," Aytchan mused that regarding "the Old Testament, people said they think that he was in there and helped to write it."[14] The deeper one travels into Patterson's circle, the more one runs into this assertion. In a conversation with Patterson's widow, Louise, she mentioned without prompting: "He knew that Old Testament."[15] Likewise, Patterson's successor and nephew Bishop Milton Hawkins described Patterson as a "Master of the Old Testment."[16] What do these similar and repeated assertions point to? What characteristics of Patterson's sermons are named by the phrase "Old Testament Preacher"? Aytchan's testimony offers the richest sense of what this trope might mean, conveying the sense that Patterson's virtuosic command of the scripture—Rivers calls it a "talmudic mastery"—and his musicality enabled the Bishop and his audiences to take residence *inside* the events recorded in a sacred text.

In a 1998 sermon, "The Departed Glory Shall Return," Patterson crafts a homiletic trajectory that exceeds his sermonic scripture, 1 Samuel 4:15–22. While the text he chooses to read has to do with the glory of God departing, nothing about the return is recorded in this passage. Patterson addresses this gap directly, even as he announces the title of this message: "I want to say from this very dismal passage, a passage that any person who in Israel that day would have wept over the saying of Phinehas's wife. And anyone who has spiritual understanding today would have to feel a bit pained to hear such report is that the glory of the Lord is departed. But I want to say to you again today, as I've said in past years, because I believe it with all of my heart, that the departed glory shall return." Waxing nostalgic, Patterson went on to vent the renewalist ethos that had animated preceding generations of his Holiness-Pentecostal denomination, detailing things in the church and society that "are not how they used to be." While these ecclesial and social problems testify to the departedness of a certain divine glory, they also clarify the situation to which this sermon speaks. Patterson suggests that the occurrences with which he is concerned can be likened to the events of a fateful day in ancient Israel's history.

Preaching in B, Bishop Patterson gives voice to the messenger who visited the ancient Israelite judge Eli with news about the death of his children and the stealing of the Ark of the Covenant [▶ **Video Example BG8**]. Then the message comes to Eli's daughter-in-law, informing her that, in addition to the death of her husband and her brother dying on the battlefield, the Philistines had taken the Ark of the Covenant, the material trace of God's presence among their people. As he reanimates these ancient conversations, Patterson hovers around B3 as a reciting tone, oscillating between B3 and D4, outlining the lowest level of his message's melodic topography. When Patterson shifts persona from the messenger talking to Eli's unnamed daughter-in-law to the woman herself, he moves into a higher range of his instrument. After expressing her decision to name the child Ichabod, which means "the glory is departed," Patterson uses amplification to explain her reasoning:

> **I'm not naming him** after his grandfather, Eli
> That's bad but that's not the worst part.
> **I'm not naming him** after his uncle, Hopni
> Because that also was heart-rending, but I could've lived through that.
> **I'm not even naming him** <u>after my husband his father,</u> Phineas because that's not the worst thing that happened today.
> But <u>when I learned</u> that the glory of God <u>had been taken</u> away from Israel: this boy will always <u>be a remembrance that the glory</u> have departed.

Punctuated by the Hammond organ, driven forward by interlocking forms of repetition, this explanation combines a three-limbed statement with an extensively reiterated three-note device. While the bolded type highlights the anaphora, the underlined text visualizes the recursive stepwise ascent from D4 to F#4 whose sonic insistence gives authority to Patterson's contention.

Then Patterson makes the homiletic turn, tracing the Ark of the Covenant across biblical history, into the reign of King David, the monarch who was able to reclaim this tangible manifestation of the glory of God. As he arrives at this defining moment of recovery, he finds his way into the highest reaches of his voice, repeatedly leaping to and reciting on B4, a transcendent version of his reciting tone, a pitch with singular importance in Patterson's oeuvre. Having unfurled his full melodic topography, he moves freely within the octave that separated B3 and B4, embedding his congregation in the world of the Old Testament/Hebrew Bible, extemporaneously calling attention to characters like "Obed-Edom" and "Zerubbabel, the son of Shealtiel, the governor of Judah"; prophets like Haggai and Zechariah; and memorized scripture like "the silver is mine, and the gold is mine." In so doing, he gives these ancient scenes a tangible and audible reality in his Memphis sanctuary. Patterson's "talmudic mastery" of scripture and his virtuosic command of his voice reversed the flow of energy that broadcast his worship service directly to the radio station. He became a channel of an eternal transmission—"an oracle of Christ."

To call Patterson an "Old Testament preacher" is to make a claim for a kind of fidelity, a homiletic pursuit of faithfulness that was inspired, in part, by Patterson's preoccupation with sound recording. While faithfulness to the text is an enduring ideal for translation, guide for interpretation, and ethic for preaching, Patterson's Broadcast Religion suggests that we might interpret his practice through the auditory lens of fidelity. I am not interested in fidelity as a scientifically measurable characteristic of sound recordings, or the early twentieth-century philosophy of reproducibility that preceded these metrics. Rather, the understanding of fidelity that elucidates Patterson's ministry concerns the relationship between both preacher and audience—transmitter and receiver—linking sermon, scripture, and the events recorded therein. This homiletic project can be illuminated by one of Sterne's contentions about the social genesis of sound fidelity: "sound reproduction is a social process . . . fidelity is a story that we tell ourselves to staple separate pieces of sonic reality."[17]

As he attends to the conditions of this adhesion, Sterne undoes the distinction between original and copy, showing that both the notion of an original or a copy is a consequence of reproducibility. There is a similar link at work between sermon and scripture in Patterson's religious imagination: scripture is defined as something from which to preach, even as the sermon is defined by its derivation from scripture. Fidelity is thus a positive assertion that a homiletic event has forged a meaningful connection between an ancient text and a contemporary context. In Patterson's Broadcast Religion this connection is defined by the transmission of spiritual power, an invisible force whose palpable presence must appear in the bodies of the believers. This homiletic fidelity might be likened to archivist Patrick Feaster's notion of "performative fidelity," which "recognizes the degree to which the social force associated with a sound is accepted as carrying over into its reproduction."[18] Fidelity also seems to be at issue in the prayer Patterson prayed before beginning his sermons: "Lord, we ask that you would allow us to speak as an oracle of Christ, and not just as a man. Hide us behind your glorious cross. Cover us with your precious blood, allowing no flesh to glory in your sight." This prayer is a literal petition to be a vanishing mediator, a static-free channel through which an eternal transmission might flow.

To call Patterson an "Old Testament Preacher" is to make a claim about religious authority, especially as it is mediated by sound reproduction—vocal and technological. Over and over, in Patterson's life and in his afterlife, the oracular memory that enabled Patterson to recall at will large swaths of sacred writ fueled his Black Pentecostal instrumentality. His pulpits were always recording studios, and while media ministry such as this is a common practice in Black churches large and small, Patterson's specific relationship to the fact of recording and to the specific kinds of vocal transcendence it enabled was distinctive. The recording of his recursive messages did not contribute to the withering of the force philosopher Walter Benjamin termed the "aura"; rather, these interlocking forms of repetition gave material durability and spiritual gravity to Patterson's proclamations.[19]

Patterson's Broadcast Religion deploys a sanctified form of what the ethnomusicologist Louise Meintjes calls "the studio's power of rarefaction," wherein the presence of technologies for the reproduction and transmission of sound contributes to the sanctuary's sense of alterity.[20] The mechanics that underlie this alterity arose when Louise Patterson described the physical proof of Bishop Patterson's technophilia to me, recalling: "You would've thought our church was CNN."[21] Uttered into microphones and cameras in a building that housed countless cassette, CD, VHS, and DVD duplicators, the Bishop's hi-fi messages were doubly authenticated. In so doing, they illuminate the production, practice, and social construction of religious authority in ways that have broader implications for studies in a host of religious traditions.

Afterliveness indexes spiritual authority; its conjunction of mediation and immediacy marshal the sermon and its many reproductions as conduits of spiritual power, whose collective effect is the ecclesial sway Patterson enjoys—in life and in death. Rather unlike the "live and direct faith" that takes the place of scripture for the Zimbabwean Apostolics with whom the anthropologist Matthew Engelke works, Patterson's broadcast religion depends on the preacher's virtuosic command of sacred writ.[22] The Afterliveness Patterson's congregations seek arises from the sonic techniques that fuel each message's Broadcast Grammar. Once inscribed and broadcast, Patterson's sermons relay both content and form, causing audiences to wonder if he really knew the individuals about whom he preached. Like the recurring musical elements, which collectively constitute eternal pitch, Patterson's homiletic fidelity, his encompassing relationship to a host of scenes from scripture, is best viewed through the kinds of comparisons that recording makes possible. The authority of Patterson's "The Departed Glory Shall Return" is strengthened by the striking similarities between this message and a 2005 sermon, "David's Day of Thanksgiving," which is analyzed in Chapter 4. As the parameter of key, the use of pace, and the verbatim characterizations of biblical actors like David and Obed-Edom clarify the connections between these two homiletic events, their shared characteristics make both messages seem close to scripture's distant scenes.

Many of those who participate in Patterson's digital afterlife wax nostalgic about his message and the authority it contained. These statements are consonant with the anthropologist Patrick Eisenlohr's analysis of the media theologies at work in the devotional practices of Mauritian Muslims, especially his claim that "sound reproduction is also important for what many view as the safeguarding of the appropriate performative style, which is as important as the textual dimension for its efficaciousness as a practice of pious transformation and spiritual intercession."[23] In an August 2020 post on Patterson's online obituary, one user wrote: "Awesome man of God they don't preach like this anymore."[24] Similarly, another user, in a 2020 YouTube comment on a video titled "Bishop GE Patterson The Dawn of a New Day," wrote: "A profound teacher and preacher of God's Word!!! They definitely don't make them like him anymore. So thankful for these videos, for they have Blessed my life exponentially! May he continue to rest in Heavenly Peace, and his sermons continue to Bless God's people."[25]

While both netizens long for the forms of religious authority Patterson embodied, Gourdine celebrated the endurance that is made possible by the recordings that were responsible for Patterson's renown. Echoing a sentiment numerous individuals have made to me during the preparation of this book, one user's November 2019 obituary post demonstrates that she is an active participant in the reproduction of Patterson's sermons. She wrote: "I will always remember him. I started watching his TV show because of my mother. She always watched his shows. Today I continue this tradition. I record all of his messages."[26] As recording and watching Patterson enables this online congregant to feel connected to the preacher and to her deceased mother, the devotional practices that sustain Patterson's afterlife come rather forcefully into view.

FIDELITY AND ETERNITY

"Focusing Your Eyes upon the Lord," a message delivered on Sunday, November 5, 2006, offers one final glimpse into Patterson's pursuit of homiletic fidelity [▶ **Video Example BG9**]. Drawn from 2 Chronicles 20, the context from which Patterson's eternal song comes, the theme of this message is drawn from the final words of King Jehoshaphat's prayer: "Our eyes are upon thee." Patterson begins by recounting the geopolitical struggles that fueled the many battles described in scripture and elsewhere, noting the promise of survival that hovered over each moment of adversity. Then he uses the idea of telephony to define prayer as a two-way conversation, an antiphonal grammar that compels the open-ended conclusion to Jehoshaphat's prayer, which doubles as the title of this message.

With ten minutes left in this sermon, as Patterson recounts the prophetic instruction to "handpick some of your singers ... and hide the army behind the choir," he makes his own expected movement toward song (Musical Example 7). Establishing E as a reciting tone and tonal center, Patterson broadcasts the scripture:

> Let the singers go before the army,
> usually you'd the think the army is gon' protect the singers, but [here the army is being protected by the singers]. (as stated: but here the singers are being protected by the army)
> Let, let, let, Let the army get in the background.
> Put the singers in the front.
> And I know they haven't had choir rehearsal, but it's a short song.
> And it won't take long for them to learn it.
> All they gotta do is say: "Praise the lord for his mercy endureth forever"
>
> Now, wait a minute that's not no whole song! Sometimes all you need is a chorus.
> Sometimes you don't need no three, don't need no three or four verses.
> All you need is just a lil tune to hum.
> Put the army behind the choir
> and let 'em march toward their enemy.
> And as they march toward their enemy just let everybody sing:
> "Praise the lord for his mercy endureth forever."

Situated in his message's heightened musical frame, Bishop Patterson marched toward his text's narrative conclusion—the improbable victory that followed this unlikely act of singing. Patterson's deliberate approach to this point of culmination was punctuated by a series of narrative asides, each of which drew members of his audience into a more intimate relationship with the ancient scriptural scene by asserting its relevance to their current circumstances. Along the way he added to the two renderings of the eternal song two contrafact utterances of its text and three articulations of the eternal riff that is theorized in Chapter 2. The admixture of this oft-preached scripture, the eternal song, and the eternal riff yoked this homiletic event to other sermonic contexts, drawing believers out of their immediate space-time into an ecstatic space where resounds an eternal transmission.

Before the last utterance of the eternal song, Patterson uses an anecdote about preparing for one of the church's recording projects to com-

Example 7. Eternal song in E major, Temple of Deliverance Church, Memphis, Tennessee, November 5, 2006.

ment on the kinds of musical scaffolding songs often require. Looking in the direction of his secretary, Evangelist O'Tanya Allen, Patterson recalled:

> And when we trying to put together that first album, you know of old songs, we were sitting in there (and if she can get a little music behind her, she don't sound so bad) but we were sitting in there [laughs] we were sitting in the conference room, and didn't have no music. And start tryna sing some old songs. And I heard her singing, and I said: "What's that?" She said, "You know that song." And then the next thing you know somebody, Brother Spight, came, but he couldn't get it together either. I think Bro. Spight came and somebody else and finally we got a little music, and I said, "Oh, yeah, I know that song." Just needed a little music to go with it. Oh, y'all not listening to me! And sometimes you gotta have music before the song makes any sense. But sometimes God puts it way down in your spirit, and if you don't have the organ, if you don't have the guitar string, if you don't have anybody to help you with some instrumental music, way down on the inside you start humming the tune.

In Patterson's memory three levels of musicality interact: song, instrumental accompaniment, and a deeper vocal instrumentality. In the first instance music seems to be what song relies on for its aural contextualization. On this point he seems to have in mind the kind of harmonic and metrical infrastructure that, though implied by a melody, might in some cases be hard to imagine. Only when accompanied do certain songs make sense. But, although it often provides the kind of context that enables song to "make sense," instrumental accompaniment is not the only source of musical clarity. Rather, Patterson contends that a different kind of musical intelligence can be accessed if a singer is willing to reach "way down on the inside" to find and hum a heightened form of song: he calls this a "tune."

Grounded in Broadcast Religion, a context where "tuning up" and "tuning in" are such essential formulations, Patterson's word of choice is instructive. Moreover, his substitution of "tune" for "song" suggests a shift in scale, a preference for smallness that Chapter 5 defines as "the logic of the prayer cloth." Patterson's comment accents the two kinds of musicality that structure his sermons: first, there is the syllabic, chanted musicality that pervades these messages; second, there are the three emblems of homiletic endurance: the eternal song, the eternal riff, and the eternal pitch. As they inject a heightened form of musicality into a message's already-musical unfolding, these musical devices help the sermon "make sense," unleashing an interworldly intelligence that seems to be inextricable from sacred writ. In the sermon at hand, the eternal song, the recurring musical exegesis of 2 Chronicles 20, brings congregants within earshot of everlasting mercy. With these ecstatic gestures Patterson does to his voice and to his previous sermons what he has made a life of doing to scripture. I refer to these routine appearances as instances of Pentecostal playback. These repetitive acts are phonogenic, creative "voicings of communicative behavior [designed] for sonic mediation across time and space."[27] Patterson's eternal song and eternal riff are self-consciously made to be recorded, reproduced, technologically disseminated along with their many other appearances.

But there is a deeper phonogenicity at work in Patterson's catalog. The ease with which Patterson recalls the smallest details of his chosen story also evidences the fidelity of his homiletic broadcast. The prodigious recall often accented by his television broadcast's text overlay shows up in this context in a host of proper names. After noting the social insignificance of the Levite discussed in the text, he tells the audience that his name was Jehaziel. Pointing down to his right, he recites the path that will be traveled by the Southern Kingdom's enemies: "They're coming up by cliff of Ziz; and ye shall find them at the end of the brook, before the wilderness of Jeruel." Though these details could have been omitted, Patterson chooses to recount them. While I might have ended the previous sentence with the phrase "from memory," it is not so clear that remembrance is what Patterson is offering his congregation. Recalling Mance Aytchan's assertion that the narrative specificity of Patterson's manuscript-less preaching made some wonder if he was *in* the Old Testament, helping to write it, I suggest that these feats of memory support his sermons' chief broadcasting aesthetic: fidelity.

It is in this context that Patterson's eternal song is extended as a valuable reproduction of the events recounted in sacred writ. Alongside Patterson's many expressions of the phrases "I hear" and "the Lord says," the eternal song, in conjunction with the eternal riff, reveals that his religious imagination and homiletic praxis is built on a phonographic conception of scripture. His technophilic Pentecostalism moves past philosopher Walter Ong's apposite and well-worn claim that sound "is the most productive [sensory source] of understanding and unity, the most personally human, and in this sense closest to the divine."[28] This phonographic conception of scripture is a central component of Patterson's Broadcast Religion, his thoroughgoing fascination with the social process of sound reproduction, which, when combined with his Pentecostal theology, yields the twin convictions that preachers can be more or less effective at relaying the eternal transmission and that sermons can be more or less faithful reproductions of the eternal message. The question of fidelity is further clarified by the eternal song, which provides a rare moment when the collective joins Bishop Patterson in song, clarifying the sociality of his Broadcast Grammar. Patterson's pursuit of homiletic fidelity derives efficacy from the audile techniques of his many audiences, believers whose practice of what I have elsewhere termed "the Gospel Imagination," leaves them convinced that musical sound can turn spiritual power into a physical reality.[29]

As this chapter has shown, Bishop Patterson's Broadcast Religion, his sermons' pursuit of ecstasy, is apparent at two levels of homiletic design. Patterson's voice lends a sounding reality to his selected sacred text by converting the sermonic theme into an experiential and musical destination and by amplifying brief ideas into viral and interworldly moments, enabling the message's transmitter and receivers to march deeper into the world of a given text. Homiletic fidelity is the prized result of this movement from tuning up to tuning in; it is a subjective evaluation of the degree of Afterliveness a sermon grants to the contents of scripture. Fueled by the interaction of a scripture's plot, a sermon's thematic trajectory, and its musical teleology, Patterson's Broadcast Grammar performs a communal acceleration that stops only after it achieves a kind of escape velocity—a moment when a message's unfolding is briefly overshadowed by the sound of an eternal transmission.

4 Broadcast Frequency, or The Politics of Key

Before beginning a 2004 sermon at COGIC's Ninety-seventh Annual Holy Convocation, Bishop Patterson turned away from the vast audience in front of him, facing the band that was situated behind him—stage right [▶ **Video Example BF1**]. Looking in the direction of the group of musicians tasked with accompanying him that night, Patterson made the following request: "Before I go to the scripture, give me B♭ back there, Brother Derrick Jackson." Jackson, one of Patterson's traveling accompanists and one of the denomination's best-known keyboardists, played a conventional organ lick, establishing B♭ as the tonal center. After pausing for a minute to orient himself in this new tonal environment, Patterson dedicated the song he was about to sing to those who "feel like you've just worked and worked in the church and the church don't appreciate you [or] your family," to those who sometimes "feel kinda like nobody cares." Patterson sang a free-flowing version of Lucie Campbell's hymn "He'll Understand, He'll Say Well Done."

The reason for the request came into focus as he rendered the first verse of Campbell's hymn: "If when you give the best of your service telling the world that the Savior is come, be not dismayed when men don't believe you. He'll understand, he'll say well done." Rather than taxing the upper reaches of the Bishop's voice, this song challenges the bottom end. Thus it is easy to imagine that Patterson might have started the song in too low a key if not for Jackson's instrumental incipit. While Patterson sang each of his many trademark congregational songs in multiple keys over the course of his career, that day he asked to be placed in B♭, grounded in a sonic environment that would help him navigate this song's wide-ranging vocal line. But asking for a key in which to sing that hymn reversed the typical flow of musical responsibility in Patterson's sermons. He would normally land on a reciting tone, a pitch class that determines the tonal context in which his band would sustain a sermon's ecstatic frame. Indeed, just a half hour after this sermonic selection, when Patterson tuned up at the end of that day's message, "Strategies for Victory," he rested on and in A♭, one of his most common keys—a familiar place from which to preach yet another sermon, a message that ends where this book begins: the eternal song.

The differing approaches Bishop Patterson takes to musical orientation during two segments of a single service raises a set of questions: What, for Patterson, is a key? How does the idea of a tonal center organize his interactive and interworldly messages? Across decades of his career, and at the level of the individual sermon, how do these musical systems shape religious experience? This chapter seeks to understand the tonal phenomenology of Patterson's sermons. I examine the interrelated and interworldly politics of key and pitch in his messages, sonic relationships that formalize the interaction between Patterson, band, and congregation, and between the material world and the realm whose presence the sermons broadcast. Key, I argue, functions as an emergent sonic infrastructure, which, when combined with an antiphonal atmosphere, produces an immersive musical environment. While the preacher's reciting tone dictates the emerging tonal center, the key intersects with the affordances of the Bishop's instrument, structuring his improvisational performance.

Across decades of Bishop Patterson's preaching, and in a host of tonal contexts, one note—B4—recurs over and over again. This reverberant pitch functions as a resonant frequency, a definable musical telos that Patterson understands as essential to his capacity to vocalize ecstasy. Given its frequent place as the highest note in, and the very last note of, Patterson's sermons, this one sonority transcends both space and time. As the last note uttered in Patterson's last sermon, it seems central to his practice of Afterliveness. Serving as an antenna that connects a specific sermon to an eternal transmission, this pitch is a sonorous channel through which Patterson brings his congregations into the presence of God.

"HE KNEW WHERE HE WANTED TO GO": TRAJECTORY AND TONALITY

I argued in Chapter 3 that Bishop Patterson's articulation of the routine movement from speech into song, characteristic of many forms of Black Christian preaching, should be understood as a Broadcast Grammar. I showed that his messages become musical just as they arrive at their central argument, allowing these two items of attention to reinforce each other. This customary emergence of homiletical song begets a musical environment that foments intimacy with a biblical scene. At the center of this new kind of audible orientation is the sense of being in a key. In Patterson's message this central aspect of tonal phenomenology acquires interworldly significance, functioning as a crucial lever with which he "turns the dial," bringing each sermon into contact with an eternal transmission.

Over the course of Patterson's musical life, he delivered sermons marshalling each of the twelve notes of the equal tempered scale as a tonal center. He settled on C as a tonal center in "God's Plan Can Be Altered but Not Cancelled" (2000) and "When the Dust Settles" (2005). D♭ functioned as a tonic for "The Password" (2001) and "Where Are Your Eyes Focused" (1997). Patterson rested in D as a sonic environment for "The Dawn of a New Day" (1990) and "There's Power in the Blood" (2001). He lighted on E♭ as a tonic for "Call His Name" (2000) and "Don't Ask God How, Just Follow His Instructions" (2003). "The Power of Preaching" (1983) and "Learn When It's Your Mail" (2006) climaxed in E. Patterson established F as a tonal center for "Lord, Let Your Glory Fill This House" (1999) and "Psalm 37" (2003). "Neither Were They Thankful" (1993) and "God in Jesus Christ Made the Difference" (1995) ended in G♭. Patterson established G as a tonal center for "Infallible Proofs" (2004) and "God Can" (2006). "The Saint's Remedy in Times of Trouble" (1998) and

"Job 42:10" (2006) both ended in A♭. He established A as a tonic in "The God of All Supply" (1989) and "Living the Abundant Life" (2004). "A Compassionate Father" (2005) and "A Second Touch" (1990) concluded in B♭. "The Next Fifteen Years" (1990) and "Philippians 2:5–11" (2006) culminated in B.

While Patterson's engagement with so many keys points to both the centrality of key to his preaching and the expansive range of his vocal instrument, his Broadcast Grammar brought him back to certain musical contexts over and over again. When I asked Mance Aytchan, Patterson's long-serving minister of music, about the tonal centers that sustained his pastor's homiletic broadcasts, Aytchan replied: "His preaching key was a COGIC key, A♭."[1] As these words illuminate Patterson's practice, they also highlight the fundamental sociality of the musical system known as the key. Knowing that A♭ was a kind of sweet spot for Bishop Patterson helped Aytchan to navigate any specific homiletic event. If Patterson began the musical phase of his sermon in an unusual location, Aytchan knew not to get comfortable in that place. "If he got somewhere that was difficult . . . I knew he wasn't gonna stay there." Often, Patterson would return from song to speech in order to reorient himself in a more advantageous tonal context. But he needed to initiate such a change, not Aytchan or any other musician. In fact, Aytchan recalled a sermon when he tried to give Bishop Patterson too much help: "The worst thing you could ever do was try to force him to a key because that musician in him would kick in." Aytchan learned this lesson the hard way: "I had that experience one time, he was in G, so I tried to put him [in A♭] where I knew he wanted to be. He said, no, go back to where I was."

When Bishop Patterson was going to sing—a song, that is, not a sermon—he took a different approach to this kind of musical orientation. As the chapter's opening vignette demonstrates, Patterson would sometimes ask to be grounded in a key, saying, in Aytchan's words, "'Give me F,' 'put me in B♭.'" Or, if Patterson was going to sing Andrae Crouch's "Through It All," he might ask for C♯. Aytchan suggests that the attention Patterson paid to key grew from his expressive intention and deep knowledge of his instrument: "He knew where he wanted to go. He knew his key." Clearly the notion of a musical key was vital to Patterson's performance as a primary channel through which he interacted with his ensemble and audiences. How to describe this dispositional force? A space for musical activity? A place from which to pursue transcendence? An occasional point of contestation? In the context of Bishop Patterson's Broadcast Religion, what kind of thing is a key?

A POLITICS OF KEY

Before reading the scripture from which he would preach on Easter Sunday 2006, Bishop Patterson decided to sing a bluesy congregational version of the hymn "How Much I Owe" [▶ Video Example BF2]. Looking behind him, in the direction of his musicians, Patterson sang "How much I owe for love divine," moving up from B♭3 to D♭4, before falling to a "worried" G3. As he sang these opening words, his band, choir, and congregation struggled to lock into this song. Since this was one of Patterson's standards—a song he in fact recorded on the first volume of *Singing the Old Time Way*—the audible difficulty could not have betrayed a lack of knowledge of the tune's rhythmic or harmonic framework. Yet there was something else that needed to be grasped.

While Patterson, undeterred by the efforts to locate his elusive tonic, continued with the hymn's second line, his body's suspended stance demonstrated the instability that reigned during this brief period of discovery. When, at the end of the song's second line, he fell from B♭3 down the blues scale to E♭3, Patterson, who was still facing the band, instructed his accompanying musicians: "Get in my key!" By the time he finished issuing this directive, the band had found their way into this performance's E♭ blues tonality. As they shuffled in this newly defined key, Patterson finally turned back to face the congregation, relaxing into the grounding force of this tightly regulated musical environment. Although much could be said about the details that complicated this brief exercise in key-finding—including the underdetermined melodic content of the song's first line and the lingering effects of the preceding song's A♭ tonality—I want to stress that this rare moment of struggle discloses the role key plays in Patterson's innumerable songs, sermons, and prayers.

Keys, I contend, functioned as musical infrastructures for Patterson's Broadcast Religion. A choice made in view of where "he wanted to go," the key simultaneously organizes the interaction of individuals and governs the motions of various sonic entities. In Patterson's sermons both the pervasive practice of "tuning up" and the distinctive, broadcast homiletic of "tuning in" depend on *tuning* itself. As Patterson settles on a reciting tone, he instructs the band about which tonal environment should house the musical phase of his sermon, a liminal space whose alterity foments a congregation's intimacy with a biblical scene. Yes, the palpable sense of being *in* a key is vital to the experience of being *inside* the scripture. When all of the interpersonal and interworldly effects of an emerging tonal center are considered together, these phenomena collectively disclose a politics of key. Of course, key is always political, inasmuch as it is both derived from and sustaining of a set of sonic power relations. As it organizes preacher, band, and congregation, key also becomes an axis of an interpersonal politics, operating both within a single sanctuary and across an expansive denomination. On this subject music theorist David Temperley refers to both metrical structure and harmony as an "'infrastructure' for tonal music," likening each to "a network of basic structure" and a means to an end.[2] To elucidate this dimension of Patterson's media concept, I follow media theorist John Durham Peters's view of infrastructures as "the habitats and materials through which we act and are."[3]

According to Peters, the media-theoretic interest in infrastructures seeks to "make environments visible," illuminating the "logistical media," whose function is to "organize and orient, to arrange people and property, often into grids." Peters contends that these media "both coordinate and subordinate, arranging relationships among people and things." While Peters discusses the infrastructural efficacy of concepts like the point and the number zero, the tonic exerted an analogous organizing force in Patterson's musical settings. As an infrastructure, key linked preacher, band, and congregation in a heightened sonic environment, an audible topography that fueled the Broadcast Grammar of Patterson's sermons. Key itself became a "sensational form," an agent of immersion that helped the sermonic broadcasts to bring believers into contact with an eternal transmission.[4]

The politics of key comes into relief through a reconsideration of Bishop Patterson's eternal song. Tracking multiple articulations of the recurring exegesis of 2 Chronicles 20, the eternal song, across years and between

Example 8. Eternal song in A♭ major, Temple of Deliverance Church, Memphis, Tennessee, 2003.

sermons offers a clearer sense of the work that key does for Patterson's preaching. While the 2001 sermon, "Dealing with Life's Battles," drew its text and focus from 2 Chronicles 20, the biblical context for Patterson's eternal song, the recurrence of this musical fragment in two sermons in 2002 and 2003 constitutes a different kind of sermonic construction. In "It's Time for You to Sing Your Song" (2002) and "Strategies for Victory" (2003), Patterson engrafts this musical set piece into a message built on a different text [▶ **Video Example BF3**]. While the shared themes of military struggle and improbable singing offer one rationale for this homiletic decision, their shared tonal environment of A♭ formed an even more important link between these messages and Patterson's eternal song. Indeed, there are other correspondences in Patterson's catalog that suggest that his engagement with a text and theme is bound up with a key. For example, two presentations of "Arrows of the Lord's Deliverance," in 1990 and 1999, both concluded with G♭ as a tonal center. In the case of Patterson's eternal song, the refrain and the key offer each other mutual forms of definition. The sonic infrastructure of A♭ grounds the falling melody, imbuing this sounding material with scale degree qualia. At the same time, the eternal song gives the A♭ tonal center a fleeting major definition (Musical Example 8).

Departing from an A♭ blues' pendular third, this melody's use of the major third precipitates several concomitant conversions: (1) a syllabic, hymnlike tune takes the place of Patterson's melismatic blues lines, while (2) the iteration and reiteration of this tune prompts band and congregation to abandon antiphony. Instead of punctuating his utterance with percussive chords, the band accompanies the eternal song as if it were a hymn, moving from I-V/ii-ii-V-I. Instead of affirming the Bishop's messages with improvised interjections, both choir and congregation sing Patterson's eternal song in time with the preacher. And this brief bit of music gives a fleeting definition to mode. In so doing, it sharpens the sense of being in a key, and this increasing tonal definition is a vital effect through which this brief bit of singing inculcates intimacy with an ancient scene. As I have argued, this increases the audible fidelity of Patterson's sermonic transmission. Like the eternal riff, this movement within the song's heightened musical frame is an important point of inflection. These recurring moments are ecstasy's ecstasy. As they join forces with other iterations in other sonic events, they announce the presence of a resonance that exists outside the spatiotemporal constraints of any single sermon. Thus these musical phenomena resound the afterlife of ecstasy.

The structuring force of musical key also helps clarify the differences between the emergence of this song in the first years of the twenty-first century and in the last months of Bishop Patterson's life. That "Focusing Our Eyes upon the Lord" and "Jehoshaphat's Prayer and God's Answer" concluded in E and F, respectively, makes for a rather arresting contrast against the three preceding versions of this musical item. Whether lowered by a major or minor third, both of these new tonal environments point to the effects of extended illness on Patterson's voice. Since the falling octave woven into the melody that would emerge at the climax of both these sermons would require that Patterson spend much more of the sermon on the higher version of his reciting tone than on the lower one, E4 and F4 would seem much more manageable places to land than A♭4. The affordances of these different tonal contexts are evident in the transposed versions of Patterson's eternal song. These sermons' arrival at this familiar place in these unfamiliar keys lends the eternal song some of the portability that had long been the defining characteristic of the eternal riff. That all this happens in the face of Patterson's declining health allows the transcendence of key to foreshadow the endurance of the sermons in question. The repetition of these ideas during Patterson's life prefigures the reverberation of his message long after the messenger went to his final rest.

ANTIPHONY IN/AND/AS ATMOSPHERE

How did the musicality that consistently fueled Bishop Patterson's movement into religious ecstasy generate the call to which his afterlife responds?

My understanding of the antiphonal relationship between the form of Patterson's sermons and the endurance of his message beyond the grave is indebted to Shana Redmond's investigation of Paul Robeson's decades-long career and even lengthier musical afterlife. In *Everything Man: The Form and Function of Paul Robeson,* Redmond writes that Robeson "lived life through melodies that often lasted less than three minutes," a musical existence that "moves quickly and appears widely," requiring the analyst to "listen to [Robeson's] antiphonal life."[5]

Fueled by media infrastructures, like-minded collectives, and a voluminous vocal instrument, Robeson continues to live in communities that span this planet. Analogous to Robeson, Patterson's lifelong preoccupation with religious broadcasting found expression on multiple scales of time, in sermons that could stretch from thirty minutes to an hour and in extraordinarily brief, but memorable moments whose ecstatic force caused them to simultaneously stand apart from their temporal surroundings while adhering to other expressions of eternal pitch. These flashes of religious ecstasy reveal a life not susceptible to ordinary death. Their apartness resonates with what Redmond calls Robeson's "antiphonal life," a presence grounded in the paradoxical endurance of brief units of performance, enactments that forged links between songs, traditions, performers, and worlds. "This connection is characteristic of the spirituals that Robeson made famous," Redmond writes, "which rely on antiphony: the call-and-response that kept him in constant communication and negotiation with new publics all over the world. This (inter)play as well as Paul's play in other forums was the antiphonal life that made him vibrate over a forty-year career."[6]

Vibration is an appropriate term for Patterson's career too. Resonance, endurance, reverberation—these three terms accurately describe the work Patterson continues to do for many believers, in the Church of God in Christ and beyond. As the sermons and songs that materialize his digital presence circulate between various virtual venues, they show that the antiphonal character of an individual performance points far beyond any single sonic retort. As Redmond notes of Robeson, "the repetition of a call is met by his response in and beyond the time of physical animation."[7] As antiphony is imagined in a "nonlinear and open-ended" fashion, it is understood as an ongoing work, an "exchange [that] is not only phonic or working as we expect phonics should but exists in complicated tension and exchange with sound and language as well as a host of other media and modalities."[8]

The response to Patterson's ministry certainly involves the tremendous efforts spent to keep him alive after his physical death—from the staff that produces weekly telecasts to social media users who upload, share, and like online videos. These affective labors constitute the mediated "after" to the Bishop's musical "life." As they relay fragments of Patterson's sermons, these followers enact forms of digital cultural production that extend the ecstatic energy emanating from the messages' accumulating layers of antiphony—emerging between Patterson and band, Patterson and congregation, and Patterson and his lead guitarist, Walter Dunlap. Building on the infrastructure provided by the musical key, this plural antiphony creates an immersive atmosphere, central to both the broadcast of a scripture's contents and the posthumous reverberation of Patterson's messages.

DAVID'S DAY OF THANKSGIVING

In a sermon delivered on Thanksgiving Day 2005, Bishop Patterson returned to one of his canonical scriptures, 2 Samuel 6:14, following a text that recounts the return of the Ark of the Covenant to the seat of ancient Israel's power: the city of David. After noting that he "sometimes liked to preach without a theme or topic," Patterson begrudgingly titled the message "David's Day of Thanksgiving." Early in the message, he recalls that while David "had had many victories as it relates to going out on the battlefield and defeating the enemies of Israel, there was a spiritual longing" to repossess what was regarded as an emblem of the divine's presence, an object of worship which had been lost during a military battle.

Patterson's sermon marshals David's embodied response to the victory of the day as a model for the kind of thanksgiving that this worship service should elicit. While this and other similar worship events represent the repurposing of an American holiday for a religious purpose, the sermon sought to build a bridge between the time of the text and the moment of its declaration. Patterson spends the early moments of the sermon winding through biblical history, setting the stage for David's ascendance to Israel's throne and for the loss of the Ark of the Covenant, both of which were preconditions for the events recorded in the sermonic text. When Patterson's historical narrative—delivered without reference to prepared notes—arrives at David's reign, his proclamation begins its gradual shift toward a discernible pitch. This characteristic inflection, this articulation of "tuning up," takes advantage of one of the scripture's discordant tones:

> Well, he made one mistake. The ark had been out of their presence for so long and many of the priests had not kept up with the law concerning how this holy vessel was to be handled. So, David takes thirty thousand people and they go to get the ark and he decides, well, maybe the best way for me to bring it back is to get a new cart. Let this presence of God ride on a new cart. But while the oxen was pulling the cart, one writer says that "he stumbled." But whatever happened to the oxen, it caused the ark to start to shake and start to look like it was gonna fall off the cart. And here was a man that wanted to do good. It's one thing to want to do good, but it's another to know the rules concerning the good you want to do. Here is a good man by the name of Uzzah. When he saw the ark looking like it was about to fall, his instinct, his concern, caused him to put out his hand, touch the ark, and try to keep it from falling. But what he didn't realize is that the ark was not supposed to be touched by human hands.

In the story Uzzah dies because his hand touches the ark. Uzzah's death interrupts the redemptive mission, necessitating a second attempt for the journey that unfolds in the sermonic text.

As this series of events is outlined, Patterson's voice settles on the B3, constructing B as a tonal center. As the forthcoming discussion will make clear, B major is another one of Patterson's recurring keys, a musical domain the preacher routinely locates even without instrumental prodding. While Patterson's turn to musicality might be thought of as a heightened response to his oration's call, antiphony becomes the sermon's prevailing musical characteristic. Indeed, antiphony seems to become the condition of his sermons' musicality. As he settles on a pitch, the preacher's pace of speech slows down, marking a contrast to the preceding speech, while creating space for his band's forthcoming instrumental interjections—musical comments that regularize the audience's manifold reactions. The rhythmic cadence that emerges joins together the congregational and instrumental responses to create an antiphonal matrix, a sonic environment that these believers use to collapse the distance between twenty-first-century Memphis and the space-time of scripture.

While the audience's shouts of praise pervade the sermon's ecstatic frame, Patterson's capacious pauses let their sound break through. The emergence of this collective utterance is amplified by the percussive snare and kick drum attack that accompanies Patterson's breathing. In this conjunction, band and audience become entrained to the preacher's cadence, iterating a flexible backbeat that helps to construct a malleable metrical environment. That this communal performance is tied to the Bishop's inhalation clarifies that this intensely social expression is an exhalation of "Blackpentecostal breath."[9] And these moments of imitation are a synchronous microrepresentation of the devotional network Patterson's voice anchors on both sides of the grave.

Soaring above this sermon's antiphonal texture are three moments when Bishop Patterson and the lead guitarist, Walter Dunlap, engage in a striking dialogue, an interchange that claims attention even amid the surfeit of call-and-response [▶ **Video Example BF4**]. This new thread in the performance's antiphonal matrix begins at 7:04, when Patterson turns to the guitarist and says, "I don't wanna ride." The next two nodal points are characterized by a movement from ordinary language. At 8:27, Patterson exclaims "mmhm mhmm" on the tenor F♯, and the lead guitarist's answer begins with the same note on a wah-wah pedal before departing into melisma. At 9:11 the Bishop makes a falsetto declaration, sliding from A♯ to B. As the guitar echoes this ascending slide, this interchange clarifies the mutual instrumentalization of voice and guitar that animates this—and many other—Patterson performances. The gesture wherein Patterson turned to face the band is paramount as a physical embodiment of this message's communal essence—its participation in a community that far surpasses boundaries of space and time, even as it makes its presence known in the bodies of believers.

In the final stage of his broadcast of this text, Bishop Patterson takes off his suit jacket, metaphorically and physically coming out of his clothes to embody the scripture's report that King David disrobed himself in a fit of ecstatic movement. Patterson danced just as David danced. As in every other aspect of the sermon, Patterson did not shout alone. Their leader's embodiment of praise is all the permission congregants needed to partake of communal corporeal ecstasy, an experience that cannot be extinguished by ordinary death.

HE CARES FOR YOU

"He Cares for You," a sermon Bishop Patterson delivered in July 2005, broadcasts gospel narratives of a storm Jesus's disciples faced while he slept. Although the message is explicitly drawn from Mark 4:35–41, Patterson moves across the versions of the story presented in the New Testament's two other synoptic gospels, Luke and Matthew. The message's drama arises from the mismatch between the storm's vehemence and Jesus's sound sleep, a tension that prompted his companions to wonder if he cared. Patterson's affirmative answer to the question, the assertion that "he cares for you," converts the storm described in scripture into encouragement for his assembled audience.

In "He Cares for You," alongside the multiparametric antiphony addressed in the previous example, a homiletic chorality emerges as Patterson moves between registers of voice, expanding the category of antiphony to also name the interaction between the multiple speakers that he is presencing. In one frame of this performance, Patterson ceases to speak to the congregants, choosing instead to speak for them. In this heightened musical space, he staggers across the cavernous pulpit, giving voice to the audience's concern, their iterative uncertainty about divine care. Giving contemporary relevance to the question posed in the sermonic text, Patterson exclaims:

> Do you care that my bills are stacked and I can't pay 'em?
> Do you care that confusion is tearing my house asunder?
> Do you care that I'm a youngster and I'm in a storm of peer pressure?
> Do you care that sickness is in my body?
> Jesus didn't open his mouth to say one word because he already had a volume of scripture—the word was already there to show how he cares.

With these four amplifying queries, Patterson, who is closing in B again, reverses the pitch contour of spoken question, using the first three words of each interrogative to climb up the scale, before falling to a cadence on the baritone B. These anaphoric statements are shaped into a narrative flow by the incipit. The first statement marches up from scale degree 3 to 5. The second iterates scale degree 5. The third reaches over 5 to resound on scale degree 6. And the fourth mirrors the second, sitting on scale degree 5. The fifth line of this segment moves still higher to the subtonic, marking that most significant word "Jesus" as a site of special emphasis. From this summit the line stays suspended until the end of the phrase, the site of melodic repose.

This section's end calls forth the next move, in which Patterson enumerates the scriptures that demonstrate Jesus's care. Audience members who were familiar with Patterson's style—and the tradition he exemplifies—could anticipate that Patterson's utterance "the word was already there" would lead to a litany of biblical recitations, echoes of an eternal transmission breaking into their sanctuary. In like manner they could expect the overall shape of the Bishop's melody to retain its basic character. True to form, as this next phrase starts, Patterson returns to the rising-and-falling melodic character of the preceding questions:

> He had already said, in Psalm 103, like a father pitieth his children, so the Lord pitieth them that fear him.
> He had already said that God is a God of compassion.
> He had already shown his love
> So he didn't say a word
> When he was asked do you care
> He gets up and wipes the sleep from his eyes
> And He didn't speak but two words
> One of them was peace
> And when he said peace
> The wind stopped blowing

Just as the story seems to end, the Bishop turns back to a more traditional declamatory register to say: "I want you to know that it may be windy in your life. It may be stormy in your life. And you're saying . . ." The ellipses mark Patterson's double movement: the Bishop goes back to speaking on the audience's behalf, but he uses well-known song lyrics to do it [▶ Video Example BF5a]. Patterson intones:

> You're saying, Master
> The tempest is raging
> The billows are tossing high
> Sky is o'ershadowed with blackness
> No shelter or hope is not
> Carest thou not that we perish
> How can thou lie asleep?
> When each moment so madly is threatening
> A grave in the angry deep
> Get up, Jesus
> Oh, the wind . . .

While it is abundantly clear that Patterson is reanimating the lyrics to "Peace Be Still," up until this point, it was not clear if he was summoning the hymn written by William Herbert Brewster, a Memphis pastor of a previous generation, or the renowned rearrangement recorded by James Cleveland and the Angelic Choir of the First Baptist Church of Nutley, New Jersey. "Get Up, Jesus," one of James Cleveland's oft-repeated ad-libs, clarifies the version Patterson had in mind through vocalic expression. But the foregoing ambiguity is productive: it multiplies the voices being brought to bear on that situation. As Patterson moves between strands of tradition, from his gospel text to the lyrics of a gospel song, the song's lyrics are braided into his overarching melodic scheme yielding a nested experience of contrafactum, an antiphonal effect that leads to a new affective peak.

After Patterson exclaims "Oh, the wind," moving syllabically from A-F♯-E-D, he staggered across the stage, enacting a gaping silence that his musicians and congregants gladly filled with praise. Again, he hollers "Oh, the wind," this time lingering on the "Oh" in a manner that some gospel singers call a "squall." Repeating this line made these words serve as their own answer. Hanging out between the fifth and flattened seventh, Patterson moved on to "and the waves" before cadencing on "will obey your will." Then he went back up to the podium, gripping the microphone, gesturing with his right hand, and hunching over. He growled "all you got to do," moving from A-G-F♯-E-F♯ before rising and falling one more time, exclaiming, "is say peace be still." Done with the song's lyrics, Patterson vamped:

Wind stop blowing
Water lay down
Everything . . .

The affect of these three equivalent declarations demonstrates the interpenetration of repetition, antiphony, and musicality in the Bishop's preaching. As he left the audience to fill in his textual elisions with "will be alright," he returns back to the podium, clarifying his intent to make another point before taking his seat. Patterson then lifts the synoptic gospels' three distinct descriptions of the disciples' faith. Before he finishes, Patterson speaks of another song that was played as an instrumental solo, noting that even though his audience may not have intuited it without lyrics, it conveys the same message: "Jesus cares for you."

Weaving in yet another thread of tradition, Patterson moved from the gospel story's description of Peter to the epistle attributed to Peter, offering a recitation that ends with Peter declaring the sermon's title: "He Cares for You." Patterson's movement between biblical traditions is amplified by the video editing that superimposes an image of each scriptural source on the screen during each of the Bishop's utterances. These postproduction impositions reveal the multitude of voices collected in any single Patterson sermon while elevating scripture as the most authoritative expression of the eternal word and Patterson's voice as an ideal vessel of truth—an oracle of Christ (Figure 7).

Antiphony is productive. What results from all this antiphony? How to describe in spatial terms what I have described as audible fidelity and affective intimacy? Atmosphere, namely an antiphonal atmosphere, is one way to think about the places that were built by Patterson's sermonic broadcasts. During these sermons interlocking forms of antiphony generate a kind of atmosphere, a polysemous phrase that for these purposes "refers to a shared sense of affective intensity and is described as occupying an immersive, resonant, and spherical spatiality, much like sound itself."[10] The notion of atmosphere is familiar in Bishop Patterson's context for, as Alisha Lola Jones notes: "Within historically African American Pentecostal worship, a minister's capability to get to God instantly and use God's present into worship seamlessly is referred to in the vernacular as 'setting the atmosphere.'"[11]

Figure 7. Screenshot of 1 Peter 5:7 from Bishop G. E. Patterson's sermon "He Cares for You," Memphis, Tennessee, Sunday, July 10, 2005.

While Patterson's atmospheric labors are more emergent than instant, it is safe to say that this concern was often on his mind. In myriad sermons and exhortations, notions of divine presence and glory were prominently featured. This palpable sense of access to God was inextricable from a deep connection to the musicians and believers with whom he shared room—both at Temple of Deliverance and "in auditoriums across America."[12] These physical structures scaffold the embodied experience of sonic intensity. As the tonal force of key grounds the mounting sonic materiality of cascading calls and responses, these audible energies produce an inhabitable musical place—an immediate sense of being-together *within* something else. What is made together envelops those who produce it, enclosing them in an encompassing exterior for, as anthropologist Patrick Eisenlohr claims, "atmospheres are distinct entities that exist independently from human subjectivity and can be felt and encountered by bodies," even as they are produced by musical interaction.[13] An antiphonal atmosphere is the sense of place that emerges at the intersection of sound and space—an ecstasy that anchors, even as it opens.

In Chapter 1, I discussed a moment from Patterson's 2005 sermon "A Vicarious Victory," when he used red lighting to "bathe the whole house in the blood of Jesus." Delivered at the apotheosis of his message's ecstatic frame, this re-illumination gave congregants an entrancing view of their redemption. Then I argued that the forceful enshrouding accomplished through the medium of light that day elucidated the striking vocal inflections that characterize Patterson's ministry on many days. I now want to clarify that both immersions—sounding and irradiating—perform the work of "atmosphering." Indeed, Gernot Bohme, one of atmosphere's most influential theorists, observes that these intensive space-times "seem to fill the space with a certain tone of feeling like a haze."[14] "Atmosphering," like the ubiquitous gerund "worlding," is a communal process of which antiphony is an unusually effective musical agent. In Bishop Patterson's sermons multiple, intersecting streams of antiphony produce an affective atmosphere buttressed by the sonic infrastructure of key.

THE ETERNAL PITCH

Even as the sonic infrastructure of key grounds an antiphonal atmosphere, creating a musical environment fit for the broadcast of religion, these modes of musical organization intersect with another structuring force. In journalist David Waters's 1997 article he mentions, almost as an aside, that "his sermons start off low and slow. He's in no hurry. He knows where he's going. The congregation knows he'll get there soon enough."[15] If "there" seems to refer to an indefinite moment in the sermons, or an interworldly experience of religious delight, Patterson's preaching puts a bit of pressure on these assumptions. Across his decades of ministry, "there" often had a definable sonic destination; his sermon's affective and musical trajectories so often pointed to a single note: the tenor B—B4. Indeed, we see this in the final moments of the 2005 sermon "He Cares for You" [▶ **Video Example BF5b**]. After building significant intensity, using A4, the flat seventh of his B tonal context, as a kind of vocal ceiling, Patterson takes the roof off in the final two-and-a-half minutes of his message. Repeatedly and emphatically reaching up to B4, Patterson proclaims:

<u>Oh</u>, the storm, the storm <u>in your life</u>, is only designed to stop you from reaching from your goal.
But oh! <u>If he said let's go to the other side. Nothing is gonna stop you from reaching your goal.</u>
<u>Oh</u>! I wish <u>you'd tell</u> somebody, <u>when the storm</u> is over, <u>I</u> have a destiny to fulfill.
When the <u>storm</u> is <u>over</u>, there's <u>something</u> that <u>God</u> has or<u>dained</u> for me
<u>Eh</u>, when the storm.
<u>Oh! Oh! Oh</u>! When the <u>storm is over</u>
I got a blessing waiting on me.
<u>Oh</u>!
<u>Hey</u>! Hey! Hey!

Each of the underlined words and phrases is delivered from this summit by Patterson, who, with increasing physical affectivity, makes a forceful movement from the narrative present into the promised future, a change of tense that is accented by this musical intensification. This very note recurs over and over again in the fieriest moments of Patterson's pyrotechnic messages, calling each homiletic event into an enduring conversation. In the final moments of a 2000 sermon, "This Is Your Year of Restoration," B4 is the very last note of a sermon delivered in D♭ [▶ **Video Example BF6**]. Similarly, in a 2005 message, "A Cry in Desperation," B4, while not the very last note of the message, is the highest pitch [▶ **Video Example BF7**]. Patterson hits a resounding "hallelujah" in this A♭ tonal environment just after uttering the cry that was the sermon's thematic destination.

Often this recurring pitch appeared after the message seemed to be over. "Your Day Will Come," a 1996 sermon, tells the story of Joseph from Genesis 50, a man whose life was marked by dramatic triumphs and struggles, all separated by a divine promise that a better day would come [▶ **Video Example BF8**]. After reaching the high part of the story, when Joseph was named prime minister to Pharaoh, Patterson delivered the musical phase of this sermon in E, using an anaphoric string of sentences to summarize Joseph's life story:

You meant it for evil, but God meant it for good.
If I hadn't been a dreamer, you never woulda hated me.
If you'd never hated me, you wouldn't put me in the pit.
If you hadn't hated me, you've wouldn't sold me into slavery.
If you hadn't sold me, I never would've met Potiphar.

If I'd never met Potiphar, I never would've met his wife.
If I hadn't met his wife, I wouldn't have ended up in prison.
If I hadn't ended up in prison, I never woulda met Pharaoh.
And if I hadn't met Pharaoh, I wouldn't be the second ruler in Egypt.
But it was all working to bring about my day.

Encouraging his congregation, Patterson says: "I don't know what you're going through. I don't know what you've been through. But your day will come." He puts the mic back on the stand, closes his Bible, turns and faces the ministers and singers behind him. Even if these actions suggested that Patterson might be done with his sermon, the fact that he continues to swing the large white handkerchief, clenched firmly in his hand throughout his sermon, suggested that he was not yet ready to let the message go. This teeming sense of possibility has a musical basis. Preaching in E, the two major sites of emphasis had been the reciting tone E4 and the minor third above it, G4. While his anaphoric run had built considerable intensity, Patterson had not yet ascended into the highest reaches of his voice.

This need to communicate the affective amplification that had made him swing the handkerchief with such abandon prompted him to turn to the microphone, exclaiming "halellu" and reaching, for the first time in this message, up to B4, which is the fifth in this key, joining the pitch's manifold iterations in his other keys. In this new phase of sermonic activity, Patterson leaves the pulpit and walks over to the church's right wing, saying, "I wanna get where I can look you in your face." Seeking a different kind of connection with those whose peripheral location might have made them seem less proximate to the message, he repeatedly reached above the previous ceiling of G4, building up to the final melismatic word "yeah," which falls from B4 down the blues scale to his reciting tone, E. Even by saying, "I'm not coming up to the balcony," Patterson expresses that the thought had come to mind. But he did not need to ascend the stairs to the balcony: having climbed to his voice's familiar apotheosis, the Bishop had already gotten his congregants to ecstasy—a place that might simply be called *there*.

Each of these sermons take place in different keys, the first in B, the second in D♭, the third in A♭, and the fourth in E. In each of these keys, at the climax of his sermon's heightened frame, Patterson finds his way to B4. In a manner of speaking, this was his golden note. Placed at the upper

Example 9. The eternal pitch, Temple of Deliverance Church, Memphis, Tennessee, 1996.

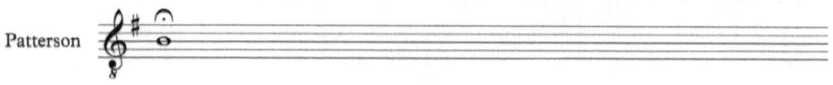

end of his broadcast medium, it optimizes both effort and ability, yielding the characteristic sound of vocalic ecstasy (Musical Example 9).

While in B this top note sounds as a transcendent tonic, it was equally as potent as a blue third above the transcendent tonic in A♭, the blue seventh in D♭, or a triumphant fifth in E. Patterson was so attached to this expression of vocal ecstasy that in a 2001 sermon, "The Password," he seems to equate access to these notes with having his full voice: "I wish I had my voice. I been preaching every night and day probably for the last seventeen or eighteen days. And I'm just a little bit stopped up. But you just don't know what's going on down on the inside." To my ears, Patterson sounds quite good this day, and there are no obvious signs of exertion, save the fact that he does not move above A♭4. What are we to make of this recurring pitch, one whose absence makes Bishop Patterson lament the limitation of his voice?

Since its consistent presence across multiple keys means we cannot refer to it in terms of scale degree qualia, we then need a different category for this singular pitch. What if we call it a "resonant frequency," approximately 494 Hz, an eternal pitch that stretches across decades of Patterson's ministry, tuning each time into a similar sonic portal, a vibrating link between the material world and another. In every homiletic event that it intensifies, this one pitch marks a movement outside the already ecstatic phase of his sermon, connecting with some enduring sonority, the same transmission captured by the eternal song and the eternal riff. Crucially, these sonic bridges do not die with Patterson's physical body, but they fund his posthumous resonance, especially as these recurring musical devices populate the various videos that circulate on television, radio, and across various digital platforms. The frequency of oscillation from which it arises and the frequency of appearance across years of Patterson's life collaborate in the production of eternal pitch.

Patterson's eternal pitch can profitably be compared to the "time-crossing tone" that ethnomusicologist Carol Robertson outlines in her scholarship on the musical practices of the Mapuche, an Andean-Argentinian indigenous group. "Pulling the ancestors," the crux of Mapuche cosmology, was the primary function of a vocal genre called "tayil." For the Mapuche with whom Robertson worked, "performances are always transported across the time barrier by the same pitch."[16] While the various subgenres of tayil are all organized around a different recurring sonority, in each of these "*Chemprali* tones bridge the temporal abyss between present and past, and between the ideals of cosmological time and the realities of mundane, daily experience."[17] Patterson's pitch might also be likened to Messiaen's much-discussed preference for F♯ major, an expressly theological project bound up with the composer's synesthesia and absolute pitch. Although Patterson did not seem to possess perfect pitch, he did have eternal pitch, an enduring capacity to find this critical band of religious ecstasy.

How, one might wonder, does Bishop Patterson remember B4 in the absence of perfect pitch? This is a matter of embodied memory, and that accessing this musical destination is what social anthropologist Paul Connerton terms an "incorporating practice." Connerton notes that these practices "cannot be well accomplished without a diminution of the conscious attention that is paid to them."[18] As such, these "bodily automatisms ... provide a particularly effective system of mnemonics," or, keeping the past in mind, "by a habitual memory sedimented in the body."[19] This recall is anchored in a sweet spot in Patterson's voice, a high B that he is able to belt throughout his life: a bright, weighty, resonant vocalization perfectly suited to his broadcasting instrument. In his sermonic environments this enduring sonic force turns on its head a common definition of key articulated by music theorist Steve Larson as "the most *Stable* pitch on which a melody can end."[20] As Patterson repeatedly finds his way to B4 to end messages in D♭, D, E, A♭, A, and B, he implies that stability is not the destination where he seeks to end. Rather, rapture, disruption, and ecstasy lie at the end of his homiletic trajectory. A 1998 sermon, "The Saint's Remedy in Times of Trouble," makes this ecstatic function especially clear [▶ **Video Example BF9**].

As I noted in Chapter 3, while a period of holy dancing typically followed Patterson's sermons, the conclusion of this particular sermon folded unusually seamlessly into a "praise break." As he foreshortens a string of anaphoric utterances, all beginning with the phrase "I've got to praise him," Patterson elongates the final "praise" and thus omits its aforementioned object. At that very second the percussionist begins to play that fast, rhythmic shouting music, drawing both Patterson and congregation into a synchronized instance of emphatically embodied praise. By the time Patterson made his way to B4, he was already dancing, entranced at the pulpit, moving both arms and legs in time with the music. As he "shouts," he utters this climactic pitch, suggesting that there is some important relationship between the holy dance and his recurring sound of vocalic ecstasy. In contrast to the notion of a tonic, the stability that makes this pitch eternal is produced by the deferral of ending, the habitual emergence of ecstasy that makes this potent sonority a recurring destination. As it transcends keys, each utterance of this kinetic pitch taps into an ongoing transmission, resounding at Patterson's Broadcast Frequency, lending an Afterliveness to his religious ecstasy.

STATION IDENTIFICATION

The idea that a single, stable, sonic force might somehow contribute to the diffusion of spiritual power is a musical and metaphorical feature of Patterson's religious imagination. It is also grounded in one of Patterson's most remarkable material possessions, the 5,000-watt radio transmitter that stands on South Mitchell Road just outside Memphis. Purchased by Patterson's Bountiful Blessings, Inc., for $462,000 in October 1990, WBBP 1480 AM went live on January 4, 1991.[21] Patterson's announcement in the souvenir journal for COGIC's 1991 Holy Convocation (Figure 8) illustrates the audience that could be reached by the station's transmission. The particularities of Memphis's geography cause the station's signal to stretch over three states: Arkansas, Mississippi, and Tennessee. While the radio station went live during the last two decades of Patterson's life and ministry, this accomplishment flowed from one of his ministry's earliest desires. Resounding at the center of a broadcasting assemblage, this transmitter's carrier frequency clarifies the function of the recurring musical devices that are so central to Patterson's eternal pitch; just as

Figure 8. Announcement published in COGIC's Holy Convocation souvenir book about the establishment of radio station WBBP 1480 AM, 1991.

modulations in the amplitude of this radio wave transmit sound to listeners in three states—and, since the station went online in 1999, around the world—the unusual systematicity of Patterson's homiletical musicality enables Patterson's voice to convey spiritual power between worlds.

Returning to Broadcast Religion's constitutive dialectic of mediation and immediacy, these musical expressions of Patterson's Black Pentecostal instrumentality might be understood in terms of station identification, intermittent reminders that auditors are participating in an ongoing broadcast. Station identification is dialectical because to make its claims for immediacy, it must also call attention to the fact of mediation. Patterson often did this quite explicitly, as in his last sermon, when he used televisual broadcasting to explain the incarnation of Jesus Christ. While the materialization of the divine word in the tangible, embodied form of Jesus was the central message of "The Gospel According to John," the ending of this final Christmas Day message hinged on the activation of spiritual power in sonic form:

> "His name shall be called." I could stop right there! His name shall be called wonderful.
> His name shall be called counselor.
> His name shall be called mighty God, everlasting father, prince of peace.
> You see his name got power. But what good is power if you don't use it?
> You can never get the maximum power unless you use it.
>
> It's not enough just to know it.
> You got to learn how to call it.
>
> Call his name!
> When trouble comes, call his name.
> When affliction is in your body, call his name.
> When the enemy is out to destroy you, call his name.
> Whatever's going on in your life, call his name.
>
> Call him! Salvation is in his name.
> Call him!

At the end of this sermon two fragments of eternal pitch emerge, sounding a fitting conclusion to a life of preaching [▶ **Video Example BF10**]. Preaching about the power in Jesus's name, Patterson exhorted his congregation that "learning how to call his name" is the way to "trigger the power." Then Bishop Patterson shows how to do it, one more time. After using the eternal riff to proclaim "I never shall forget," rising from B2 to B3, he leaps, in mere seconds, from B3 to B4, repeatedly uttering the phrase "call him."

Given the vocal demands of this climactic pitch, it is not surprising that Patterson, whose physical weakness required him to preach while seated in his chair, was a bit under the pitch the first time he reached for it. But the second and third time, he locked into the note that had linked so many of his sermons to another world. As he contemplated his own absence from the world he had occupied for more than sixty-five years, Patterson found his way back to the register of voice, the resonance in body, and the realm of spirit that had so often emerged at the intersection of time and eternity. As the last note enunciated in Bishop Patterson's last sermon, the eternal pitch injected a final call into the ongoing resonance that this book defines as Afterliveness.

CONCLUSION

When he spoke at the second of Patterson's three funerals, Shelby County mayor A. C. Wharton seemed to have WBBP AM 1480's radio transmitter in mind. "Bishop Patterson has signed off but he didn't shut down," Wharton suggested. "He's moved on up and will broadcast on a much higher frequency."[22] As he marshalled radio broadcasting as a synecdoche for Patterson's life and afterlife, Wharton used one of the most conspicuous features of Broadcast Religion to describe one of its most ethereal. Afterliveness, the enduring efficacy and Black social life that arises from the immersive power of Patterson's sermons, resonates at the Bishop's Broadcast Frequency, both through the specific sonic techniques that shape Patterson's preaching and the repetitiveness with which they appear.

As this chapter has illustrated, Bishop Patterson's sermonic broadcasts are held together by a politics of key and the affective atmospheres produced by antiphony. The musical key, as an idea and a sounding reality, links preacher, band, and congregation, using their multilayered call-and-responses to organize the ritual participants into something more than the sum of their parts. In the midst of this felt togetherness, an experience of religious ecstasy emerges, a sharpening sense of intimacy with any number of scenes from scripture. When the sermon moves from tuning up to tuning in, the experience of being in a key, shaped by the recurrence of musical devices that point past both sermon and key, enables each homiletic event to come into contact with a gripping transmission of the eternal word. As Patterson's preaching finds eternal pitch, his Broadcast Religion helps his audiences to access ecstasy.

5 Broadcast Ensemble

THE LOGIC OF THE PRAYER CLOTH

In a May 3, 2015, Instagram post then Superintendent Linwood Dillard posted what might have been an unremarkable image of him holding a microphone, dressed in a black robe with red piping. This Memphis-area COGIC minister's caption, however, describes the image as a representation of "one of the most awesome and humbling experiences in my entire life." Dillard was so moved, he explained, because that day he had the opportunity to "minister in the robe that was one worn by one of the greatest preachers that ever lived, THE BISHOP G. E. PATTERSON."[1]

Given as a gift by Patterson's widow, Louise, this robe induced awe in the one who wore it because it offered an experience of closeness with a deceased cleric whom Dillard clearly held in high esteem. The form of this Instagram post materializes the proximity Dillard must have felt that day by juxtaposing images of Dillard wearing the robe with screenshots of Patterson bedecked in the same garment when he preached "After the Dust Settles" on Sunday, June 11, 2006 (Figure 9). Transcending space, time, and person, this robe's afterlife gives new meaning to the title of the sermon Bishop Patterson preached that day. The rapid changes that occurred in Patterson's body during the last year of his life suggest that this occasion was the last time he would don this vestment during this

Figure 9. Instagram post by Linwood Dillard, depicting Dillard ministering in a robe worn by Bishop G. E. Patterson, May 3, 2015.

period of physical animation. Yet as the Instagram post demonstrates, Patterson's robe is reanimated through the ministry of now Bishop Linwood Dillard, an emerging denominational leader for whom Patterson's garment functions as source of spiritual authority.

It would be impossible to pin down all of the pieces—and I do mean pieces—of Patterson's clothing that have been disseminated during his life and after his death: robes bestowed on preaching protégés, neckties mailed to ministers across the country, and swatches of Patterson's garments, cut up, anointed, and shared with believers as "prayer cloths"—tactile extensions of his spiritual power. Alongside these fabrics, which literally bear traces of Patterson's genetic material, are other objects that are said to convey Patterson's anointing, including innumerable bottles of oil that were produced, dedicated, and distributed to congregants throughout his life. The widespread circulation of materials associated with Patterson's physical presence is, I argue, a form of religious broadcasting. How, exactly, does the circulation of Patterson's clothing, or fragments of it, fit into the system we have come to know as Broadcast Religion? What does this material economy reveal about the form and function of the musical gestures that appear again and again in Patterson's sermons? And how does this network of devotional objects—sermons and recordings, oil and cloth—bind together Patterson's life and afterlife?

This chapter uncovers the links between the musical dimensions of Broadcast Religion and the material regimes that scaffold the experience of Patterson's "anointing" on both sides of the grave. To do so, I develop two phrases that encapsulate the workings of Patterson's Broadcast Religion: the logic of the prayer cloth and the idea of Broadcast Ensemble. What I call "the logic of the prayer cloth"—the production and dissemination of spiritual power through the practice of fragmentation—holds together the diverse media of Bishop Patterson's Broadcast Ensemble: the sermon, the song, and the human voice stand on similar footing with microphones, cameras, oil, cloth, television, radio, and the internet as potential conduits of divine power. On the logic of Eucharistic transformation, a single garment fragments into scores of prayer cloths and enables the diffusion of curative energy and the formation of a religious micropublic. So too, the miniaturization of Patterson's sermons, both by his ministry's engineers and countless social media users, enables these sermon clips to travel further than the wholes from which they were extracted. The logic of the prayer cloth also affects the form of Patterson's messages: the brief musical gestures whose recurrence fuels eternal pitch are uttered and apprehended as audible fragments. Paradoxically, the transcendence of these extensively repeated musical entities depends on their minute scale and the resulting sense that they belong to some other moment.

While Pentecostal materiality, religious broadcasting, and musical preaching are all practices Bishop Patterson inherited, his Broadcast Ensemble brought these fabrics of tradition into a particularly salient configuration. As it placed bluesy Black preaching at the center of a Pentecostal broadcasting imaginary, Patterson's Black Pentecostalism assembled an emerging and evolving constellation of religious media that worked together to inculcate intimacy between his messages, his audiences, and various scenes from scripture. This intimacy is ongoing. This intimacy is Afterliveness. Bishop Patterson's Broadcast Ensemble is a Black Pentecostal assemblage, which represents a distinctive contribution to religious broadcasting in the United States. The unusual systematicity of Patterson's homiletic musicality makes his ministry an ideally representative bridge between the practices of first-century Christians, twentieth-century Healing and Charismatic Revivalists, and twenty-first-century social media users. Powered by today's various forms of internet sociality,

Patterson's ecstatic vocality offers thousands of believers an occasion to live religion online, turning countless social media users into a new kind of religious broadcaster.

"A MORE RADICAL APPROACH"

In a 1975 article in the Memphis-area *Tri-State Defender,* then Apostle G. E. Patterson's ministry was contrasted with the church-building efforts of his preaching relatives. Written soon after G. E. Patterson left the denomination to protest the feud between his father, Bishop W. A. Patterson, and his uncle, Bishop J. O. Patterson Sr., the article asserts that "Patterson, a member of the famed Patterson family of the Church of God in Christ, is an alleged 'rebel' of his relatives' teachings."[2] Having "pulled away from the church," Patterson was said to have "developed a more 'radical' approach" to Black Pentecostalism.[3] Rather than shunning this diagnosis of difference as inaccurate or as a relic of a bygone era, Patterson embraced this "more radical approach" in a 1990 sermon, "A Second Touch"—a message delivered two years after he returned to the denomination as a Jurisdictional Bishop [▶ **Video Example BE1**]. That day, Patterson recalled: "I've always had to endure that criticism, and most of us that believe in healing from the laying on of hands and anointing with oil, that in the early infancy of the Bountiful Blessings ministry that was how they distinguished this church—they distinguished this ministry. You know, there've always been a whole lot of Pattersons in town. And then, whenever my name was called: 'Now, which one is that? Is that the one with them little ole bottles of oil?'"

After summarizing the critics' sentiments—"I don't want nobody greasing me with that oil"—Patterson asserts that his approach to anointing was consonant with early Christian practices: "But I found out that the Word of God, in the fifth chapter of James, the prayer of faith includes not only calling for the elders of the church, but it says let them pray over him, anointing him with oil in the name of the Lord." In contrast to those who say, "I don't believe in oil, I just believe in the Word," Patterson argues for a religious assemblage of scripture and sacrament, claiming: "It's the Word that tells you to use the oil." His sense that access to divine power depends on the interaction of "the Word" and "the oil" is a Pentecostal articulation of archaeologist Chris Fowler's more general contention that "an assemblage acts, and acts in a way that none of its components can without being in such a configuration."[4] In this scene, and throughout his life, Patterson locates obedience and efficacy in assemblage, contending that "when you want something from God, you've got to learn to do it God's way."

Taken together, the journalistic criticism and the homiletic response reveal a debate about form, a disagreement about the proper arrangement of the things that scaffold religious practice, a controversy that hinges on the degree to which things matter in a spiritual economy. The intermedial aspects of Patterson's religious practice affirm the philosopher James K. A. Smith's proposal that "that there is a kind of sacramentality of Pentecostal worship that sees the material as a good and necessary mediator of the Spirit's work and presence."[5] Patterson's little bottles of oil—a "more radical" articulation of the widespread Christian practice of anointing—distill one of the numerous "sensational forms" housed within his Broadcast Ensemble. The little bottles of oil that were so central to Memphian/Pattersonian lore constitute what anthropologist Birgit Meyer more generally refers to as a "relatively fixed mode for invoking and organizing access to the transcendental, offering structures of repetition to create and sustain links between believers in the context of particular religious regimes."[6]

The fixity of anointed oil-bearing containers in Pentecostal and Charismatic circles is well-documented, and its grounding beliefs are helpfully elucidated in the writings of one of the twentieth century's most prominent exponents of faith healing, Oral Roberts. In his most famous healing treatise, *If You Need Healing, Do These Things*, Roberts outlines the material circuits that are most central to accessing the divine's curative energy. In answer to the question of how to "reach" God, "the only true Healer," Roberts responds, "*by establishing a point of contact. Faith is the meeting ground between your limited self and your limitless God. A point of contact is given as a means of steadying and helping you to release your faith.*"[7] The anthropologist Anderson Blanton refers to "point of contact," the phrase Roberts made famous, as a "theologico-technical" term, "both a specific theurgical technique that augments or amplifies the efficacy of the prayer, as well as a theological claim upon the nature of divine communication and faith."[8] The historian David Edwin Harrell Jr. wrote extensively about the theological, infrastructural, and financial weight that was affixed to tiny pieces of cloth in Roberts's ministry—the paradigmatic points of contact.[9] Early versions of these cloths were emblazoned with the following script:

> I prayed over this cloth for God to deliver you—use as a point of contact (Acts 19:11–12). It is not necessary to wear the cloth unless you feel you should. It can be used more than once or for more than one person. If you wish to request more, I will be glad to send them to you. The important thing is to use the cloth as a point of contact for the release of your faith in God, so that when you pray and put the cloth on your body, you will believe the Lord will heal you at that moment. I have prayed over this cloth in the name of Jesus of Nazareth and asked Him to heal you when you apply it to your body.[10]

The sheer machinery required to produce and disseminate more than one hundred thousand prayer cloths as early as 1949 clarifies the scale of the enterprise that took shape around Oral Roberts at midcentury, a bully pulpit that allowed his beliefs to travel widely. To be clear, Roberts did not invent the idea of "blessed handkerchiefs," which dates to nineteenth-century Protestant movements and has a logic of contact and holiness that finds articulation even in ancient Christianity. These prayer cloths became a centerpiece of Pentecostal devotion in the early twentieth century. Still, Roberts's mid- and late-century prominence made his theory of the "point of contact" an especially influential force across a broad religious field.

Moving past the prayer cloth, the radio also functioned as a theurgical device for Roberts—and for earlier Pentecostal innovators. Building on a practice that was key to Aimee McPherson's Foursquare Church radio broadcasts (as early as the 1920s), Roberts claimed that "many lay their hands on their radio as a point of contact during our Healing Waters broadcast. Through this means they release their faith and through faith they are healed during the 'prayer-time' of the broadcast."[11] While Roberts's proclamation of the term gave clarity to the uses of prayer cloths, radios, and other devotional objects during the mid-twentieth-century Healing Revival, the phrase "point of contact" also brings us back to Bishop

Patterson's little bottles of oil, for it was in the nineteenth-century evangelist Andrew Murray's 1884 book on *Divine Healing* that this formulation first appeared, referring to the use of anointing oil and the "laying-on of hands" during healing prayer. Murray contended that the oil should be regarded "not as a remedy but as a pledge of the mighty virtue of the Holy Spirit, as a means of strengthening faith, and as a point of contact and communion between the sick person and the members of the church who are called to anoint him or her with oil."[12] Thus, when Patterson argued that combining oil and word represented "God's way" to seek healing, he was envisaging little bottles of oil as points of contact.

As he sought to do ministry "God's way," Patterson followed the model found in Acts 19:11–12, a tradition that holds that first-century Christians "did extraordinary miracles through Paul, so that when the handkerchiefs or aprons that had touched his skin were brought to the sick, their diseases left them, and the evil spirits came out of them." While important differences of production, dissemination, and affordance distinguish prayer cloths and anointed oil, this chapter focuses on the similar ways these materials are deployed in a host of religious traditions. Like the "little bottles of oil," many fragments of Patterson's clothing still circulate as prayer cloths, textile extensions of an eternally curative energy. In a 2014 interview "Remembering Bishop G. E. Patterson," Pastor John Brown, who served as one of Patterson's associate ministers and as a nurse who cared for Patterson at the end of his life, observed that his wife—a breast cancer survivor—"wears one of Bishop G. E. Patterson's prayer cloths every single day of her life" [▶ **Video Example BE2**]. Rehearsing Patterson's teaching, Brown described each piece of sanctified fabric as "a connection." With the help of his fellow panelists, Brown recalled the technical term, calling the prayer cloth "a point of contact for your faith to trust God, according to his word." The Brown family's engagement with Patterson's prayer cloth complicates political scientist R. Marie Griffith's emphasis on the immediacy of prayer cloths, which "may not be active six months later if something else comes up."[13]

In contrast, Blanton rightly contends that it is only through "habituation and perpetual use of the prayer cloth that this object makes its (re)appearance with the most compelling force of faith." The force of faith happens over time, animated by "the movement of the testimony *and* the physical circulation of the devotional object."[14] Like his wife, Pastor Brown incorporates Patterson into his daily ensemble; when he was interviewed, he was wearing a fabric bracelet, produced by Patterson's ministry, emblazoned with one of the late Bishop's famous phrases: "Jesus is a habit-breaker." This garment is itself an ensemble that assembles a strip of fabric and a pithy Pattersonian proclamation. In order to prove the truth of Patterson's claim and the efficacy of Patterson's utterance, Brown made an even more emphatic turn toward material corroboration of spiritual power, noting that many who came to Patterson's tent revivals "put cigarette packages and liquor bottles in the trash," overcoming addiction through the power of Patterson's preaching and the power of Jesus to break habits. During this same interview Pastor Antonio Buckley, another of Patterson's adjutants, detailed the material microhistory of Patterson's prayer cloth: "A lot of people don't realize where a lot of the prayer cloths came from. They actually came from the clothing of Bishop Patterson. He would actually take one of his suits or robes and cut it up and give it out to people as a point of contact."[15]

In an interview Mance Aytchan, Patterson's long-serving minister of music, told me about one such occasion. Before a Sunday service, Patterson instructed Aytchan to call the missionaries into the pastor's office. Aytchan continued:

> He told them to go in there and get thirty shirts out of his closet and cut them up into strips. (I want you to follow me now.) [They] cut the shirts up in strips, and then he dismissed them, and dipped all those strips in . . . you know, he made his own oil . . . nobody still knows what that oil was cause it was red on the top and green on the bottom: the blood and prosperity. And I think I still have two bottles. He dipped those shirt strips in that oil and prayed over it.[16]

As Aytchan remembers it, hundreds of parishioners came to the altar, bearing offerings, clamoring "to get a strip of one the shirts he had sweated in and preached in and then put on oil on it and prayed over it." Through this assemblage of fabric, oil, sweat, and prayer, Patterson's prayer cloths fulfilled his stated purpose: "I want you to have a piece of my anointing." When Aytchan recalled that phrase, he gestured affectedly before confessing: "I feel something right now."

The ritual efficacy unleashed through Patterson's textile fragmentation, an extension of millennia of Christian healing practices, also appears in the videographic context. Buttressing Patterson's assertion that the presence of God felt in a given worship service could be transmitted to his far-flung audiences, Pastor John Brown claimed that viewers would often heed Patterson's healing exhortation: "People would watch the TV, catch hold to faith, and be healed." In so doing, Brown and Patterson extend the "radio tactility" of Roberts and McPherson to television.[17] In Brown's discussion of Patterson's Broadcast Religion, faith is something of which to catch hold. In Roberts's view, faith is something to be released. And in Murray's treatise, faith is described as something in need of strengthening. That healing in Christian faith is described here in nearly opposite ways as something of which one should "catch hold" and something that must be "released," through oil and cloth, on radio and TV, shows the textures of confessional discourse that depend on the interaction of an equally assorted array of devotional objects. In each case the activation of the faith that enables the operation of divine healing comes to depend on the material regimes that surround it.

THE LOGIC OF THE PRAYER CLOTH

Although I do not possess one of Patterson's prayer cloths, I do have three items of his clothing. After hearing, on YouTube, a talk I gave about her husband, Evangelist Louise Patterson mailed me three of Bishop G. E. Patterson's neckties, each of which arrived in a long white box, emblazoned with the logo of Patterson's Bountiful Blessings, Inc. Inside each box lies one necktie covered in a thin sheet of protective paper, framed by a folded card that contains an overtly hagiographical image (Figure 10).

The card's claim that "this tie connects you to the anointing of the one who wore it" is buttressed by the visible presence that the picture—taken at Paterson's second inauguration—lends to the deceased Bishop. If, as this card contends, these ties connect their holders to Patterson's anointing, then they must quite literally be ties that bind: points of contact. Even if the scale of a necktie seems quite different from that of the robe depicted

Figure 10. Folded card included in a package from Bountiful Blessings, Inc. containing three of Bishop G. E. Patterson's neckties, 2022.

in this chapter's opening vignette, both kinds of apparel shared a common existence in Patterson's wardrobe, out of which they could emerge as constituents of any given day's sartorial ensemble. Louise Patterson's decision to share pieces of her late husband's wardrobe with men all over the country—and presumably around the world—seems motivated by her sense of what these fabrics could convey: a form of spiritual power that has somehow soaked into the material traces of Patterson's life.

Although at first glance Patterson's penchant for circulating textiles might seem to have little to do with the technological infrastructures described in Chapter 1, I argue that the logic of the prayer cloth lies at the very foundation of Broadcast Religion. In Patterson's religious imagination, points of contact like oil and cloth function alongside the distinctive sonorous dimensions of Broadcast Religion: sound also follows the logic of the prayer cloth. Patterson's theory of religious communication came to the fore the last two times he preached from 2 Chronicles 20. When

Bishop Patterson preached "Focusing Our Eyes upon the Lord" on Sunday, November 5, 2006, he called attention to the brevity and potency of the material we have come to know as the eternal song:

> And I know they haven't had choir rehearsal, but it's a short song.
> And it won't take long for them to learn it.
> All they gotta do is say: "Praise the Lord for his mercy endureth forever"
> Now, wait a minute that's not a whole song! Sometimes all you need is a chorus.
> Sometimes you don't need no three, don't need no three or four verses.
> [▶ Video Example BE3]

One week later, at the Ninety-ninth Annual Holy Convocation, when Patterson delivered "Jehoshaphat's Prayer and God's Answer," the sermon with which this book's introduction begins, he again pondered the illogical instruction to sing this little scrap of a song while marching into battle [▶ Video Example BE4]. He emphasized the enormity of the enmity with which Ancient Judah was confronted, telling his congregants: "You mean to tell me that there are three nations—Ammon, Moab, Mount Seir—and you want us to go up against them, saying, 'Praise the Lord for his mercy endureth forever?'" Responding to his own inquiry, Patterson thunders: "But let me tell you: if that's all God gives you, that's what's gon' work." This gift, this tool, this resource, this weapon should, Patterson suggests, be Judah's sole focus: "Don't worry about what you don't have. Use what you do have. Use what he gave you for this battle. And for this battle he gave you, what? 'Praise the lord for his mercy endureth forever.'" The scene and its music summarize an elemental moment for Patterson's preaching and for the musicality that sustained it. As he proclaims the apotropaic power of this musical fragment, he hints at the role the eternal song, the eternal riff, and the eternal pitch played across the decades of his ministry, foreshadowing the work these three resonant devices would do even after his death.

In previous chapters I traced the eternal song as far back as a 2001 sermon, "Dealing with Life's Battles." But this musical fragment has an even deeper history. By then this recurring musical exegesis of 2 Chronicles 20 was well-established in Patterson's sermonic catalog. Near the end of a 1995 sermon, "It's Not Your Battle," Bishop Patterson mused: "I've

Example 10. Eternal song in G major, Temple of Deliverance Church, Memphis, Tennessee, August 20, 1995.

preached it so many times" [▶ **Video Example BE5**]. With this phrase he launched into the now-familiar set piece, telling of the powerful enmity that confronted the ancient Judahite king Jehoshaphat and the musical solution that was prescribed by the young prophet Jehaziel. As Patterson repeatedly sang the words "praise the Lord for his mercy endureth forever" in the chanted manner of the rest of the sermon, it seemed as if he would conclude the sermon without summoning the heightened musical moment that we have come to know as the eternal song. But then he made his characteristic move, urging the congregation to join him in singing the eternal song in G major (Musical Example 10).

The reemergence of this marked musical figure clarifies what Patterson meant by "I've preached it so many times." The eternal song does not sound like the kind of phrase to be uttered only one time. It is a sonic fragment with enduring power. What links the musical dimensions of Broadcast Religion to the tactile and textile devotional objects that are at work in a host of Pentecostal contexts? The ensemble of material deployed in Broadcast Religion is paradoxically held together by a theory of the power of fragmentation, which I refer to as "the logic of the prayer cloth." The fragments that are most central to Patterson's religious imagination are those stitched and quilted into the sonic tapestry of his sermonic utterances. These homiletic fragments are not the scattered remains of some other, more intentionally produced object: they are designed. Produced through countless acts of musical repetition and textile fragmentation, these pieces of Patterson's Broadcast Ensemble give lie to a misconception that is often appended to the very idea of a fragment. Literary scholar Heather Bamford, writing about the role fragments played in medieval Iberian manuscript culture, works against the "commonplace notion that fragments came about accidentally. The majority of manuscript fragments were created on purpose, as a result of the use of manuscript material for a wide variety of practical, intellectual, and spiritual purposes—from binding material to excerpting for an anthology, to talismans. These fragments are thus created rather than born."[18]

Leaning into the medieval resonances at work here might prompt one to understand Patterson's points of contact—textile and audile—as contact relics. Like seeds tucked into the soil of an ongoing sermon, or like relics of dust or bone that sanctify or heal even after a saint's death, these homiletic fragments contain the potential energy of Patterson's afterlife. Yet the function of these devotional objects preceded Patterson's physical death, even if their posthumous endurance seems to clarify something about their transcendent ontology. Given their strategic placement both during Patterson's period of physical animation and after the messenger went to sleep, they might be understood as anticipatory relics or antiphonal relics: musical calls whose responses reverberate on both sides of the grave.

The will to relay spiritual energy through textiles of various sorts, while obviously in deep sympathy with a host of Pentecostal, Christian, and world religious practices, also forms a crucial link to the forms that are most central to this study: the recurring musical devices that collectively constitute Patterson's eternal pitch. When placed in conversation with the making and dissemination of prayer cloths during Patterson's life, and with the division and distribution of Patterson's clothing after his death, the function of the repeated articulation of the eternal song, the eternal riff, and the eternal pitch comes into clearer focus. Although it was not possible to share the textile fragments that we have come to know as prayer cloths with every member of his manifold in-person and mediated congregation, it was possible to give each of his listeners an ensemble of audible fragments, enduring musical moments that transcend the individual sermon, connecting each homiletic event to an eternal transmission.

Like the eternal song, the eternal riff—the ascending octaval melisma that moves from scale degree 1 to 3 to 5 to 6 to 1 in the higher octave—epitomizes the logic of the prayer cloth. At the end of a 1998 sermon, "You Can Depend on God," Patterson's penchant for musical and rhetorical amplification was on full display, when he turned the conjunction "if" into an emphatic musical anchor, rhythmically uttered on the tenor A♭ (set in bold in the text that follows) [▶ **Video Example BE6**]. Anaphorically constructing a vamp of conditional phrases, Patterson thundered:

> **If** he didn't fail Jehoshaphat when three kings and three armies came up against him...
> **If** he didn't fail Daniel in a den of lions...
> **If** he didn't fail Shadrach, Meshack, and Obednego in the fiery furnace..
> **If** he didn't fail Paul when the ship broke up...
> **If** he didn't fail John on the Isle of Patmos...
> He won't fail me!
> He won't fail you!
> You can depend!
> Oh!
> You can
> (I got to close), but you can: you can depend on God!
> Uh...

Patterson's delayed arrival at this sermonic destination, the given title of this sermon, distills the homiletic trajectory that we discussed in Chapter 3. The musical intensity built in the first five lines of this sermon's final minute reaches its climax in the interrupted statement of the message's title: from the reciting tone (the tenor A♭), Patterson interjects "oh" on the tenor B, the note we have come to know as the eternal pitch. After completing the statement "you can depend on God," Patterson dramatically descends an octave to the lower A♭, only to sing his way back to his sermonic register on the eternal pitch. Although it is hard to tell exactly which vocable is being uttered on this melisma, the message of ecstatic conclusion is far from ambiguous.

Posted by one user in the Facebook group "In loving memory of Bishop G. E. Patterson," this one-minute video is itself a product of fragmentation. Extracted from a seventy-two-minute sermon recording, this clip allows the most affecting sections of this sermon to circulate more widely, and the eternal riff to be ingested more easily, than the message from which it is taken, even as it raises curiosity about the rest of what transpired during the homiletic event. Certain social-networking platforms, including TikTok and Instagram, place firm limits on the duration of the files that can traffic thereon. In these instances fragmentation is a necessary condition for Bishop Patterson's afterlife. But this practice of distillation is not unprecedented: his radio and television broadcasts and the affordances of albums, cassettes, VHS, and DVD formats also placed temporal limits on his presentations. There is an important resonance between the clips that social media users excerpt from Patterson's sermons and the recurring devices he chose to reproduce in unfolding messages.

Patterson's audiences across time and space sometimes indicate that they understand the significance of the musical fragment and its transitory power, its ability to float away from one sermon and embed itself in the next. In doing so, they extend the power of the musical/sermonic fragment that manifests in online commentary that contributes to Patterson's digital afterlife. Consider a March 15, 2021, social media post by one Facebook user. Responding to a video excerpt shared by another Facebook user, a clip that shows Patterson engaged in the heightened musical phase of a sermon, this netizen argued that "ANY preacher in the past 30 years that does the 1-3-5-6-1 riff in their whoop owes it to Bishop Patterson. That's his."[19] While I do not wish to evaluate the veracity of his statement, I do want to highlight his insight that the brief bit of music that we have come to know as the eternal riff functions as a point of contact for, to, and from Bishop Patterson. Confidently, he delimits a historical period during which Patterson's voice becomes so synonymous with this musical fragment that to repeat it is to invoke him.

It was in 2021 that this Facebook user made this claim about thirty years of preaching. At this point Patterson had been deceased for fully half of this temporal span. This assertion points to the tradition-making quality of Patterson's broadcasts—those that flow from his ministry's headquarters and those that circulate between a host of social media users. Moreover, this claim highlights the preoccupation with transcendence that is expressed by each of the three configurations of Patterson's eternal pitch. Although a key facet of my project's musicohistorical work has been to track down and to attempt to pin down very early articulations of the eternal song, the eternal riff, and the eternal pitch, what matters most about these fragments—besides the fact of their uncommon endurance and consistency—is the transcendent purposefulness vented by each articulation. Return, for example, to Patterson's wanton utterance of the eternal riff at the end of the 1993 sermon "Neither Were They Thankful"
[▶ Video Example BE7].

The hard-to-identify "yeah" delivered through this series of notes stands apart from the rest of the melodic formulae that were uttered in this message, musical figures that were defined by their hovering relationship to the sermon's tonal center, and by the amplifying arc that built larger sermonic units from these musical cells. The eternal riff, in contrast, is a singular entity, distinguished by its octaval contour, and by the fact that it starts and ends on the tonal center. This Pattersonian leitmotif arrests sympathetic attention through its obvious virtuosity and audacity. It sounds equally spontaneous and practiced, simultaneously ready-at-hand and sent-from-above.

While the eternal riff clearly functions as a melodic fragment, it manages to feel like a full statement of something. It is so conclusory that it has been used to mark the end of many one-minute viral clips of Patterson sermons that circulate across social media platforms. That is, those who distill the long sermon to a one-minute epitome very often chose a section that contains one of Patterson's famous fragments. These religious fragments, audible and tangible, are not to be understood merely in terms of their origins: the robe from which the cloth is cut, or the first sermon in which a riff is articulated. Instead, presence and absence mix as, beyond Bishop Patterson's earthly lifetime, his sermons are edited and epitomized and his eternal riff is clipped to offer a conclusion. The paradoxical situation of the whole from which the fragment seems to come is helpfully glossed by literary theorist Hans Gumbrecht: "We certainly cannot perceive it because, by definition, it cannot be present together with the fragment." While it cannot be apprehended, its existence is announced by "the intuition of a lack coming from the contemplation of a present object."[20]

Yet the prayer cloth does not beg to be reunited with the rest of the towel, shirt, robe, or sheet from which it was abstracted, nor do the eternal song, eternal riff, or the eternal pitch yearn to be rejoined to any single sermon. The prayer cloth's emphatic incompleteness fuels its paradoxical ontology as a point of contact: it so effectively enables connection because of the act of fragmentation by which it was produced. This is the logic of the prayer cloth, applicable to the materiality of fabric and to the seemingly ephemeral materiality of sound. While Patterson's prayer cloths clearly exemplify the tactile mediation of spiritual power, his homiletic fragments do something more: they locate energy and power in the process of fragmentation itself. These fragments synthesize radio tactility and textile tactility, wedding the logic of the prayer cloth to the invisible transmission of sonic power.

BLACK PENTECOSTAL ASSEMBLAGE

The spiritual economy that sustains Bishop Patterson's eternal pitch depends on the combination of devotional fragments into ensembles of varying form and scale. The stakes of these combinatorial processes came to light during the 2014 panel discussion "Remembering Bishop G. E. Patterson," when Pastor Stephen Smith, another of Patterson's mentees, described watching various displays of miraculous healing with his own eyes. This leads Pastor John Brown to claim that "Bishop Patterson had a similar anointing to [COGIC founder] Bishop [Charles Harrison] Mason" [▶ Video Example BE2].

No higher praise could ever have been given to Patterson than to be likened to the founder of the denomination, one known for his capacity to act as an instrument of divine healing and other miraculous phenomena. In Chapters 1 and 2, I discussed the way Patterson's incorporation of a segment of the "Yes, Lord" chant into his television broadcast's opening scene asserts a closeness to Bishop Mason. Having outlined the logic of the prayer cloth, I want to push this argument one step further. In the opening montage of Patterson's still-airing television broadcasts, the singing of "Yes, Lord" is closely linked to Patterson's homiletic utterance of his most famous exhortation: "I command you to be healed, be delivered, and be set free." "Yes, Lord," the chant attributed to Mason, is one of the best-known pieces of Black sacred music, and it is to this song that Patterson conjoins his own best-known phrase [▶ Video Example BE8].

Even if Patterson's exhortation "I command you to be healed, be delivered, and be set free" is less ubiquitous than Mason's tune, it does enjoy wide circulation. For example, consider the banner than hangs behind the pulpit of the Trinity Temple Church of God in Christ in New Haven, Connecticut (Figure 11).[21] The phrase was also the subtitle of the resolution that the Congressional Black Caucus entered into the *Congressional*

Record on Tuesday, March 28, 2007, eight days after Patterson died.[22] Whether embroidered on a bracelet, printed on a banner, or edited into a video, the broadcasting of Patterson's exhortation simultaneously incarnates a theology of healing, a philosophy of media, and a theory of divine communication. Each of these claims—be healed, be delivered, be set free—is buttressed by the proximity the broadcast's opening montage provides to COGIC's best-known musical fragment.

All this points to another key assumption of the logic of the prayer cloth: fragmentation, a vital musical process and essential expression of tactile devotion, depends for its coherence on various acts of recombination. The integration of the prayer cloths into devotional practices and the engrafting of homiletic fragments into an ongoing sermon are essential to Broadcast Religion. While it would be impossible to put a whole sermon on a cloth bracelet, or to squeeze an entire message into a broadcast's opening scene, processes of fragmentation and miniaturization enable recombination and widespread dissemination. Indeed, this is crucial to understanding the logic from which these devotional objects emerge, a conception that summons the etymology of broadcasting itself. For well before it was taken up as a name for the transcendence of space and time in mass communications, broadcasting referred to the wide dispersal of material, especially small items like seeds in agricultural contexts. This agricultural formulation is strikingly germane for the present discussion because it raises the issue of life—potential and realized. In so doing, it helps us think about the relation between the form and function of Patterson's ministry on both sides of the grave.

The exhortative fragments that continue to appear in the opening seconds of Patterson's *Bountiful Blessings* broadcast also fill the banner that hangs in a New Haven sanctuary. This echoing shows that the practices that made Patterson especially fit for remediation on television also sustain his afterlife, whether in church edifices or on a host of social media platforms. Patterson, the preacher who oversaw the fragmentation and dispersal of his clothing, also served as executive producer of his television broadcasts, supervising the conversion of ninety-minute-long worship service into roughly twenty minutes of broadcast content for a half-hour television slot. Patterson was similarly responsible for selecting material to be broadcast during his fifteen-minute radio segments. Patterson's

Figure 11. Members of Trinity Temple COGIC's congregation gathered beneath a banner containing images of Bishop G. E. Patterson and his ubiquitous exhortation: "Be Healed, Be Delivered, and Be Set Free," March 5, 2018.

hands-on involvement in all the facets of Broadcast Religion—crafting the sermons and supervising the broadcasts, selecting the apparel, and overseeing its segmentation—motivates this book's free movement between media in search of a unifying epistemology.

As a name for the individual constellations of oil, fabric, and various sounding and recorded media through which Bishop Patterson disseminated spiritual power, I coin the term Broadcast Ensemble. It holds together tangible, sonorous, and digital expressions of his technophilic Pentecostalism. The theory of religious mediation that is evidenced through oil, cloth, and in a host of pithy proclamations is also manifest in the unusual systematicity of Patterson's homiletic musicality. The consistency and virtuosity with which Patterson weaves granular, musical, and rhetorical amplification into intensifying musical arcs recalls my earlier claim that as much as he was anything else, Bishop Patterson was a media theorist. His media theory, his extension of the logic of the prayer cloth, is incarnate in the repeated musical devices that form a fleeting configuration (or ensemble) in each sermon.

Like a short utterance printed on a cloth bracelet, or a prayer cloth tucked inside one's outfit, the eternal song, the eternal riff, and especially the eternal pitch arises in scores of individual sermons, governed in each instance by the text, title, and key that gives each homiletic event its musical structure. The coming-together of an ongoing sermon and one or more of these three musical gestures is assemblage, both the process that yields various Black Pentecostal assemblages and their collective form: Bishop Patterson's Broadcast Ensemble. In Broadcast Religion, the copresence of oil, cloth, sermons, and various recordings shows that "the parts that are fitted together are not uniform either in nature or in origin, and that the assemblage actively links these parts together by establishing relations between them."[23]

Patterson's homiletic fragments sensitize us to the mechanics of this coherence: neither the singular pitch, the five-note riff, or the recurring song are meaningful devotional objects apart from their emplotment in specific sermons. While the sermon's key dictates the notes that the eternal riff and song will occupy, the eternal pitch transcends the governmentality of the musical key. Yet its transcendence can only be gleaned by recognizing its appearance in a host of musical environments. Moreover, even as the sonic infrastructure of the individual sermon influences the specific form these recurring figures take, the fact of their reiteration draws each message together with scores of other Patterson sermons. Through these audible fragments, Patterson brings the logic of the prayer cloth to bear on the most important Pentecostal instrument, the human voice, whose capacity for modulation—linguistic and tonal—offers evidence of the spirit's indwelling and a divine desire to be voiced in the world.

Patterson's homiletic articulation of the logic of the prayer cloth makes a transformative intervention in American religious broadcasting. His homiletic fragments resound at the intersection of musical Black preaching, Pentecostal material devotion, and religious broadcasting. Although anointed oil, prayer cloths, and recorded sermons are widely shared features of Pentecostal practice, something happens to Pentecostalism when bluesy Black musicality is placed at its center. Something happens to religious broadcasting when such a forceful formal consonance emerges between the sermon and its material scaffolding. While the claims of televangelists like Oral Roberts, who in the 1950s asserted that his *Healing*

Waters broadcasts could transmit spiritual power into the homes of viewers is consonant with a host of Pentecostal convictions, Patterson's claims of spiritual conductivity gain greater veracity from the form of his vocal instrumentality. Patterson's Broadcast Ensemble—emerging and evolving constellations of radio, television, oil, textile, and sermon—embody many of the key characteristics of assemblages. The logic of the prayer cloth holds together this "multiplicity which is made up of many heterogenous terms and establishes liaisons, relations between them . . . the assemblage's only unity is that of a co-functioning: it is a symbiosis, a 'sympathy.'"[24]

The sympathy these objects enjoy arises from their shared functioning as points of contact—material extensions of divine potency. The Black Pentecostalism that is Broadcast Religion depends on and is an assemblage, "a specific arrangement of diverse, heterogenous, interacting components that has specific *effects*."[25] It is not that Black Pentecostalism stands apart from its co-constitutive materials, waiting for articulation. No, it is the circulation of oil, cloth, scripture, sermon, song, and prayer that constitutes the living tissue of belief. The transmission and experience of spiritual power, the assemblage's desired effect, is fundamentally altered by the addition of Patterson's musical fragments to this religious economy.

BROADCAST ENSEMBLE

Broadcast Ensemble is both the practice and the means of dissemination for the particular and peculiar form of Black Pentecostalism that Bishop G. E. Patterson developed in his community and that the community continues to develop for itself—even after his death. Broadcast Ensemble is a Black Pentecostal assemblage: its contents and their configuration articulate the logic of the prayer cloth. The ongoing remediation of Patterson's final sermon, "The Gospel According to John," brings into focus many of the terms of this assemblage. Originally delivered on Christmas Day 2006, clips from this message are especially visible in the days and weeks surrounding December 25. Individual posts are typically collected in Facebook groups like "In Loving Memory of Bishop G. E. Patterson."[26] Created on February 1, 2009, this group boasts 95,832 members and is home to daily posts of and about Patterson's preaching. On December 7, 2018, one Facebook user posted a video of the last three minutes and forty-four seconds of this final homiletic event, writing: "Bishop G. E. Patterson preached his last message on Christmas Morning, Dec. 25th 2006! This is a short clip of it! Powerful!!!"[27]

This short clip is quite predictably drawn from the final minutes of Patterson's sermon, the moment when, after making the characteristic turn from speech toward song, Patterson is tuning up for the last time [▶ **Video Example BE9**]. About fifty seconds before the end of this sermon, Patterson exclaims: "I got to quit! I just got to let this thing go." As he calls attention to the climactic section that we have discussed throughout this book, Patterson clips his own sermon, announcing that, even though he was already well into the heightened frame of the sermon, this next phrase would represent the conclusion of his final message. Set in italicized bold, this richly intertextual phrase serves as the title or key lyric for multiple gospel songs and hymns:

I never shall forget, when I was on my way down to a devil's hell.
I wasn't fit to live. I was scared to die. But I heard somebody say:
Call him! He'll come to your rescue.
Call him! He'll wash you from your sins.
Call him!

As Patterson preaches about the importance of calling on the name of Jesus, in the final thirty seconds of this message, he assembles several homiletic fragments. He begins by uttering the lyrics "I Never Shall Forget." And he delivers this phrase through the eternal riff, rising from B2 to B3 on the five-note melisma. Then he repeats one of his stock phrases: "I wasn't fit to live. I was scared to die" (italicized). Finally, he reaches up to the eternal pitch (bolded) three times, to deliver the words "call him." Preached with full knowledge of his frailty and mortality, it is as if knew that believers would return to this final sermon and its final moments again and again. In this sonic mosaic Patterson condenses decades' worth of pyrotechnic preaching into a seconds-long homiletic assemblage.

But when did this video first appear online, and where? On October 28, 2016, nearly a decade after Patterson's death, YouTube user MusicMan 78414 posted a sixty-two-minute long video titled "Bishop GE Patterson

Christmas 2006."[28] This is the earliest online posting of Patterson's final message. And it is not a solitary addition to YouTube's online repository. Rather, MusicMan 78414's video is linked to an expansive YouTube playlist titled "Bishop GE Patterson sermons."[29] This playlist includes 184 videos posted by numerous YouTubers but collected by MusicMan 78414. A caption clarifies the logic around which this ensemble is organized: "A chronological list of Bishop's sermons starting in the 1980s and continuing to his final Sermon on Christmas Day 2006." Since the time MusicMan 78414 published this playlist, the caption has lost some of its explanatory value: more recent additions to the playlist have abandoned the chronological conceit. But this user's earliest intentions continue to merit analysis.

As Patterson's lifecycle is worked out through the hypertextual affordances of this social-networking platform, the very idea of a sermon catalog—that thing Patterson asserts through his marketing infrastructure and by his incessantly repeated musical fragments—acquires a digital materiality. Scrolling through the playlist, even without playing any of the videos, allows viewers to traverse Patterson's maturation and his decline, tracing his ministry as it moves between sanctuaries, making use of an ever-modernizing ensemble of communications technologies. What MusicMan 78414 does for Patterson sermons, he also does for numerous live performances of music by composers of Western art music, including Mendelssohn, Beethoven, and Bach. Patterson is the only Black musician and the only preacher of any race to be treated to this digital collection.

MusicMan 78414's collecting efforts also disclose an analytic orientation. On at least one occasion, he employed YouTube's time-stamping capacities to name and interpret the key moments in Patterson's penultimate sermon, "The Purpose of the Four Gospels."[30] As Figure 12 shows, MusicMan 78414 uses the affordances of this medium to amplify the details of this sermon. He discusses the content, form, and ecstatic behavior that the sermon elicited, inviting viewers to attend to a fragment of this message instead of the entire recording. In this way MusicMan 78414 does to this message what this message does to scripture, extending a cycle of remediation that stretches between Patterson's physical life and his mediated afterlife, and offering a new kind of chapter and verse structure to Patterson's sermon: not Matthew 11:8 but Patterson 11:08 and so on.

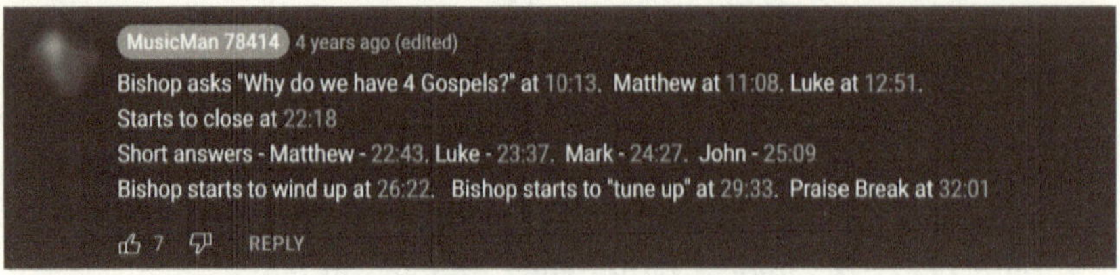

> **MusicMan 78414** 4 years ago (edited)
> Bishop asks "Why do we have 4 Gospels?" at 10:13. Matthew at 11:08. Luke at 12:51. Starts to close at 22:18
> Short answers - Matthew - 22:43. Luke - 23:37. Mark - 24:27. John - 25:09
> Bishop starts to wind up at 26:22. Bishop starts to "tune up" at 29:33. Praise Break at 32:01
>
> 👍 7   👎   REPLY

Figure 12. A YouTube user's annotations and time stamps of Bishop G. E. Patterson's sermon "The Purpose of the Four Gospels," October 28, 2016.

Like the evangelists and communities whose collective narratives and traditions turn into the New Testament's gospels, this YouTube user scours the platform to find and organize recordings of Patterson's sermons, connecting each homiletic event to those that precede and follow it. The making of a catalog, this hypertextual act, also mimics the effects of Patterson's recurring musical devices, each of which forms a link between many Patterson sermons, accessing an efficacy that transcends the event. This is Afterliveness.

ASSEMBLING AFTERLIVENESS

Patterson's Black Pentecostal assemblage endures not only through the efforts of MusicMan 78414 but because of the labor and logics of an ensemble of believers, ranging in power and proximity from his widow, Louise Patterson, to anonymous social media users who had scarcely reached elementary school age by the time of Patterson's death. Louise Patterson serves as the CEO of Bountiful Blessings, Inc., the organization that manages WBBP 1480 AM, produces radio and television broadcasts, sells recordings of Patterson's CDs, and owns the rights to Patterson's likeness. While much of the broadcasting landscape has changed since Bishop Patterson died in 2007, Bountiful Blessings, Inc. continues to be guided by an enduring theory of religious mediation. The logic of the prayer cloth is at work in Louise Patterson's dissemination of neckties as points of contact for her late husband's anointing. Similarly, this logic is articulated as social media users produce online content in ways that mimic the fragmentary procedures that enabled the diffusion of Patterson's messages during his life. Consider a post from the COGIC International Mass Choir Group Facebook page, an excerpt of a Patterson service, captioned: "Today we remember the iconic, Presiding Bishop G. E. Patterson. A man who is yet winning souls from the grave. His legacy lives on! #WeRemember."[31]

Posted on March 20, 2018—eleven years after Bishop Patterson's death—this caption illustrates the memorial work performed by this video, which at the time of writing this has been viewed more than eight hundred thousand times. While the interconnected labors of mourning, eulogy, and remembrance are essential functions of social media platforms, as previous chapters have demonstrated, Patterson's posthumous circulation is animated by a rhetoric of Afterliveness. This post features a video that comes from a 2006 service which, instead of a typical sermon-focused event, is cataloged by Bountiful Blessings, Inc. as a "Healing Service" [▶ **Video Example BE10**]. The video shows the aftermath of Patterson taking up Donald Lawrence's gospel song "I Speak Life," to encourage those who, like him, were struggling with illness. Patterson sang: "I speak life. You're gonna live, oh my brother, my sister. I speak life. You are the head and not the tail, you will prevail. I speak life. Don't give up the fight for your life. You shall live and not die." He argued that "a spirit of life" was present in the sanctuary, a presence that should call forth a performance of holy dancing: a shout.

The "spirit of life" of which Patterson spoke did not simply convey ordinary, physical life but another kind of persistence that asserts itself in the face of mortality. More than fifteen years after his death, Patterson's presence persists, especially on platforms like Facebook and especially through online contributions like the anniversary post. His virtual afterlife is helpfully elucidated by the analysis of Jed R. Brubaker, Gillian R. Hayes, and Paul Dourish, scholars of communication, who write: "SNS [Social Network Services] users craft profiles to represent their identities while they are alive, yet these digital identities continue to persist after death. Moreover, these identities grow as friends add content to the deceased's profile and weave them into their social networks with images, tags, and evidence of SNS activities."[32]

While Bishop Patterson was not a social media user in any traditional sense, Broadcast Religion, and the multitude of high-quality recordings resulting from it, provide the raw material for his online remediation. In many ways Patterson is even more pervasive postmortem than during his physical life. In 2007 there were not yet one hundred full-length Patterson sermons available for free on YouTube, Facebook, and other platforms. By the late 2010s, however, hundreds of Patterson sermons had become available for viewing whenever desire, device, and connectivity were present, with no need to wait for the regularly scheduled television or radio broadcasts. YouTube's function as a cultural archive thus plays a particularly important role in the participatory cultural production of Patterson's life.[33] Given the centrality of preaching to the departed Bishop's public identity, an increasingly pervasive technologized co-presence makes Patterson's message more alive after his death than before.

The members of Patterson's virtual congregation work together to navigate the pieces of his message that populate various online venues. In the comments section of a January 31, 2020, Facebook post, one Facebook user responded to a clip of Patterson preaching: "What a message. Where can I buy the complete DVD OR CD?"[34] While the Facebook member who posted his video on the COGIC History Page Facebook Group responded with links to Patterson's website, his reply was insufficient given that neither the one-minute clip nor the caption contained the title of the sermon from which the excerpt is taken. Recognizing this, another user commented: "Sermon is entitled 'Healing in the Temple'; Tape #718. You can contact Bountiful Blessings to purchase." The commenter replies to the post, tagging the original poster and saying, "Thank you so much." The conversation that unfolds beneath this post resonates with the chain of communication within it. While the video was shared with the Facebook Group on January 31, 2020, this version of the video was originally shared on September 22, 2017, in the Jude 3 Project's Facebook page.[35]

Furthermore, this brief excerpt is taken from a nearly thirty-minute-long version of the sermon posted on Facebook by one of the poster's above interlocutors, the user whose reply is just discussed.[36] And finally, this thirty-minute version of this sermon is a concatenated form of the original video, an artifact that runs more than one hour. The interplay that unfolds here between three individuals, two Facebook Groups, two sharings of a video excerpt, the longer sermon video, and the full recording of that Sunday's service offers only one window into the digital mechanism of Patterson's afterlife. Like the dialogic shape of these conversations,

Patterson's virtual existence resonates with the way musical and homiletic fragments were trafficked between numerous sermons during Patterson's period of physical animation. His movement between performance, TV, YouTube, and Facebook, is an especially intermedial manifestation of what media scholar Henry Jenkins calls "convergence culture."[37]

The afterlife that is sustained by Bishop Patterson's Black Pentecostal assemblage forms a peculiar kind of community, evidencing what musicologists Jason Stanyek and Benjamin Piekut call the "interpenetration between worlds of living and dead, arrangements that might best be termed *intermundane*." In intermundane existence "the living do not one-sidedly handle the dead, but participate in an inter-handling, a mutually effective co-laboring."[38] Even as Patterson's congregants—former congregants they are not—proclaim "the messenger sleeps but the message lives on," they seem to convey an explanation for the intensity of this intermundane arrangement.[39] Like Patterson's widow, those who view, share, and upload his videos on various social media platforms and those who send donations to fund the broadcasts play essential roles as living devotees of his "living" preaching. This devotion is animated by a sense that there is something breathing in those recordings, some force that persists past death. If, as COGIC leader Frances Kelley asserts, Patterson has "saved more folks from the grave than some do alive," then his preaching must be both affective and effective, characteristics that require us, following Stanyek and Piekut, to move past notions of agency centered on living humans. Stanyek and Piekut propose a "notion of effectivity, where 'having' an effect is not understood in a proprietary sense, but rather as the enactment of agencies that make a difference—through making a difference, by having an effect, an agency is delineated."[40] Their insights in some ways update the old story: there is resurrection; there is a power of saints beyond the grave. But Stanyek and Piekut's conception also prompts a question: What difference does Patterson make? What might it mean for the sermons of a deceased messenger to move, persuade, and convict? What—or who—acts in such a situation?

A set of protocols for managing the material traces of a recently deceased Bishop's life are outlined in the 2015 teaching manual for the national adjutancy of the Church of God in Christ. Hidden away among reference materials on the denomination's structure, liturgy, the administration of sacraments, and organization, there is a course titled "Sanctity and Servitude." This section, written by Bishop Robert L. Perry Jr., a COGIC pastor, funeral director, and the denomination's senior deputy adjutant general, begins with the following preface:

> As Adjutants, we are taught to "Sanctify our Leaders in the eyes of the people." That same degree of commitment should be evident at their passing. We must strive to adequately provide the same degree of respect and reverence during this very solemn time as during the tenure of a Bishop. He is not a fallen leader but a promoted one. II Kings 13:21 says ... "And it came to pass as they were burying a man, that behold, they spied a band of men; and they cast the man into the sepulcher of Elisha: and when the man was let down, and touched the bones of Elisha, he revived, and stood up on his feet." This passage leads me to believe that our commitment to serve our Bishops should continue, even after death.
>
> If the bones of the Prophet Elisha could bring life back to the body of the unrighteous, the remains of the leaders of our church must be viewed and handled with upmost respect and reverence. Therefore, we feel compelled to continue assisting the Adjutancy in its challenge to provide dignity and service to our Bishops to the very end.[41]

Perry's directs adjutants on how to prepare for the death of a Bishop, what to do at the time of death, instructing them to serve as a conduit between mortuaries and the office of the Adjutant General, whose designee would convey guidance concerning the proper process of preservation. While the church's interests most centrally pertain to the mortician's care for the Bishop's remains, their carefulness has a revealing extension into the realms of materiality—sonorous and tangible.

According to Bishop Perry, adjutants are to "accompany the remains to the funeral home and remain on the premises during the embalming of the body (outside of the embalming room) making certain that the Bishop's presence in their facility is noted and properly respected. There should be NO SMOKING, USE OF PROFANITY OR PLAYING OF UNSACRED MUSIC IN THE ROOM(S) where the Bishop's remains are placed."[42] The presence of a Bishop's body enforces his denomination's holiness code on all who share its space. The Prelate's postmortem governmentality, though enforced by the "living" adjutant who serves as the denomination's proxy, draws its authority from the decedent. Certainly this devotion to the material dimensions of the Bishop's existence flows from beliefs about the cleric's spiritual power, their role as mediators of the holy. If such attention is customarily given to the remains of any COGIC Bishop, it would be hard to overstate the care afforded to the body of the Presiding Bishop, the denomination's chief apostle.

I am interested in what the denomination's funeral mandates teach about Bishop Patterson's afterlife. I especially want to stress the resonances between the COGIC decedent protocol and Pastor John Brown's claim that many tent-revival attendees placed alcohol and cigarettes into trash cans in response to Bishop Patterson's anointing. Given the doubled mediation of Patterson's spiritual effect and physical body through sound, and of sound through recording, one might want to appropriate media theorist Jonathan Sterne's contention that such technologies "preserve the bodies of the dead so that they could continue to perform a social function after life."[43] Yet Patterson's afterlife is motivated by a sense that his voice never stopped being both active and agential, resonating through "an arrangement of technologies and bodies that is less about preservation than it is about complex forms of rearticulation."[44] As COGIC's funeral mandates draw a connection between recorded music and cigar smoke, they show how holiness and sanctity are produced—during life and after death. The manual makes two linked assertions: (1) There are some materials through which the power, anointing, and presence of a spiritual leader can be apprehended—even, and especially, after death. (2) There are other materials with which the body of a Bishop must not assemble—even when it is no longer alive.

One Legacy.com user confessed in a 2017 post that she did not know Bishop Patterson was dead, despite his passing a full decade earlier.[45] She thus testified to the success with which a community has labored to keep Patterson's message alive and as part of a larger Broadcast Ensemble of riffs, cloths, videos, and humans who appear in various assemblages and support Patterson's Afterliveness. Patterson's pervasive online presence and his ongoing national television broadcasts lend credence to his ministry's claim that "the messenger sleeps; the message lives on."[46] But the production of Afterliveness began long before Patterson's death, evident whenever he worked to make the traces of his physical presence and the experience of spiritual power available to audiences spread across space and time. Across the decades of his life, little pieces of cloth, little bits of music, and little bottles of oil gave fuel to the aforementioned pursuit.

This chapter has clarified the links between the musical dimensions of Broadcast Religion and the tangible materialities that mediate Bishop Patterson's spiritual power on both sides of the grave. "The logic of the prayer cloth," which produces and disseminates spiritual power through the practice of fragmentation, animates the various facets of Patterson's Broadcast Ensemble, braiding the sermon, the song, and the human voice together with microphones, cameras, oil, cloth, television, radio, and the internet as potential conduits of divine power. While Pentecostal material devotion, religious broadcasting, and musical preaching all far predate Patterson's ministry, his Broadcast Religion brought Pentecostalism's most important instrument, the human voice, under the influence of the logic of the prayer cloth, yielding a set of audible fragments whose transcendence fuels eternal pitch.

In so doing, Patterson made a signal contribution to American religious broadcasting, a significance that is evidenced by the ecclesial power he attained during his life and the religious authority he enjoys even after his death. When bluesy Black preaching is placed at the center of Pentecostal practice, a distinctive efficacy emerges from an evolving constellation of religious media that work together to inculcate intimacy between Patterson's messages, his audiences, and various scenes from scripture. These Eucharistic practices convert whole garments and full sermons into energetic fragments whose circulation across space and time produces Afterliveness, the interworldly efficacy that arises from Black Pentecostal assemblage. Long after Patterson's 2007 death, his Broadcast Ensemble offers thousands of believers an occasion to live religion online, turning countless social media users into a new kind of religious broadcaster.

Eternal Life

AN EPILOGUE

After fifteen years as the public face of Bountiful Blessings, Inc., Evangelist Louise Patterson passed away on Sunday, November 20, 2022. While her death prompted a host of memorials and two heavily attended and widely livestreamed funerals, the most illuminating responses to her death have come from those who worked most closely with her. Just as the posthumous remediation of Bishop G. E. Patterson's message continues to clarify the meanings of his ministry, Bountiful Blessings's grappling with Louise Patterson's death sheds light on her centrality to this religious economy. This epilogue opens and closes with the ministry's attempts to come to grips with her passing because this moment of contingency reveals with particular clarity the intercalation of Blackness, belief, and technology in Broadcast Religion.

One week after Louise Patterson died, on Sunday, November 27, the first *Bountiful Blessings* broadcast aired in the ministry's assigned venues [▶ **Video Example EP1**]. After the opening montage, which has remained unchanged since the late 1990s, the camera cut to a tight scene of Temple of Deliverance's old church, located at 547 Mississippi Boulevard, the sanctuary from which Bishop Patterson first rose to national prominence. In a voice-over, two members of Bountiful Blessings's staff introduced themselves and shared an official announcement of their leader's passing:

> MICHAEL: Hello, I'm James O. Michael.
>
> ADAMS: And I'm Tabitha Adams. On last Sunday, November 20, our president and CEO, Evangelist Louise Patterson, went home to be with the Lord.
>
> MICHAEL: For the past fifteen years, Mother Patterson has made it her life's endeavor to continue spreading the gospel by hand selecting every message heard on the Bishop G. E. Patterson broadcast. Because of that we are healed, delivered, and set free.
>
> ADAMS: General manager of AM 1480 WBBP, former first lady of the Church of God in Christ, author of *A Rare Pearl*, mother, teacher, and friend, our beautiful queen, Louise Patterson, will be greatly missed. But her legacy will live on just as she planned it. And now . . .
>
> ADAMS AND MICHAEL: Welcome to the *Bountiful Blessings* broadcast with Bishop G. E. Patterson!

While Adams and Michael spoke, a picture of Louise Patterson appeared, along with a banner at the bottom of the screen that read: "We will always remember Evangelist Louise Patterson." Chief among the things Adams and Michael pledged to remember was her hand in shaping each week's broadcast. During her tenure atop the ministry, Evangelist Patterson frequently assured viewers that "we do not haphazardly select tapes," asserting this choice as an act of prayerful devotion, analogous to the labor and wisdom by which Bishop G. E. Patterson decided what to preach on a given Sunday. Adams and Michael insist that the "intermundane" partnership between G. E. Patterson's proclamations and Louise Patterson's curation was more than an analogy.[1] She helped enact Bishop Patterson's famous exhortation to "be healed, be delivered, and set free." She accentuated the power that is Afterliveness.

Evangelist Patterson's life was celebrated in two homegoing services, which took place on Thursday and Friday, December 1–2, 2022. Both gatherings illustrated her influence, drawing together elected officials, the leaders of virtually every Black church in Memphis, the leaders of COGIC's

ETERNAL LIFE: AN EPILOGUE

Department of Women, the Bishops' wives circles, numerous Bishops, and the sitting Presiding Bishop of COGIC, the Rt. Rev. J. Drew Sheard. Many gospel artists—including Bishop Marvin Winans, Myrna Summers, Judith McAllister, and Pastor Carlis Moody Jr.—gathered to lead the assembly in song. I, too, flew to Memphis to attend the Thursday night and Friday morning services to honor the significance of Louise Patterson's contributions to the Black church and the personal kindness she had shown to me. Thus, while I have only witnessed recordings of the final viewing with which this book began—the moment when the Bishop G. E. Patterson's bier was sealed—I was there, in Temple of Deliverance, when Louise Patterson's casket was closed for the last time.

Being there really mattered. Being there attuned me to the problematics of presence that were provoked by the need to say goodbye to a human body—"the remains." What a phrase: "the remains." Over and over that Thursday and Friday, I heard ushers and attendants beseech congregants: "Do not take any pictures of the remains." Having spent so much time thinking and writing about technology's place in the endurance of Bishop Patterson's Black life, I was gripped by this aversion to photographic reproduction—and by the forcefulness of its assertion. What a phrase: "the remains."

When I walked toward the casket before the Thursday night service, with my iPhone in my hand, hanging by my side, one of the ushers kindly asked me to put my phone away, reminding me that no photographs were to be taken of "the body." While I easily complied with this request, given my lack of interest in taking such a picture, not everyone found this instruction so actionable. During the Friday morning national homegoing service, one mourner managed to sneak in a picture of Evangelist Patterson—or so they thought. Bishop Dickerson Wells, the Adjutant General of the Church of God in Christ, who presided over this final viewing, saw this photograph being taken. As the covert photographer walked away from the casket, Bishop Wells interrupted the choir that had been singing the vamp of Richard Smallwood's "I Love the Lord (He Heard My Cry)" to enforce the technological protocol: "I'm going to ask that there be no picture-taking of the remains. Please don't do that. And, if our adjutant brothers will follow them back to their seats regarding that photograph ..." Wells did not need to complete his instruction because the implication was clear enough: the adjutants would make sure that the forbidden image would be deleted.

How does this iconoclastic Pentecostalism relate to the technophilia that I have theorized throughout this book? What conceptions of life are revealed by these encounters with death? While photographing the deceased is the subject of great disagreement in Black funeral culture, the Black Pentecostals who were responsible for Louise Patterson's final public appearances clarified that picture-taking was not allowed. Two details add complexity to these funereal technoethics. First, her body was clearly visible on the livestream of both homegoing services. Given the established excellence of Temple of Deliverance's media ministry, there is no reason to understand this as an error. Second, those who selected her final apparel arranged for Evangelist Patterson to be dressed in two different outfits for the two homegoing services: green on Thursday and white, for all eternity. This Aretha Franklin-esque wardrobe change was a fitting honor for one known, throughout COGIC and many other sectors of the Black church, for her impeccable sense of fashion.

Indeed, the Uber driver who drove me from my hotel to the church for the Friday service recalled being sure that Patterson was somebody "important"—even before being introduced to her—simply because of how "sharp a dresser" she was. Her final wardrobe change did not go unnoticed by those who livestreamed the funeral. One YouTube user wrote: "Beautiful outfit change. I expected nothing less." And another commented: "They did a fine job of taking care of mother Patterson even down to the different outfit. May mother Patterson rest in peace." This change in fashion, this "expected" expression of "care" was in a sense unnecessary—so extra, so excessive, so Black. So Black that it must be read as an instance of what literary scholar Christina Sharpe calls "wake work," ways of attending to the Black dead and dying that insist on "the largeness that is Black life."[2]

But this wake work was meant to be seen, not reproduced. Indeed, the prohibition on photography at Louise Patterson's homegoing reflects transformations in the media environment since her husband's transition. When Bishop Patterson died in March 2007, the iPhone had not yet become available for popular purchase. Fifteen years later, virtually everyone in the sanctuary had some version of a smartphone, bringing with it the capacity to preserve anything—including death. Even as this new technological regime, which prompted the injunctions against funereal picture-taking, puts pressure on the Black Pentecostal technophilia that funds Afterliveness, it clarifies this vernacular philosophy's archetypically Black relationship to death. Despite pictures of Evangelist Patterson cycling across the church's large projection screens before both services and, despite videos of the late Pattersons speaking, singing, and preaching, it was not appropriate to take a picture of the remains. In response to a life spent resisting the ephemerality of sound, the fact of ordinary death does not merit repeating—only death surpassed, only death undone is worthy of dissemination. Only something living should be reproduced because nothing less than life itself—Afterliveness—is available for transmission. The aversion to photography for such a frequently photographed person reveals a desire to make death ephemeral, not life.

CO-PASTORING

The most prominent evangelist of Patterson's Afterliveness was his widow, Louise, who played a crucial role in both phases of Bishop G. E. Patterson's ministry. Chapter 5 illustrates how Louise Patterson enacted the logic of the prayer cloth by disseminating articles of her late husband's clothing along with the claim that this apparel connected recipients with the late Bishop's anointing. This form of religious broadcasting, however, was only evident to those she chose to "bless" with one or more garments. Her role in the still-airing *Bountiful Blessings* television broadcast enacted this process on a much grander scale—visible to millions through Word Network, local television stations, Facebook, YouTube, or the ministry's website, www.bbless.org. From 2007 to 2022 the opening scene of each *Bountiful Blessings* broadcast quickly cut from the standard opening to footage of Evangelist Patterson standing or sitting in her living room, proclaiming: "From the beautiful city of Memphis, Tennessee, I'm Evangelist Louise Patterson" [▶ **Video Example EP2**].

Unlike the many introductory scenes that Bishop G. E. Patterson taped in various sanctuaries and offices, Louise Patterson's welcome was situated domestically, producing a forceful symmetry with the setting in which her viewing congregation would participate in the broadcast. As she welcomed viewers to the broadcast and into her home, she thanked them for tuning in, for granting her access to their dwellings, and for the gifts that enabled *Bountiful Blessings* to stay on air. After offering a mixture of exhortation and encouragement, she introduced the theme of the forthcoming sermon, before leading listeners into a service that was "already in process."

Bishop G. E. Patterson and Evangelist Louise Patterson served as the public face of Bountiful Blessings national television ministry for nearly equivalent spans of time. The seventeen years between Bishop G. E. Patterson's arrival on national TV and his 2007 death only barely exceed the fifteen years that Louise Patterson presided over the broadcast—itself a forum for producing religious authority and transmitting spiritual power. During her tenure she repeatedly asserted that through the ongoing television programming, "People are being saved. They are being healed. And they are being delivered. That is what the message is all about." She prefigured this partnership during her message to the 2005 COGIC International Women's Conference, a gathering that followed closely on the heels of the first indications of Bishop Patterson's faltering health [▶ **Video Example EP3**].

She said: "Some of us feel like Job's wives. All we know about Job['s wife] is that they say she was a foolish woman. Job told her she talked like a foolish woman. But what I don't understand about that whole scenario: You don't hear nothing. She doesn't even have a name, Bishop." Looking to her left, in the direction of the (male) Bishops sitting on the stage, Evangelist Patterson leans into her critique of this sense of namelessness. "Just Job's wife. Job's children. Job's this and Job's that. But I come to tell you, tonight, women, you have a name! You have name, women! You are virtuous, the virtuous women of God. And God has placed you strategically where you are to do what you do." Then she turns to the topic of ecclesial titles—a charged one in a denomination whose official policy excludes women from ordained leadership, even if exceptions are made in practice.[3] She said: "They don't have to give you no title. They don't have to give you no title. [They don't have to] call you administrative assistant. Don't have to call me co-pastor. But I been co-pastoring [as] long as he been pastoring. Yes, I have! Yes, I have! Amen! I been co-pastoring long as he been pastoring. Amen!"

After making this forceful assertion of her centrality to the ministry of her husband, who was then one of the most powerful religious leaders in the United States, Louise Patterson buttressed her claim, arguing that if "anything go[es] wrong" in the church, members knew where to find resolution. "If you can't get to him, 'Let me get to Sister Blake. Let me get Sister Owens. Let me get to Sister White.' We been co-pastors all the time. Y'all just didn't know what to call us!" As thousands leapt to their feet, responding to the form and content of her message, Louise Patterson clapped demonstratively for her own message, as if to say, "I said what I said." While her arguments that day described her past contributions to Temple of Deliverance, Bountiful Blessings, Inc., and the Church of God in Christ, no domain of ministry has made the partnership of these Pattersons clearer than her stewardship of the media ministry after Bishop Patterson went to sleep. Leading the *Bountiful Blessings* broadcasts allowed Louise Patterson to operate in the ether in ways that subverted patriarchal elements of the denomination's structure, building on the influence she enjoyed during G. E. Patterson's life as the instrument of his ministry's afterlife. But stewardship is an insufficient term for Louise Patterson's place in this religious economy. She, more than anyone else, clarifies that Broadcast Religion was not G. E. Patterson's alone.

AN ETERNAL FLAME: THE PENTECOSTAL NETWORK

A few months after Bishop Patterson died, Evangelist Patterson led several hundred relatives and parishioners in a service of dedication for a commemorative installation that had been erected outside Temple of Deliverance: an eternal flame [▶ **Video Example EP4**]. In this machinic ensemble a curved metal dish, supported by a tall metal beam, nourishes an indefatigable flame—a blaze designed to burn for all eternity. During the dedication of this burning memorial, Louise Patterson observed: "From this day forward we'll be able to tell children what these flames mean and about Bishop G. E. Patterson and his magnitude in Memphis and all over the world."[4]

The meaningfulness of this flame and this preacher meld particularity and exemplarity. While the eternal flame that honors Bishop Patterson participates in a widespread custom for celebrating endurance and commitment, this installation derives salience from three features of Patterson's life and ministry, which I have theorized in Chapter 5 as Broadcast Ensemble: his assemblage of Black musicking, Pentecostal preaching, and religious broadcasting. The symbol of fire visualizes the Pentecostal theology that shaped his ministry, materializing the "tongues of fire" that are so central to the biblical understandings that buttress the most distinctive form of Pentecostal speech: glossolalia. Moreover, this flame incarnates the intensity achieved in Patterson's sermons, embodying the telos of the pyrotechnic messages that hold the key to his renown. Finally, inasmuch as this eternal flame exemplifies perpetual ongoing, it illuminates Bishop Patterson's musical afterlife, the posthumous resonance studied in the foregoing pages. Through his virtuosic recombination of these widely shared materials, Bishop Patterson built something that ordinary death could not dismantle.

While Evangelist Patterson's fiery argument referenced the blaze that stands outside her church, this book has been equally concerned with a different set of enduring, symbolic flames—the ones that fill this representative comment on a one-minute Instagram video of a Patterson sermon.[5] In the comments below this video—and countless other videos—one finds emojis representing fire, a commonplace visible declaration used by social media users when they find an online object particularly powerful. While this fire-invoking clip derives from a much longer video, a 1993 sermon titled "Neither Were They Thankful," its current form reflects the limits and logics of Instagram and other social-networking platforms on which it circulates. When compared to the eternal flame installed in front of Temple of Deliverance, these bits of digital materiality might seem resolutely insignificant at first glance. After all, these tiny virtual objects are dwarfed by the fiery assemblage that stands outside Patterson's temple, just as the Instagram clip is (in only one sense) dwarfed by the scale of the full sermon.

But considered through the framework of Broadcast Religion, a different interpretation comes into view. Like the mechanical assemblage that sustains the fire outside Temple of Deliverance, a vast network of belief, technologies, and ritual practices kindles these flames online (Figure 13). When attached to the pieces of Patterson sermons circulating across vari-

Figure 13. Instagram users' comments depicting Bishop G. E. Patterson's eternal flame, October 4, 2020.

ous social networking platforms, these little flames materialize the rhetoric of Afterliveness, asserting that fragments of Bishop Patterson's technophilic Pentecostalism are still quite alive and that this life has always been most evident in the fragments (Figure 14).

All this raises a counterfactual question: What if Bishop Patterson *were* still alive—alive in the conventional, embodied sense? What if his period of physical animation extended into the 2010s, the moment when social-networking platforms became as central to the practice of faith as radio, television, anointed oil, and prayer cloths had long been? How might this technophilic religious broadcaster have engaged these new virtual venues? How would these new formats influence the shape of the disseminated content? If Patterson had to select a one-minute excerpt from one of his many sermons, might they resemble the fragments that contemporary users have selected, or would he have highlighted something altogether different? While precise answers to these questions cannot be ascertained, the material facts of Bishop Patterson's life and ministry offer solid ground from which to hypothesize. As such, these speculative questions cast the central research question of this book in a new light.

Figure 14. Instagram users' comments depicting Bishop G. E. Patterson's eternal flame, in response to a post by @Preachernation, April 17, 2022.

Although I cannot prove it, I am persuaded that there would be significant overlap with the homiletic fragments Patterson would have chosen to disseminate online and those that are routinely shared by members of his virtual congregation. The formalism of Black Pentecostalism is evident in "the logic of the prayer cloth," the theory of religious communication that links Patterson's voice to a network of believers, practices, and devotional objects, while structuring his digital remediation. As it turns out, the keeping-alive of Bishop Patterson is a very Black Pentecostal thing to do. When social media users fragment and disseminate audible traces of Patterson's "anointing," they are inhabiting a creative space analogous to what Patterson himself occupied when he repeated musical tropes, transformed his utterances into broadcasts, and captured them on various media. These traces include cassette recordings of prayers and sermons in the 1960s and 1970s, VHSs of worship services in the 1980s, CDs of gospel songs in the 1990s, and DVDs of sermons in the 2000s.

Akin to deciding which sermon to broadcast on a given Sunday, the analytical labor being performed by those who extract fragments from longer Patterson videos is also argumentative. Like the emoji flames that spread beneath them, these posts assert that this excerpt is an especially important and affectively potent moment of the sermon. As pieces of Patterson's power are engrafted onto the devotional practices of various audiences, his lifelong pursuit of technologically mediated vocal presence is realized through his uncommon endurance, reiterated in his recurring prayer for the power "to speak as an oracle of Christ." Indeed, at least one Patterson broadcast has materialized on radio, television, or the internet nearly every day since the early 1960s, even though he has been deceased for a quarter of this time span.

One of the most striking aspects of the digital Patterson catalog is the degree to which the eternal riff pervades these clips. It is anything but coincidental that the eternal riff appears so often: given the great quantity of possible material, the digital reiteration of this musical device vents a deep understanding of Patterson's project. Indeed, beyond Patterson's catalog, the heightened, ecstatic frame of a characteristically Black sermon is the most likely moment to be captured on YouTube and the moment a Facebook user is most likely to "go live." The emphatic, climactic moment most often captured in Patterson's sermons, like all Black sermons, is precisely the moment in which he routinely articulated his riff. Patterson's recurring gestures enact an ongoing affront against the ephemerality of sound that Chapter 1 theorizes as "Pentecostal playback," the practice in which Patterson records himself, instrumentalizing his voice to conduct scripture's eternal transmission. The presence of these riffs in these digital devotional objects suggests that Patterson's eternal song, eternal riff, and eternal pitch collectively constitute a homiletic, musical hint about the most crucial moments to repeat. The riff was always already viral—a recursive highlight, an ecstatic moment. Its afterlife—like his afterlife—takes place in these virtual venues. Its repetition in the ever-burgeoning video clips is evidence of a shared theocultural logic, Broadcast Religion's logic of the prayer cloth of which Patterson has been an exemplar.

The recursive, fragmentary, and convergent character of Patterson's Pentecostal network offers an occasion to think about how ritual unfolds in the digital age. While the argument advanced in the foregoing pages is informed by countless Facebook posts, YouTube comments, and obituary remembrances, one of the most telling observations emerged from a brief telephone conversation. When she discovered I was writing this book, a senior Black churchwoman told me: "Every time I open up YouTube on my iPhone, Bishop Patterson comes right up." This comment connects Patterson, a device, a platform, and his frequency of occurrence: it highlights the digital mechanics of eternal pitch. Trained by her viewing habits, YouTube's recommendation algorithms guide a path through its voluminous video library, lending a predictable structure to her personal devotional practices. In so doing, the platform links this virtual congregant to Patterson's ministry, other viewers, and the users who contribute to Patterson's ever-expanding catalog. These moments of encounter between "Black women and everyday struggles of faith," to summon anthropologist Marla Frederick's words, point to the productive resonance between the spiritual magnetism of Patterson's preaching and the invisible agencies that facilitate digital ritualization.[6]

THE AFTERLIVES OF ECSTASY

When I describe Bishop G. E. Patterson's Afterliveness as an archetypically Black and Pentecostal unfolding, I am claiming that this phenomenon is only thinkable in conjunction with the nonlinear temporalities that both structure and arise from Black musicking, Black religion, and Black social life.[7] These Black temporalities frequently come into focus in relation to various kinds of death. In the weeks following Evangelist Patterson's passing, the Bountiful Blessings, Inc. television staff experimented with several ways of opening and closing the television program, recognizing that her death, like that of her husband, required a reanimation of Broadcast Religion. For the first few weeks the ministry's producers filled Louise Patterson's introductory segment with a version of the death announcement [▶ **Video Example EP5**].

The next couple of broadcasts evaded introduction altogether, jumping directly from the opening montage into the recording of that day's selected sermon. Remarkably, the ministry's rebroadcast of Patterson's 2000 sermon "Call His Name" on Sunday, December 18, 2022, opened with the original introduction Patterson filmed before airing this sermon for the first time [▶ **Video Example EP6**]. It had been more than fifteen years since his likeness was deployed in this way, yet this reanimation seemed newly plausible as the ministry grappled with the meanings of Louise Patterson's recent death. The weeks thereafter featured another striking shift to a string of vintage sermons, each of which was originally recorded by a young Apostle G. E. Patterson during the mid-1980s in Temple of Deliverance's original sanctuary.

Born again at the intersection of 2022 and 2023, the ministry's response to Evangelist Patterson's passing offers a window into the ways Broadcast Religion has responded to a host of evolving circumstances. Much about the late 2022 TV broadcasts resembles the ways that Bountiful Blessings, Inc. grappled with technological change, the emergence of new audiences, and historical exigencies like physical death—with and without the two Pattersons. An expansive distance separates Elder G. E. Patterson's recorded telephonic prayers in the 1960s from the emphatic opposition to smartphone photographs of Evangelist Patterson's remains in late 2022. But a stronger thread, which I earlier termed "a lifelong pursuit of technologically mediated vocal omnipresence," connects the phases of broadcast religion. This pursuit is Afterliveness.

The proximity of Louise Patterson's death to the first Sunday of December in 2022 prompted the ministry to interrupt one of the rituals she established. On the first Sunday of each month, she would lead the television audience in celebrating communion: the Lord's Supper. During the introductory segment of these broadcasts, she would instruct viewers to "go and get your wafer and grape juice and prepare yourself for having communion with the saints of God." At the end of that day's sermon the broadcast would turn to footage of a communion service held during Bishop Patterson's life, cutting back and forth between the recording and footage of Louise Patterson consuming communion elements of "bread and wine" in her living room. By intertwining these two events, the producers enabled Louise Patterson to join both the original congregation and her television audience in celebrating this Christian ritual.

While the broadcast of Sunday, December 4, was the rare first Sunday program without a communion celebration, the ministry more than made up for it during the first broadcast of 2023, on Sunday, January 1. This New Year's Day telecast had specific significance: the ministry's split screen synchronization of Bishop Patterson and Evangelist Patterson drinking consecrated juice—in different years but at the same time—materialized the suggestion that they are together again. Unfolding at the intersection of ritual and history, belief and technology, this new communion pressed the claim that broadcasting technology occasions the transmission of spiritual power—an eternal flame—around the world and between visible and spiritual realms [▶ **Video Example EP7**]. Alongside Evangelist Louise Patterson and the staff of Bountiful Blessings, Inc., countless members of Patterson's Broadcast Ensemble have played vital roles in Bishop G. E. Patterson's afterlife. Thus as much as this book has been about Patterson's virtuosic vocality, institutional savvy, and broadcasting acumen, it is equally concerned with another kind of religious broadcaster: those who purchased, recorded, and disseminated hard copies of sermons and songs during his life, and those who cut, post, and share fragments of these messages long after his death. This network is animated by the rhetoric of Afterliveness.

I have described Afterliveness as the enduring affect that Broadcast Religion's practitioners locate in the posthumous circulation of Patterson's recorded messages—paradoxically, an affect central to his preaching during his lifetime. Afterliveness is multivalent. As an experience, Afterliveness names a certain sense of proximity, both to events recorded in scripture and the moment when Patterson's proclamations of these events were captured on tape. As a rhetorical tool, Afterliveness holds together tens of thousands of individual assertions about the peculiar potency of Patterson's messages—in person and online, unveiling a network of reception and remediation that we have come to know as Broadcast Religion. As a homiletic aim, Afterliveness is expressed in Patterson's customary pre-sermonic prayer, the repeated appeal for power with which "to speak as an oracle of Christ." As a formal practice, Afterliveness is a logic at work across the entire catalogue of Patterson's sermons, most evident in the set of recurring gestures this book has collected under the rubric of "eternal pitch."

Like the genesis and evolution of notions of liveness, the production of Afterliveness is a thoroughly technological feat, one occasioned by interactions between Black music and sound technologies. If this book's assertion that Black Pentecostalism is a technophilic formation seems counterintuitive, its grounding in the central beliefs of Black Pentecostals should by now be clear. Black Pentecostalism is a set of sound techniques that respond to the expectation that the human voice should and must become a vehicle of divine speech—an ensemble of sonic tools that manage the relationship between the material world and the spiritual realm. In this way Broadcast Religion contradicts a pervasive tendency of ignoring the theoretical and practical innovations of Black religious subjects.

With his combination of technological sophistication, Pentecostal instrumentality, and Black musicality, Patterson made an enduring contribution to religious broadcasting. When members of Patterson's Broadcast Ensemble use digital tools to relay the musical logic of the prayer cloth, they join in a Black technopoetic genealogy. In offering their own Pattersonian interventions, they further highlight the impact this religious figure has made on both sides of the grave. Like a devotional fragment holding together a network of believers, material, and convictions, Patterson's distinctive combination of tradition and innovation makes his oeuvre an ideal site from which to study Black music, digital culture, and lived religion. The longer his voice resounds, the truer it seems to be that Bishop G. E. Patterson's ministry is endowed with an eternal pitch.

Notes

INTRODUCTION

1. adeddao, "GEP Focusing Our Eyes upon the Lord," YouTube video, 43:49, June 11, 2015, https://youtu.be/dekN3jFVoIU.

2. Official Bishop G E Patterson Channel, "Bishop G. E. Patterson—Focusing Your Eyes upon the Lord," YouTube video, 2:16, July 1, 2016, https://youtu.be/rIZgRVYEdLM.

3. Gordon Palmer, "GE Patterson Focusing Your Eyes upon the Lord," YouTube video, 1:04:24, April 17, 2020, https://youtu.be/YsMtI3gLW18.

4. This concept is inspired by Shana Redmond's work on Paul Robeson's musical afterlives—a project that extends Saidiya Hartman's discussion of "the afterlives of slavery" in *Lose Your Mother: A Journey Along the Atlantic Slave Route* (New York: Farrar, Straus and Giroux, 2007), 6.

5. See Philip Auslander, *Liveness: Performance in a Mediatized Culture* (New York: Routledge, 1999). See Paul Sanden, "Rethinking Liveness in the Digital Age," in *The Cambridge Companion to Music and Digital Culture*, ed. Nicholas Cook, Monique Ingalls, and David Trippett (Cambridge, UK: Cambridge University Press, 2019), 178–92.

6. On the topic of "lived religion," see Heidi A. Campbell, "The Rise of the Study of Digital Religion," in *Digital Religion: Understanding Religious Practice in New Media Worlds*, ed. Heidi A. Campbell (Routledge: New York, 2012), 1–22; and Heidi A. Campbell, "Understanding the Relationship between Religion

Online and Offline in a Networked Society," *Journal of the American Academy of Religion* 80, no. 1 (2012): 63–93.

7. As the following chapters demonstrate, this project is thoroughly engaged with Alexander Weheliye, *Phonographies: Grooves in Sonic Afro-Modernity* (Durham, NC: Duke University Press, 2005); and Louis Chude-Sokei, *The Sound of Culture: Diaspora and Black Technopoetics* (Middletown, CT: Wesleyan University Press, 2016).

8. John Guillory, "Genesis of the Media Concept," *Critical Inquiry* 36, no. 2 (2010): 346.

9. Shana Redmond, *Everything Man: The Form and Function of Paul Robeson* (Durham, NC: Duke University Press, 2020), 8.

10. Ruth Prince, *The Whole Truth: Official Magazine of the Church of God in Christ*, August 1959, front page.

11. "Bishop Gilbert Earl Paterson: Reflections—the Life of a Visionary," *Whole Truth: The Official Magazine of the Church of God in Christ*, April/May/June 2007, 18–19; Dennis Hevesi, "Bishop G. E. Patterson, 67, Who Led Church of God in Christ, Dies," *New York Times*, March 22, 2007, www.nytimes.com/2007/03/22/obituaries/22patterson.html?_r=0.

12. John Giggie, *After Redemption: Jim Crow and the Transformation of African American Religion in the Delta, 1875–1917* (New York: Oxford University Press, 2008), 168.

13. Giggie, *After Redemption*, 169.

14. Giggie, *After Redemption*, 175.

15. James Dowd, "G. E. Patterson: Redefined Role as COGIC's Presiding Bishop," *Memphis Commercial Appeal*, March 21, 2007.

16. "Patterson Is Upheld on Action as Bishop," *Memphis Press-Scimitar*, December 21, 1974.

17. Valerie G. Lowe, "God's Man in Memphis," *Charisma*, September 2001, www.charismamag.com/spirit/devotionals/daily-breakthroughs?view=article&id=436:gods-man-in-memphis&catid=146.

18. BrothaRollins, video of sermon by Gilbert Patterson, "Divine Worship" (Temple of Deliverance COGIC, Memphis, TN, March 16, 1997), YouTube video, 3:02, September 23, 2010, www.YouTube.com/watch?v = A_BwmzZUiE4.

19. Owens quoted in Corrie Cutrer, "Church of God in Christ: COGIC Presiding Bishop Ousted," *Christianity Today*, January 8, 2001, www.christianitytoday.com/ct/2001/january8/16.22.html?start=2.

20. Cutrer, "Church of God in Christ."

21. BrothaRollins, video of Patterson, "Divine Worship."

22. Jonathan L. Walton, *Watch This! The Ethics and Aesthetics of Black Televangelism* (New York: New York University Press, 2009), 199.

23. "Bishop G. E. Patterson Elected New Leader of Church of God in Christ," *Jet Magazine*, December 18, 2000.

24. Marla Frederick, *Colored Television: American Religion Gone Global* (Stanford, CA: Stanford University Press, 2015), 187fn33.

25. Kate Bowler, *Blessed: A History of the American Prosperity Gospel* (New York: Oxford University Press, 2013), 115.

26. Calvin White, *The Rise to Respectability: Race, Religion, and the Church of God in Christ* (Fayetteville: University of Arkansas Press, 2012).

27. Exceptions include Anthea Butler, *Women in the Church of God in Christ: Making a Sanctified World* (Chapel Hill: University of North Carolina Press, 2007).

28. Jill Lepore, "Historians Who Love Too Much: Reflections on Microhistory and Biography," *Journal of American History* 88, no. 1 (2001): 133.

29. Butler, *Women in the Church of God in Christ*; Giggie, *After Redemption*; Cheryl J. Sanders, *Saints in Exile: The Holiness-Pentecostal Experience in African American Religion and Culture* (New York: Oxford University Press, 1996); Estrelda Alexander, *Black Fire: One Hundred Years of African American Pentecostalism* (Downers Grove, IL: IVP Academic, 2011); Amos Yong and Estrelda Alexander, eds., *Afro-Pentecostalism: Black Pentecostal and Charismatic Christianity in History and Culture* (New York: New York University Press, 2010).

30. Grant Wacker, *Heaven Below: Early Pentecostals and American Culture* (Cambridge, MA: Harvard University Press, 2001); James K. A. Smith, *Thinking in Tongues: Pentecostal Contributions to Christian Theology* (Grand Rapids, MI: William B. Eerdmans Pub. Co., 2010); David Edwin Harrell Jr., *All Things Are Possible: The Healing and Charismatic Revivals in Modern America* (Bloomington: Indiana University Press, 1975); David Edwin Harrell Jr., *Oral Roberts: An American Life* (Bloomington: Indiana University Press, 1985); Nicholas Harkness, *Songs of Seoul: An Ethnography of Voice and Voicing in Christian South Korea* (Berkeley: University of California Press, 2014); Nicholas Harkness, *Glossolalia and the Problem of Language* (Chicago: University of Chicago Press, 2021).

31. Frederick, *Colored Television*; Tona J. Hangen, *Redeeming the Dial: Radio, Religion, and Popular Culture in America* (Chapel Hill: University of North Carolina Press, 2002); Quentin J. Schultze, "Evangelical Radio and the Rise of the Electronic Church, 1921-1948," *Journal of Broadcasting and Electronic Media* 32 (Summer 1988): 289-306; Quentin J. Schultze, "The Invisible Medium: Evangelical Radio," in *American Evangelicals and the Mass Media*, ed. Quentin J. Schultze, 171-95 (Grand Rapids, MI: Academie Books, 1990); Quentin J. Schultze, "The Mythos of the Electronic Church," *Critical Studies in Mass Communication* 4 (September 1987): 245-261; Walton, *Watch This!*.

32. David Buttrick, *Homiletic: Moves and Structures* (Philadelphia: Fortress Press, 2007); Henry Mitchell, *Celebration and Experience in Preaching* (Nashville, TN: Abingdon Press, 1990); William Turner, "The Musicality of Black Preaching: A Phenomenology," in *Performance in Preaching: Bringing the*

Sermon to Life, ed. Jana Childers and Clayton Schmitt, 191–209 (Grand Rapids, MI: Baker Academic, 2008); Martha Feldman and Judith Zeitlin, eds., *The Voice as Something More: Essays toward Materiality* (Chicago: University of Chicago Press, 2019).

33. Anderson Blanton, *Hittin' the Prayer Bones: Materiality of Spirit in the Pentecostal South* (Chapel Hill: University of North Carolina Press, 2015); Birgit Meyer, "Mediation and Immediacy: Sensational Forms, Semiotic Ideologies, and the Question of the Medium," *Social Anthropology* 19, no. 1 (2011): 23–39; Patrick Eisenlohr, *Sounding Islam: Voice, Media, and Sonic Atmospheres in an Indian Ocean World* (Oakland: University of California Press, 2018); Charles Hirschkind, *The Ethical Soundscape: Cassette Sermons and Islamic Counterpublics* (New York: Columbia University Press, 2006); Matthew Engelke, *A Problem of Presence: Beyond Scripture in an African Church* (Berkeley: University of California Press, 2007).

34. John Durham Peters, *Marvelous Clouds: Toward a Philosophy of Elemental Media* (Chicago: University of Chicago Press, 2015); John Durham Peters, *Speaking into the Air: A History of the Idea of Communication* (Chicago: University of Chicago Press, 1999); Jonathan Sterne, *The Audible Past: Cultural Origins of Sound Reproduction* (Durham, NC: Duke University Press, 2003); Jonathan Sterne, *MP3: The Meaning of a Format* (Durham, NC: Duke University Press, 2012); Gavin Feller, *Eternity in the Ether: A Mormon Media History* (Urbana: University of Illinois Press, 2023); Pamela Klassen, *The Story of Radio Mind: A Missionary's Journey on Indigenous Land* (Chicago: University of Chicago Press, 2018).

35. Spencer Miller Jr., "Radio and Religion," *Annals of the American Academy of Political and Social Science* 177, no. 1 (1935): 135–140.

36. Hangen, *Redeeming the Dial*, 2.

37. See Jeffrey Sconce, *Haunted Media: Electronic Presence from Telegraphy to Television* (Durham, NC: Duke University Press, 2000); John Durham Peters, "Phantasms of the Living, Dialogues with the Dead," in Peters, *Speaking into the Air: The History of the Idea of Communication* (Chicago: University of Chicago Press, 1999): 137–177.

38. Norman Spaulding, "History of Black Oriented Radio in Chicago, 1929–1963," PhD dissertation, University of Illinois at Urbana-Champaign, 1981, 101.

39. For more on early Black radio broadcasting in Chicago, see Robert Marovich, *A City Called Heaven: Chicago and the Birth of Gospel Music* (Urbana: University of Illinois Press, 2018).

40. Edgar T. Rouzeau, "'Happy Am I': Millions Listen to Elder Michaux, the Radio Evangelist," *New York Amsterdam News*, September 29, 1934, 9.

41. While many radio preachers were quite controversial figures, Michaux was especially problematic. Lerone Martin has uncovered evidence that Michaux collaborated with the Hoover-era FBI in their campaign against Martin Luther

King Jr. See Lerone Martin, "Bureau Clergyman: How the FBI Colluded with an African-American Televangelist to Destroy Dr. Martin Luther King Jr.," *Religion and American Culture* 28, no. 1 (2018): 1–51.

42. Abram Hill, "Elder Horn," August 24, 1939, Schomburg Center for Research in Black Culture at New York Public Library, Black New Yorkers Collection, https://blacknewyorkers-nypl.org/wp-content/uploads/2016/06/horn_elder.pdf.

43. See Nick Salvatore's classic treatment of C. L. Franklin: Nick Salvatore, *Singing in a Strange Land: C. L. Franklin, the Black Church, and the Transformation of America* (New York: Little Brown, 2005).

44. Salvatore, *Singing in a Strange Land*, 123.

45. Lerone Martin, *Preaching on Wax: The Phonograph and the Shaping of Modern African-American Religion* (New York: New York University Press, 2014).

46. Martin, *Preaching on Wax*, 90.

47. Walton, *Watch This!*, 47–74; and Frederick, *Colored Television*, 31–60.

48. Jason Miccolo Johnson, conversation with the author, January 2023.

49. Louise Patterson, conversation with the author, February 2021.

50. Walton, *Watch This!*, 65.

51. Frederick, *Colored Television*, 44.

52. See Frederick's discussion of Pearson in *Colored Television*, chapter 2.

53. Ashon Crawley, *Blackpentecostal Breath: The Aesthetics of Possibility* (New York: Fordham University Press, 2016).

54. Crawley, *Blackpentecostal Breath*, 176.

55. Harkness, *Glossolalia and the Problem of Language*.

56. Harkness, *Glossolalia and the Problem of Language*, 7.

57. Harkness, *Glossolalia and the Problem of Language*, 9.

58. This is a classic example of the phenomenon Webb Keane defined as a "semiotic ideology" in Webb Keane, "Semiotics and the Social Analysis of Material Things," *Language and Communication* 23, no. 3 (2003): 419.

59. Harkness, *Glossolalia and the Problem of Language*, 17.

60. Crawley, *Blackpentecostal Breath*, 224.

61. See Chapter 2 for extended discussion.

62. Crawley, *Blackpentecostal Breath*, 163.

63. William Turner, "The Musicality of Black Preaching: A Phenomenology," in *Performance in Preaching: Bringing the Sermon to Life*, ed. Jana Childers and Clayton Schmitt, 191–209 (Grand Rapids, MI: Baker Academic, 2008).

64. They include the skill with which Patterson musicalizes phrases turning single lines into transcendent sermonic moments; the consistency with which he marshals the octave as an agent of sonic and spiritual transduction; and the moments in which he engages in specific musical discourse, instructing an organist to put him in a particular key, etc.

65. Harkness, *Glossolalia and the Problem of Language*, 13.

66. Weheliye, *Phonographies*, 7.

67. Anthony Pinn, *Interplay of Things: Religion, Art, and Presence Together* (Durham, NC: Duke University Press, 2021), 1.

68. Kathy Howell, June 5, 2022, comment on "A Call to be Different, 'Pentecost' Bishop G. E. Patterson," YouTube, www.YouTube.com/watch?v=ZpotrGCs_M0&t=2231s.

69. Auslander, *Liveness*; Sanden, "Rethinking Liveness in the Digital Age."

70. Kevin Quashie, *Black Aliveness, or a Poetics of Being* (Durham, NC: Duke University Press, 2021), 26.

71. Maurice Wallace, *King's Vibrato: Modernism, Blackness, and the Sonic Life of Martin Luther King Jr.* (Durham, NC: Duke University Press, 2022), 6, italics in original.

72. Alondra Nelson, "Future Texts" and "Afrofuturism," ed. Alondra Nelson, *Social Text* 71 (Summer 2002): 5–6.

73. Kathryn Lofton, *Consuming Religion* (Chicago: University of Chicago Press, 2017), 10.

74. Vaughn Booker, *Lift Every Voice and Swing: Black Musicians and Religious Culture in the Jazz Century* (New York: New York University Press, 2020); Crawley, *Blackpentecostal Breath*; Alisha Lola Jones, *Flaming? The Peculiar Theopolitics of Fire and Desire in Black Male Gospel Performance* (New York: Oxford University Press, 2020).

75. Weheliye, *Phonographies*, 4; Chude-Sokei, *Sound of Culture*, 11.

76. Tsitsi Elia Jaji, *Africa in Stereo: Modernism, Music, and Pan-African Solidarity* (New York: Oxford University Press, 2014); Anthony Reed, *Soundworks: Race, Sound, and Poetry in Production* (Durham, NC: Duke University Press, 2021).

77. Reed, *Soundworks*, 7; Chude-Sokei, *Sound of Culture*, 8.

78. Steven Feld, "Waterfalls of Song: An Acoustemology of Place Resounding in Bosavi, Papua New Guinea," in *Senses of Place*, ed. Steven Feld and Keith Basso (Santa Fe, NM: School of American Research Press, 1996): 91–135.

79. Reed, *Soundworks*, 23.

CHAPTER 1: BROADCAST RELIGION

1. This concept is inspired by Shana Redmond's work on Paul Robeson's musical afterlives, a project that extends Saidiya Hartman's discussion of "the afterlives of slavery" in *Lose Your Mother: A Journey along the Atlantic Slave Route* (New York: Farrar, Straus and Giroux, 2007), 6.

2. See Philip Auslander, *Liveness: Performance in a Mediatized Culture* (New York: Routledge, 1999). Paul Sanden, "Rethinking Liveness in the Digital Age,"

in *The Cambridge Companion to Music and Digital Culture*, ed. Nicholas Cook, Monique Ingalls, and David Trippett (Cambridge, UK: Cambridge University Press, 2019), 178–192.

3. International Youth Congress of the COGIC, Souvenir Book and Official Program, 1966, Pentecostal and Charismatic Research Archive, University of Southern California Digital Library.

4. Avital Ronell, *The Telephone Book: Technology, Schizophrenia, Electric Speech* (Lincoln: University of Nebraska Press, 1989), 20.

5. Jonathan Walton, *Watch This!: The Ethics and Aesthetics of Black Televangelism* (New York: New York University Press, 2009), 2.

6. Sixty-second Annual Holy Convocation of COGIC, Souvenir Book and Official Program, November 4–14, 1969, Pentecostal and Charismatic Research Archive, University of Southern California Digital Library.

7. Jonathan Chism, *Saints in the Struggle: Church of God in Christ Activists in the Memphis Civil Rights Movement, 1954–1968* (Lanham, MD: Lexington Books, 2019), 114–127.

8. "Church News: Voices of Bountiful Blessing in Concert," *Tri-State Defender* (Memphis, TN), March 17, 1979.

9. "WBBP Radio Station: Where Bible Believers Praise God All Day," WBBP 1480 AM, *Bountiful Blessings*, https://bbless.org/wbbp.htm (accessed June 24, 2022).

10. Walton, *Watch This!*, 199.

11. These performance schedules are drawn from advertisements published in COGIC's Holy Convocation souvenir journal from 1988 to 1999.

12. Anthony Reed, *Soundworks: Race, Sound, and Poetry in Production* (Durham, NC: Duke University Press, 2021), 22.

13. Marla Frederick, *Colored Television: American Religion Gone Global* (Stanford, CA: Stanford University Press, 2015), x–xi.

14. Ashon Crawley, *Blackpentecostal Breath: The Aesthetics of Possibility* (New York: Fordham University Press, 2017).

15. Alexander Weheliye, *Phonographies: Grooves in Sonic Afro-Modernity* (Durham, NC: Duke University Press, 2005), 4.

16. Lindsay V. Reckson, *Realist Ecstasy: Religion, Race, and Performance in African American Literature* (New York: New York University Press, 2020), 17.

17. David Waters, "He's One of the Best Preachers in the World," *Memphis Commercial Appeal*, April 20, 1997.

18. Waters, "He's One of the Best Preachers in the World."

19. Marshall McLuhan, *Understanding Media: The Extensions of Man* (New York: McGraw Hill, 1964), 80.

20. John Durham Peters, *The Marvelous Clouds: Toward a Philosophy of Elemental Media* (Chicago: University of Chicago Press, 2015), 4.

21. Patrick Eisenlohr, "Technologies of the Spirit: Devotional Islam, Sound Reproduction, and the Dialectics of Mediation and Immediacy in Mauritius." *Anthropological Theory* 9, no. 3 (2009): 273–296, 287.

22. Walter Ong, *Orality and Literacy* (London: Methuen & Co., 1982).

23. Bishop G. E. Patterson, "Lord, Touch Me Again" sermon delivered in Memphis, TN, Sunday, August 7, 2005.

24. Louis Chude-Sokei, *The Sound of Culture: Diaspora and Black Technopoetics* (Middletown, CT: Wesleyan University Press, 2016).

25. McLuhan, *Understanding Media*, 9; Jonathan Sterne, *The Audible Past: Cultural Origins of Sound Reproduction* (Durham, NC: Duke University Press, 2003), 289.

26. Crawley, *Blackpentecostal Breath*, 3.

27. Lerone A. Martin, *Preaching on Wax: The Phonograph and the Shaping of Modern African American Religion* (New York: New York University Press, 2014).

28. Yolanda Jones, "Bishop Sees All Races in COGIC's New Temple," *Memphis Commercial Appeal*, May 29, 1999, A12; "Show of Faith," *Memphis Commercial Appeal*, May 30, 1999, B6; and Syneetra A. Williams, "Bountiful Blessings COGIC Moving into New," *Memphis Commercial Appeal*, May 27, 1999, CC2.

29. Birgit Meyer and Jeremy Stolow, "Light Mediations: Introduction," *Material Religion* 16, no. 1 (2020): 4.

30. Meyer and Stolow, "Light Mediations," 6.

31. Jonathan Sterne, *MP3: The Meaning of a Format* (Durham, NC: Duke University Press, 2012), 7.

32. Sterne, *MP3*.

33. Birgit Meyer, "Mediation and Immediacy: Sensational Forms, Semiotic Ideologies, and the Question of the Medium," *Social Anthropology* 19, no. 1 (2011): 29.

34. Weheliye, *Phonographies*, 3.

35. Meyer, "Mediation and Immediacy," 35.

36. Chude-Sokei, *Sound of Culture*, 11.

37. Mark J. Butler, *Playing with Something That Runs: Technology, Improvisation, and Composition in DJ and Laptop Performance* (New York: Oxford University Press, 2014), 115; Reckson, *Realist Ecstasy*, 17.

38. Weheliye, *Phonographies*, 7.

39. Weheliye, *Phonographies*.

40. Sanden, "Rethinking Liveness in the Digital Age," 178.

41. This concept is inspired by Shana Redmond's work on Paul Robeson's musical afterlives, a project that extends Hartman's discussion of "the afterlives of slavery."

42. See Auslander, *Liveness*; see Sanden, "Rethinking Liveness in the Digital Age."

43. Hartman, *Lose Your Mother*, 6; Shana Redmond, *Everything Man: The Form and Function of Paul Robeson* (Durham, NC: Duke University Press, 2020)

44. Redmond, *Everything Man*, 8

45. Comment on "Bishop G. E. Patterson: Guest Book and Obituary," Legacy.com, March 17, 2017, www.legacy.com/guestbooks/commercialappeal/guestbook-premium-v2.aspx?n=ge-patterson&pid = 86879443.

46. Jed R. Brubaker, Gillian R. Hayes, and Paul Dourish, "Beyond the Grave: Facebook as an Expansion of the Site of Death and Mourning," *The Information Society* 29, no. 3 (2013): 152.

47. Bobby White, "BISHOP G. E. PATTERSON SHARES A MESSAGE ON THE CORONAVIRUS PANDEMIC . . .," Facebook post (video), March 23, 2020, www.facebook.com/bobbywhitememphis/videos/10218865727967930/.

CHAPTER 2: BROADCAST MEDIUM

1. Marian Milom, "I did not know . . .," October 27, 2020, comment on G. E. Patterson Obituary, www.legacy.com/us/obituaries/commercialappeal/name/g-e-patterson-obituary?pid=86879443.

2. Emily Wilbourne, "Demo's Stutter, Subjectivity, and the Virtuosity of Vocal Failure," *Journal of American Musicological Society* 68, no. 3 (2015): 663.

3. Steven Rings, "Speech and/in Song," in *The Voice and Something More: Essays Toward Materiality*, ed. Martha Feldman and Judith Zeitlin (Chicago: University of Chicago Press, 2019), 38.

4. Brian Kane, "The Model Voice," *Journal of American Musicological Society* 68, no. 3 (2015): 672.

5. Kane, "Model Voice," 673.

6. David Waters, "He's One of the Best Preachers in the World," *Memphis Commercial Appeal*, April 30, 1997.

7. Waters, "He's One of the Best Preachers in the World."

8. Kane, "Model Voice," 674.

9. Aaron Fox, *Real Country: Music and Language in Working Class Culture* (Durham, NC: Duke University Press, 2004), 272.

10. George Lakoff and Mark Johnson, *Metaphors We Live By* (Chicago: University of Chicago Press, 1980), 3.

11. Braxton Shelley, *Healing for the Soul: Richard Smallwood, the Vamp, and the Gospel Imagination* (New York: Oxford University Press, 2021).

12. Anthony Reed, *Soundworks: Race, Sound, and Poetry in Production* (Durham, NC: Duke University Press, 2021), 2.

13. Nathaniel Mackey, *Late Arcade* (San Francisco: City Lights Press, 2017), 182.

14. Wilbourne, "Demo's Stutter," 660.

15. Ralph Ellison, "Richard Wright's Blues," *The Antioch Review* 5, no. 25 (Summer 1945): 61–74.

16. Steven Connor, "Choralities," *Twentieth-Century Music* 13, no. 1 (2016): 6.

17. Synan as quoted in Waters, "He's One of the Best Preachers in the World."

18. Adam Fitzgerald, "Interview with Fred Moten. Part 1: In Praise of Harold Bloom, Collaboration, and Book Fetishes," *Literary Hub*, August 5, 2015, https://lithub.com/an-interview-with-fred-moten-pt-i/ (emphasis in the original).

19. Martha Feldman, "Voice Gap Crack Break" in *The Voice as Something More: Essays toward Materiality*, ed. Martha Feldman and Judith Zeitlin (Chicago: University of Chicago Press, 2019), 188.

20. Carolyn Abbate, "Music—Drastic or Gnostic?" *Critical Inquiry* 30 (Spring 2004): 535.

21. James Q. Davies, "Voice Belongs," *Journal of American Musicological Society* 68, no. 3 (2015): 681.

22. Wilbourne, "Demo's Stutter," 663.

23. Roland Barthes, "The Grain of the Voice," in *The Sound Studies Reader*, ed. Jonathan Sterne (London: Routledge, 2012). 504–511.

24. Nina Sun Eidsheim, "Maria Callas's Waistliine and the Organology of Voice," *Opera Quarterly* 33, no. 3-4 (2017): 249–268.

25. Ashon Crawley, *Blackpentecostal Breath: The Aesthetics of Possibility* (New York: Fordham University Press, 2017).

26. elderkbaronsmith, "Yes Lord Praise Convocation Featuring Bishop G. E. Patterson," YouTube video, 3:05, May 9, 2007, https://youtu.be/eV0OAQiGQJc.

27. Pearl Williams-Jones, "The Musical Quality of Religious Folk Ritual," *Spirit* 1, no. 1 (1977): 29.

28. Crawley, *Blackpentecostal Breath*, 162.

29. Kay Kaufman Shelemay, *Let Jasmine Rain Down: Song and Remembrance among Syrian Jews* (Chicago: University of Chicago Press, 1998), 218.

30. Indeed, the sound recording from which this audio was extracted was posted on YouTube on the tenth anniversary of Bishop Patterson's first funeral. 2 Cor. 7:1—Isaiah M. T., "Bishop G. E. Patterson singing COGIC Yes Lord Praise," YouTube video, 3:35, March 30, 2017, https://youtu.be/SibWmvEMd3c.

31. Blake's quote is cited in James Dowd, "G. E. Patterson: Redefined Role as COGIC's Presiding Bishop," *Memphis Commercial Appeal*, March 21, 2007.

32. A conversation featuring Pastor Stephen F. Smith, Dr. Ronald E. Rolfe, Pastor Antonio M. Buckley, and Pastor John Glen Brown appeared on Smith's YouTube channel on March 30, 2014.

33. Carolyn Abbate, *Unsung Voices: Opera and Musical Narrative in the Nineteenth Century* (Princeton, NJ: Princeton University Press, 1991), 12.

CHAPTER 3: BROADCAST GRAMMAR

1. Henry Mitchell, *Celebration and Experience in Preaching* (Nashville, TN: Abingdon Press, 1990).

2. See Hortense Spillers, "Fabrics of History: Essays on the Black Sermon," PhD dissertation, Brandeis University, 1974. Wallace Best, "The Frenzy, The Preacher, and The Music," in Wallace Best, *Passionately Human: No Less Divine: Religion and Culture in Black Chicago, 1915-1952* (Princeton, NJ: Princeton University Press, 2007), 94–117. Braxton D. Shelley, "'A Balm in Gilead': 'Tuning Up' and the Gospel Imagination," in Shelley, *Healing for the Soul: Richard Smallwood, The Vamp, and the Gospel Imagination* (New York: Oxford University Press, 2021), 38–91.

3. Eugene Lowry, *Homiletical Plot: Sermon as Narrative Art Form* (Atlanta, GA: John Knox Press, 1980); and David Buttrick, *Homiletic: Moves and Structures* (Philadelphia: Fortress Press, 1987).

4. Mitchell, *Celebration and Experience in Preaching*, 30.

5. Daniel Fisher, "Radio," in *Keywords in Sound*, ed. David Novak and Matt Sakakeeny (Durham, NC: Duke University Press, 2015), 152.

6. This is one of Heidegger's descriptions of radio's effects in Martin Heidegger, *Being in Time* (New York: HarperCollins, 1962), 139.

7. Jonathan Sterne, *The Audible Past: Cultural Origins of Sound Reproduction* (Durham, NC: Duke University Press, 2003), 22.

8. Quote taken from Patterson's final sermon, "The Gospel According to John," delivered on December 25, 2006.

9. Elizabeth Hellmuth Margulis, *On Repeat: How Music Plays the Mind* (New York: Oxford University Press, 2014), 162.

10. Margulis, *On Repeat*, 162.

11. Shelley, *Healing for the Soul*, chapter 3.

12. Eugene Rivers, interview with the author, August 28, 2020.

13. Mance Aytchan, interview with the author, January 11, 2021.

14. Aytchan, interview.

15. Louise Patterson, conversation with the author, January 2021.

16. Milton Hawkins, interview with the author, January 11, 2022.

17. Sterne, *Audible Past*, 219.

18. Patrick Feaster, "Phonography," in *Keywords in Sound*, ed. David Novak and Matt Sakakeeny (Durham, NC: Duke University Press, 2015), 144.

19. Walter Benjamin, "The Work of Art in the Age of Mechanical Reproduction," in *The Work of Art in Its Age of Technological Reproducibility and Other Writings on Media*, ed. Michael W. Jennings, Brigid Doherty, and Thomas Y. Levin (Cambridge, MA: Belknap Press, 2008), 19–55.

20. Louise Meintjes, *Sound of Africa!: Making Music Zulu in a South African Studio* (Durham, NC: Duke University Press, 2003), 74.

21. Louise Patterson, conversation with the author, February 2021.

22. Matthew Engelke, *A Problem of Presence: Beyond Scripture in an African Church* (Berkeley: University of California Press, 2007), 46–78.

23. Patrick Eisenlohr, "Technologies of the Spirit: Devotional Islam, Sound Reproduction, and the Dialectics of Mediation and Immediacy in Mauritius," *Anthropological Theory* 9, no. 3 (2009): 273–296, 283.

24. Anthony Hill, "Awesome man of God," comment on "Bishop G. E. Patterson: Guest Book and Obituary," Legacy.com, August 25, 2020, www.legacy.com/guestbooks/commercialappeal/guestbook-premium-v2.aspx?n=ge-patterson&pid=86879443.

25. Cheryl Gourdine, "A profound teacher," comment on MusicMan 78414, "Bishop GE Patterson The Dawn of a New Day," YouTube video, October 28, 2016, https://youtu.be/OEgZj75mB0Q.

26. Rosa Hopgood, "I will always remember him," comment on "Bishop G. E. Patterson: Guest Book and Obituary," Legacy.com, November 15, 2019, www.legacy.com/guestbooks/commercialappeal/guestbook-premium-v2.aspx?n=ge-patterson&pid=86879443.

27. Feaster, "Phonography," 145.

28. Walter Ong, *The Presence of the Word: Some Prolegomena for Cultural and Religious History* (New Haven, CT: Yale University Press, 1967), 324.

29. Shelley, *Healing for the Soul*.

CHAPTER 4: BROADCAST FREQUENCY, OR THE POLITICS OF KEY

1. Mance Aytchan, interview with the author, January 11, 2021.

2. David Temperley, *The Cognition of Basic Musical Structures* (Cambridge, MA: MIT Press, 2001), 3.

3. John Durham Peters, *The Marvelous Clouds: Toward a Philosophy of Elemental Media* (Chicago: University of Chicago Press, 2015), 15.

4. Birgit Meyer, "Mediation and immediacy: Sensational Forms, Semiotic Ideologies and the Question of the Medium," *Social Anthropology* 19, no. 1 (2011): 23–39.

5. Shana Redmond, *Everything Man: The Form and Function of Paul Robeson* (Durham, NC: Duke University Press, 2020), 8.

6. Redmond, *Everything Man*, 51.

7. Redmond, *Everything Man*, 8.

8. Redmond, *Everything Man*.

9. Ashon Crawley, *Blackpentecostal Breath: The Aesthetics of Possibility* (New York: Fordham University Press, 2017).

10. Andrew McGraw, "Atmosphere as a Concept for Ethnomusicology: Comparing the Gamelatron and Gamelan," *Ethnomusicology* 60, no. 1 (2016): 131.

11. Alisha Lola Jones, *Flaming? The Peculiar Theopolitics of Fire and Desire in Black Male Gospel Music Performance* (New York: Oxford University Press, 2020), 1.

12. This phrase is uttered by Mance Aytchan in the opening scene of Patterson's still-airing television broadcasts—and has been since 1999.

13. Patrick Eisenlohr, *Sounding Islam: Voice, Media, and Sonic Atmospheres in an Indian Ocean World* (Berkeley: University of California Press, 2018), 17.

14. Gernot Bohme, "Atmosphere as the Fundamental Concept of a New Aesthetics," *Thesis Eleven* 36, no. 1 (1993): 113–114.

15. David Waters, "He's One of the Best Preachers in the World," *Memphis Commercial Appeal*, April 30, 1997.

16. Carol Robertson, "'Pulling the Ancestors': Performance Practice and Praxis in Mapuche Ordering," *Ethnomusicology* 23, no. 3 (1979): 411.

17. Robertson, "'Pulling the Ancestors.'"

18. Paul Connerton, *How Societies Remember* (Cambridge, UK: Cambridge University Press, 1989), 101.

19. Connerton, *How Societies Remember*, 102.

20. Steve Larson, *Musical Forces: Motion, Metaphor, and Meaning in Music* (Bloomington: University of Indiana Press, 2012), 327; emphasis in the original.

21. "Church Buys Radio Station," *Memphis Commercial Appeal*, January 5, 1991, www.newspapers.com/clip/101620479/church-buys-radio-station/, 10; and "For the Record: Actions," *Broadcasting*, November 1990, https://worldradiohistory.com/Archive-BC/BC-1990/BC-1990-11-19.pdf, 59.

22. Be Revived with Pastor Keith Martin, "The Homegoing Celebration of Presiding Bishop Gilbert Earl Patterson: Local Celebration Part 2" (recorded March 30, 2007), YouTube video, 1:45:02, December 15, 2021, https://youtu.be/FuusmUUiUOU.

CHAPTER 5: BROADCAST ENSEMBLE: THE LOGIC OF
THE PRAYER CLOTH

1. Linwood Dillard (@linwooddillard), "Today I had one of the most awesome and humbling experiences in my entire life," Instagram photo, May 3, 2015, www.instagram.com/p/2PJsXbQ_Yo/.

2. "Patterson: I Know Why Suspect Fired at Me," *Tri-State Defender* (Memphis, TN), July 5, 1975, ProQuest.

3. "Patterson: I Know Why Suspect Fired at Me."

4. Chris Fowler, "Relational Typologies, Assemblage Theory, and Early Bronze Burials," *Cambridge Archaeological Journal* 27, no. 1 (2017): 96.

5. James K. A. Smith, *Thinking in Tongues: Pentecostal Contributions to Christian Philosophy* (Grand Rapids, MI: William B. Eerdmans Pub. Co., 2010), 81–82.

6. Birgit Meyer, "Mediation and Immediacy: Sensational Forms, Semiotic Ideologies, and the Question of the Medium," *Social Anthropology* 19, no. 1 (2011): 29.

7. Oral Roberts, *If You Need Healing, Do These Things* (Tulsa, OK: Oral Roberts, 1947), 32.

8. Anderson Blanton, *Hittin' the Prayer Bones: Materiality of Spirit in the Pentecostal South* (Chapel Hill: University of North Carolina Press, 2015), 22.

9. David Edwin Harrell Jr., *Oral Roberts: An American Life* (Bloomington: Indiana University Press, 1985).

10. David Edwin Harrell Jr., *All Things Are Possible: The Healing and Charismatic Revivals in Modern America* (Bloomington: Indiana University Press, 1975), 119n52.

11. Roberts, *If You Need Healing*, 35.

12. Andrew Murray, *Divine Healing: He Gave Them Power Against Unclean Spirits, to Cast Them Out and to Heal All Manner of Sickness and All Manner of Weakness—Matthew 10:1*, revised ed. (Abbotsford, WI: Aneko Press, 2016), 119.

13. R. Marie Griffith, "Material Devotion: Pentecostal Prayer Cloths." *Material History of American Religion Newsletter* (Spring 1997), www.materialreligion.org/journal.html.

14. Blanton, *Hittin' the Prayer Bones*, 90.

15. Pastor John Brown and Pastor Antonio Buckley, comments on *The Stephen Smith Show*, video clip, March 30, 2014, www.dropbox.com/s/uuc8hcrmke8vbxu/BE2.mp4?dl=0.

16. Mance Aytchan, interview with the author, January 11, 2021.

17. Blanton, *Hittin' the Prayer Bones*, 26.

18. Heather Bamford, *Cultures of the Fragment: Uses of the Iberian Manuscript, 1100–1600* (Toronto, ON: University of Toronto Press, 2018), 7.

19. O. Christopher Buckner, "This is one of my favorite texts," comment on Jamar A. Boyd II, "Bishop Gilbert E. Patterson, I'd argue, is one of the least-studied," Facebook (video), March 15, 2021, www.facebook.com/jboydii/videos/10225568976796310.

20. Hans Ulrich Gumbrecht, *The Powers of Philology: Dynamics of Textual Scholarship* (Urbana: University of Illinois Press, 2003), 13.

21. Trinity Temple COGIC, "Sunday March 4, 2018 we climaxed our Pastor Charles H. Brewer," Facebook (photo), March 5, 2018, www.facebook.com/TRINITYTEMPLECT/photos/a.207782369271404/1591990374183923.

22. Rep. Carolyn C. Kilpatrick, "Resolution in Honor of Bishop Gilbert Earl Patterson—'Be Healed, Be Delivered, and Be Set Free,'" 110th Congress, 1st sess., *Congressional Record* 153, no. 54 (March 28, 2007): E659, www.congress.gov/110/crec/2007/03/28/CREC-2007-03-28-pt1-PgE659.pdf.

23. Manuel DeLanda, *Assemblage Theory* (Edinburgh: Edinburgh University Press, 2016), 2.

24. Gilles Deleuze and Claire Parnet, *Dialogues II*, trans. Hugh Tomlinson and Barbara Haberjam (New York: Columbia University Press, 2007), 69.

25. Deleuze and Parnet, *Dialogues II*, 69.

26. "In Loving Memory of Bishop G. E. Patterson," Facebook Group, February 1, 2019, www.facebook.com/groups/2260901341/.

27. Akins Christopher, "Bishop G. E. Patterson preached his last message on Christmas morning, Dec. 25th, 2006!" Facebook (video), 3:44, December 7, 2018, www.facebook.com/bishopakins/videos/10156058073283108.

28. MusicMan 78414, "Bishop GE Patterson Christmas 2006," YouTube video, 1:01:58, October 28, 2016, www.YouTube.com/watch?v=zIpIKjFAbTg&list=PL3u5nURrYKG_YxUJIleB2yc7mbSCeRPP4&index=174.

29. MusicMan 78414, "Bishop GE Patterson sermons," YouTube playlist, 184 videos, last updated February 2, 2022, www.YouTube.com/playlist?list = PL3u5nURrYKG_YxUJIleB2yc7mbSCeRPP4.

30. MusicMan 78414, "Bishop GE Patterson The Purpose of the Four Gospels Christmas Eve 2006," YouTube video, February 16, 2017, www.YouTube.com/watch?v = 2z4tqyaW0Nc.

31. COGIC International Mass Choir Facebook Group, "Remembering Bishop G. E. Patterson," Facebook post, March 20, 2018, www.facebook.com/watch/?v = 1792194674164080

32. Jed R. Brubaker, Gillian R. Hayes, and Paul Dourish, "Beyond the Grave: Facebook as an Expansion of the Site of Death and Mourning," *The Information Society* 29, no. 3 (2013): 153.

33. Jean Burgess and Joshua Green, *YouTube: Online Video and Participatory Culture* (Cambridge, UK: Polity Press, 2009).

34. Mary Truesdale, "What a message," comment on John Wright, "Yes Lord!," Facebook (video), posted on COGIC History Page, Facebook Group, January 31, 2020, www.facebook.com/groups/COGICHistoryPage/permalink/654582018416593/?__tn__=H-R.

35. Jude 3 Project Facebook Group, "Bishop G. E. Patterson #inthenameofjesus," Facebook (video), September 22, 2017, www.facebook.com/jude3project/videos/1568415919845572/.

36. Jamar A. Boyd II, "Remembering and celebrating the man, Bishop G. E. Patterson," Facebook (video), March 20, 2019, www.facebook.com/jboydii/videos/10218983301678548/.

37. Henry Jenkins, *Convergence Culture: Where Old and New Media Collide* (New York: New York University Press, 2006).

38. Jason Stanyek and Benjamin Piekut, "Deadness: Technologies of the Intermundane," *The Drama Review* 54, no. 1 (2010): 14.

39. Boyd, "Remembering and celebrating the man."

40. Stanyek and Piekut, "Deadness," 18.

41. Bishop Robert L. Perry Jr., "COURSE G—Sanctity and Servitude," in *2015 Training Manual: National Adjutancy, the Servant Ministry of the Church of God in Christ* (AIMS Convention, June 23, 2015), 22.

42. Perry, "COURSE G—Sanctity and Servitude," 23.

43. Jonathan Sterne, *The Audible Past: Cultural Origins of Sound Reproduction* (Durham, NC: Duke University Press, 2003), 292.

44. Stanyek and Piekut, "Deadness," 16.

45. Marian Milom, "I did not know . . .," comment on "G. E. Patterson: Guest Book and Obituary," Legacy.com, October 27, 2020, www.legacy.com/us/obituaries/commercialappeal/name/g-e-patterson-obituary?pid = 86879443.

46. Boyd, "Remembering and celebrating the man."

ETERNAL LIFE: AN EPILOGUE

1. Stanyek and Piekut, "Deadness: Technologies of the Intermundane," *TDR: The Drama Review* 54, no. 1 (2010): 14–38.

2. Christina Sharpe, *In the Wake: On Blackness and Being* (Durham, NC: Duke University Press, 2016), 17.

3. Even as he upheld the denomination's official policy, Bishop G. E. Patterson, for his part, used the titles "Mother" and "Pastor" interchangeably when referring to one of his pastoral assistants, Deola Wells Johnson.

4. Louise Patterson as quoted in James Dowd, "Eternal Flame, Montage Mark Legacy of Bishop G. E. Patterson," *Memphis Commercial Appeal*, November 5, 2007, www.pressreader.com/usa/the-commercial-appeal/20071105/281500746895498.

5. Noah Rivers (@noeycreole), "Happy Sunday y'all. Be thankful today," Instagram post, October 4, 2020, www.instagram.com/p/CF7cx5jDW5C/; and PREACHER NATION (@preachernation), "I've Been Washed * Bishop GE Patterson," Instagram post, April 17, 2022, www.instagram.com/tv/Ccd5m_Upmw7/.

6. Marla Frederick, *Between Sundays: Black Women and Everyday Struggles of Faith* (Berkeley: University of California Press, 2003).

7. Habiba Ibrahim and Badia Ahad, "Introduction: Black Temporality in Times of Crisis," *South Atlantic Quarterly* 121, no. 1 (2022): 1–10.

Bibliography

Abbate, Carolyn. "Music–Drastic or Gnostic?" *Critical Inquiry* 30 (Spring 2004): 505–536.

———. *Unsung Voices: Opera and Musical Narrative in the Nineteenth Century.* Princeton, NJ: Princeton University Press, 1991.

Alexander, Estrelda. *Black Fire: One Hundred Years of African American Pentecostalism.* Downers Grove, IL: IVP Academic Publishing, 2011.

Auslander, Philip. *Liveness: Performance in a Mediatized Culture.* New York: Routledge, 1999.

Bamford, Heather. *Cultures of the Fragment: Uses of the Iberian Manuscript, 1100-1600.* Toronto, ON: University of Toronto Press, 2018.

Barthes, Roland. "The Grain of the Voice." In *The Sound Studies Reader,* edited by Jonathan Sterne, 504–511. London: Routledge, 2012.

Benjamin, Walter. "The Work of Art in the Age of Mechanical Reproduction." In *The Work of Art in Its Age of Technological Reproducibility and Other Writings on Media,* edited by Michael W. Jennings, Brigid Doherty, and Thomas Y. Levin, 19–55. Cambridge, MA: Belknap Press, 2008.

Best, Wallace. *Passionately Human: No Less Divine: Religion and Black Culture in Black Chicago, 1915-1952.* Princeton, NJ: Princeton University Press, 2007.

"Bishop G. E. Patterson Elected New Leader of Church Of God In Christ." *Jet Magazine,* December 18, 2000.

"Bishop G. E. Patterson: Guest Book and Obituary." Legacy.com. Last modified March 17, 2007. www.legacy.com/guestbooks/commercialappeal/guestbook-premium-v2.aspx?n=ge-patterson&pid=86879443. Accessed April 6, 2023.

"Bishop Gilbert Earl Patterson: Reflections—the Life of a Visionary." *Whole Truth: The Official Magazine of the Church of God in Christ*, April/May/June 2007, 18–19.

Blanton, Anderson. *Hittin' the Prayer Bones: Materiality of Spirit in the Pentecostal South*. Chapel Hill: University of North Carolina Press, 2015.

Bohme, Gernot. "Atmosphere as the Fundamental Concept of a New Aesthetics." *Thesis Eleven* 36, no. 1 (1993): 113–126.

Booker, Vaughn. *Lift Every Voice and Swing: Black Musicians and Religious Culture in the Jazz Century*. New York: New York University Press, 2020.

Bowler, Kate. *Blessed: A History of the American Prosperity Gospel*. New York: Oxford University Press, 2013.

Brubaker, Jed. R., Gillian R. Hayes, and Paul Dourish. "Beyond the Grave: Facebook as an Expansion of the Site of Death and Mourning." *The Information Society* 29, no. 1 (2013): 152–163.

Burgess, Jean, and Joshua Green. *YouTube: Online Video and Participatory Culture*. Cambridge, UK: Polity Press, 2009.

Butler, Anthea. *Women in the Church of God in Christ: Making a Sanctified World*. Chapel Hill: University of North Carolina Press, 2007.

Butler, Mark J. *Playing with Something That Runs: Technology, Improvisation, and Composition in DJ and Laptop Performance*. New York: Oxford University Press, 2014.

Buttrick, David. *Homiletic: Moves and Structures*. Philadelphia: Fortress Press, 1987.

Campbell, Heidi A. "The Rise of the Study of Digital Religion." In *Digital Religion: Understanding Religious Practice in New Media Worlds*, edited by Heidi Campbell, 1–22. New York: Routledge, 2012.

———. "Understanding the Relation between Religion Online and Offline in a Networked Society." *Journal of the American Academy of Religion* 80, no. 1 (2012): 64–93.

Chism, Jonathan. *Saints in the Struggle: Church of God in Christ: Activists in the Memphis Civil Rights Movement, 1954–1968*. Lanham, MD: Lexington Books, 2019.

Chude-Sokei, Louis. *The Sound of Culture: Diaspora and Black Technopoetics*. Middletown, CT: Wesleyan University Press, 2016.

"Church Buys Radio Station." *Memphis Commercial Appeal*, January 5, 1991, 10. www.newspapers.com/clip/101620479/church-buys-radio-station/.

"Church News: Voices of Bountiful Blessing in Concert." *Tri-State Defender* (Memphis, TN), March 17, 1979.

COGIC Holy Convocation Souvenir Journals, 1988–1996. Pentecostal and Charismatic Research Archive, University of Southern California Digital Library.
Connerton, Paul. *How Societies Remember.* Cambridge, UK: Cambridge University Press, 1989.
Connor, Steven. "Choralities." *Twentieth-Century Music* 13, no. 1 (2016): 3–23.
Crawley, Ashon. *Blackpentecostal Breath: The Aesthetics of Possibility.* New York: Fordham University Press, 2017.
Cutrer, Corrie. "Church of God in Christ: COGIC Presiding Bishop Ousted." *Christianity Today,* January 8, 2001. www.christianitytoday.com/ct/2001/january8/16.22.html?start=2.
Davies, James Q. "Voice Belongs." *Journal of American Musicological Society* 68, no. 3 (2015): 677–686.
DeLanda, Manuel. *Assemblage Theory.* Edinburgh: Edinburgh University Press, 2012.
Deleuze, Gilles, and Claire Parnet. *Dialogues II.* Translated by Hugh Tomlinson and Barbara Haberjam. New York: Columbia University Press, 2007.
Dowd, James. "Eternal Flame, Montage Mark Legacy of Bishop G. E. Patterson." *Memphis Commercial Appeal,* November 5, 2007. www.pressreader.com/usa/the-commercial-appeal/20071105/281500746895498.
———. "G. E. Patterson: Redefined Role as COGIC's Presiding Bishop." *Memphis Commercial Appeal,* March 21, 2007.
Eidsheim, Nina Sun. "Maria Callas's Waistline and the Organology of Voice." *Opera Quarterly* 33, no. 3–4 (2017): 249–268.
Eisenlohr, Patrick. *Sounding Islam: Voice, Media, and Sonic Atmospheres in an Indian Ocean World.* Oakland: University of California Press, 2018.
———. "Technologies of the Spirit: Devotional Islam, Sound Reproduction, and the Dialectics of Mediation and Immediacy in Mauritius." *Anthropological Theory* 9, no. 3 (2009): 273–296.
Ellison, Ralph. "Richard Wright's Blues." *The Antioch Review* 5, no. 2 (1945): 61–74.
Engelke, Matthew. *A Problem of Presence: Beyond Scripture in an African Church.* Berkeley: University of California Press, 2007.
Feaster, Patrick. "Phonography." In *Keywords in Sound,* edited by David Novak and Matt Sakakeeny, 139–150. Durham, NC: Duke University Press, 2015.
Feld, Steven. "Waterfalls of Song: An Acoustemology of Place Resounding in Bosavi, Papua New Guinea." In *Senses of Place,* edited by Steven Feld and Keith Basso, 91–135. Santa Fe, NM: School of American Research Press, 1996.
Feldman, Martha. "Voice Gap Crack Break." In *The Voice as Something More: Essays toward Materiality,* edited by Martha Feldman and Judith Zeitlin, 188–208. Chicago: University of Chicago Press, 2019.

Feldman, Martha, and Judith Zeitlin, eds. *The Voice as Something More: Essays toward Materiality*. Chicago: University of Chicago Press, 2019.

Feller, Gavin. *Eternity in the Ether: A Mormon Media History*. Urbana: University of Illinois Press, 2023.

Fisher, Daniel. "Radio." In *Keywords in Sound*, edited by David Novak and Matt Sakakeeny, 151–164. Durham, NC: Duke University Press, 2015.

Fitzgerald, Adam. "An Interview with Fred Moten. Part 1: In Praise of Harold Bloom, Collaboration, and Book Fetishes." *Literary Hub*. August 5, 2015. https://lithub.com/an-interview-with-fred-moten-pt-i/.

Fowler, Chris. "Relational Typologies, Assemblage Theory, and Early Bronze Burials." *Cambridge Archaeological Journal* 27, no. 1 (2017): 95–109.

Fox, Aaron. *Real Country: Music and Language in Working-Class Culture*. Durham, NC: Duke University Press, 2004.

Frederick, Marla. *Between Sundays: Black Women and Everyday Struggles of Faith*. Berkeley: University of California Press, 2003.

———. *Colored Television: American Religion Gone Global*. Stanford, CA: Stanford University Press, 2015.

Giggie, John. *After Redemption: Jim Crow and the Transformation of African American Religion in the Delta, 1875–1917*. New York: Oxford University Press, 2008.

Griffith, R. Marie. "Material Devotion: Pentecostal Prayer Cloths." *Material History of American Religion* (Spring 1997). www.materialreligion.org/journal.html.

Guillory, John. "Genesis of the Media Concept." *Critical Inquiry* 36, no. 2 (2010): 321–362.

Gumbrecht, Hans Ulrich. *The Powers of Philology: Dynamics of Textual Scholarship*. Urbana: University of Illinois Press, 2003.

Hangen, Tona J. *Redeeming the Dial: Radio, Religion, and Popular Culture in America*. Chapel Hill: University of North Carolina Press, 2002.

Harkness, Nicholas. *Glossolalia and the Problem of Language*. Chicago: University of Chicago Press, 2021.

———. *Songs of Seoul: An Ethnography of Voice and Voicing in Christian South Korea*. Berkeley: University of California Press, 2014.

Harrell Jr., David Edwin. *All Things Are Possible: The Healing and Charismatic Revivals in Modern America*. Bloomington: Indiana University Press, 1975.

———. *Oral Roberts: An American Life*. Bloomington: Indiana University Press, 1985.

Hartman, Saidiya. *Lose Your Mother: A Journey along the Atlantic Slave Route*. New York: Farrar, Straus and Giroux, 2007.

Heidegger, Martin. *Being in Time*. New York: HarperCollins, 1962.

Hevesi, Dennis. "Bishop G. E. Patterson, 67, Who Led Church of God in Christ, Dies." *New York Times*, March 22, 2007. www.nytimes.com/2007/03/22/obituaries/22patterson.html?_r=0.

Hill, Abram. "Elder Horn." August 24, 1939. Schomburg Center for Research in Black Culture at New York Public Library, Black New Yorkers Collection.

Hirschkind, Charles. *The Ethical Soundscape: Cassette Sermons and Islamic Counterpublics*. New York: Columbia University Press, 2006.

Ibrahim, Habiba, and Badia Ahad. "Introduction: Black Temporality in Times of Crisis." *South Atlantic Quarterly* 121, no. 1 (2022): 1–10.

International Youth Congress of the COGIC Souvenir Book and Official Program, 1996. Pentecostal and Charismatic Research Archive, University of Southern California Digital Library.

Jaji, Tsitsi Elia. *Africa in Stereo: Modernism, Music, and Pan-African Solidarity*. New York: Oxford University Press, 2014.

Jenkins, Henry. *Convergence Culture: Where Old and New Media Collide*. New York: New York University Press, 2006.

Jones, Alisha Lola. *Flaming? The Peculiar Theopolitics of Fire and Desire in Black Male Gospel Music Performance*. New York: Oxford University Press, 2020.

Jones, Yolanda. "Bishop Sees All Races in COGIC's New Temple." *Memphis Commercial Appeal*, May 29, 1999.

Kane, Brian. "The Model Voice." *Journal of American Musicological Society* 68, no. 3 (2015): 671–676.

Keane, Webb. "Semiotics and the Social Analysis of Material Things." *Language and Communication* 23, no. 3 (2003): 409–425.

Kilpatrick, Rep. Carolyn C. "Resolution in Honor of Bishop Gilbert Earl Patterson—Be Healed, Be Delivered, and Be Set Free." 110th Congress, 1st Session. *Congressional Record* 153, no. 54 (March 28, 2007): E69. www.congress.gov/110/crec/2007/03/28/CREC-2007-03-28-pt1-PgE659.pdf.

Klassen, Pamela. *The Story of Radio Mind: A Missionary's Journey on Indigenous Land*. Chicago: University of Chicago Press, 2018.

Lakoff, George, and Mark Johnson. *Metaphors We Live By*. Chicago: University of Chicago Press, 1980.

Larson, Steve. *Musical Forces: Motion, Metaphor, and Meaning in Music*. Bloomington: University of Indiana Press, 2012.

Lepore, Jill. "Historians Who Love Too Much: Reflections on Microhistory and Biography." *Journal of American History* 88, no. 1 (2001): 129–144.

Lofton, Kathryn. *Consuming Religion*. Chicago: University of Chicago Press, 2017.

Lowe, Valerie G. "God's Man in Memphis." *Charisma*, September 2001. www.charismamag.com/spirit/devotionals/daily-breakthroughs?view=article&id=436:gods-man-in-memphis&catid=146.

Lowry, Eugene. *Homiletical Plot: Sermon as Narrative Art Form*. Atlanta, GA: John Knox Press, 1980.

Mackey, Nathaniel. *Late Arcade*. San Francisco: City Lights Press, 2017.

Margulis, Elizabeth Hellmuth. *On Repeat: How Music Plays the Mind*. New York: Oxford University Press, 2014.

Marovich, Robert. *A City Called Heaven: Chicago and the Birth of Gospel Music*. Urbana: University of Illinois Press, 2018.

Martin, Lerone A. "Bureau Clergyman: How the FBI Colluded with an African American Televangelist to Destroy Dr. Martin Luther King Jr." *Religion and American Culture* 28, no. 1 (2018): 1–51.

———. *Preaching on Wax: The Phonograph and the Shaping of Modern African American Religion*. New York: New York University Press, 2014.

McGraw, Andrew. "Atmosphere as a Concept for Ethnomusicology: Comparing the Gamelatron and Gamelan." *Ethnomusicology* 60, no. 1 (2016): 125–147.

McLuhan, Marshall. *Understanding Media: The Extensions of Man*. New York: McGraw Hill, 1964.

Meintjes, Louise. *Sound of Africa!: Making Music Zulu in a South African Studio*. Durham, NC: Duke University Press, 2003.

Meyer, Birgit. "Mediation and Immediacy: Sensational Forms, Semiotic Ideologies, and the Question of the Medium." *Social Anthropology* 19, no. 1 (2011): 23–39.

Meyer, Birgit, and Jeremy Stolow. "Light Mediations: Introduction." *Material Religion* 16, no. 1 (2020): 1–8.

Miller Jr., Spencer. "Radio and Religion." *Annals of the American Academy of Political and Social Science* 177, no. 1 (1935): 135–140.

Mitchell, Henry. *Celebration and Experience in Preaching*. Nashville, TN: Abingdon Press, 1990.

Murray, Andrew. *Divine Healing: He Gave Them Power against Unclean Spirits, to Cast Them Out, and to Heal All Manner of Sickness and All Manner of Weakness—Matthew 10:1*. Revised edition. Abbotsford, WI: Aneko Press, 2016.

Nelson, Alondra. "Future Texts" and "Afrofuturism." *Social Text* 71 (Summer 2002): 5–6.

Ong, Walter. *Orality and Literacy*. London: Methuen & Co., 1982.

———. *The Presence of the Word: Some Prolegomena for Cultural and Religious History*. New Haven, CT: Yale University Press, 1967.

"Patterson Is Upheld on Action as Bishop." *Memphis Press-Scimitar*, December 21, 1974.

"Patterson: I Know Why Suspect Fired at Me." *Tri-State Defender* (Memphis TN), July 5, 1975. ProQuest.

Perry Jr., Bishop Robert L. "COURSE G—Sanctity and Servitude." In *2015 Training Manual: National Adjutancy, the Servant Ministry of the*

Church of God in Christ. Auxiliaries in Ministry (AIM) Convention, June 23, 2015.

Peters, John Durham. *Marvelous Clouds: Toward a Philosophy of Elemental Media.* Chicago: University of Chicago Press, 2015.

———. *Speaking into the Air: A History of the Idea of Communication.* Chicago: University of Chicago Press, 1999.

Pinn, Anthony. *Interplay of Things: Religion, Art, and Presence Together.* Durham, NC: Duke University Press, 2021.

Prince, Ruth. "Front Page." *The Whole Truth: Official Magazine of the Church of God in Christ,* August 1959.

Quashie, Kevin. *Black Aliveness, or a Poetics of Being.* Durham, NC: Duke University Press, 2021.

Reckson, Lindsay V. *Realist Ecstasy: Religion, Race, and Performance in African American Literature.* New York: New York University Press, 2020.

Redmond, Shana. *Everything Man: The Form and Function of Paul Robeson.* Durham, NC: Duke University Press, 2020.

Reed, Anthony. *Soundworks: Race, Sound, and Poetry in Production.* Durham, NC: Duke University Press, 2021.

Rings, Steven. "Speech and/in Song." In *the Voice and Something More: Essays toward Materiality,* edited by Martha Feldman and Judith Zeitlin, 37–53. Chicago: University of Chicago Press, 2019.

Roberts, Oral. *If You Need Healing Do These Things.* Tulsa, OK: Oral Roberts, 1947.

Robertson, Carol. "'Pulling the Ancestors': Performance Practice and Praxis in Mapuche Ordering." *Ethnomusicology* 23, no. 3 (1979): 395–416.

Ronell, Avital. *The Telephone Book: Technology, Schizophrenia, Electric Speech.* Lincoln, NE: University of Nebraska Press, 1989.

Rouzeau, Edgar T. "'Happy Am I': Millions Listen to Elder Michaux, the Radio Evangelist." *New York Amsterdam News,* September 9, 1935.

Salvatore, Nick. *Singing in a Strange Land: C. L. Franklin, the Black Church, and the Transformation of America.* New York: Little Brown, 2005.

Sanden, Paul. "Rethinking Liveness in the Digital Age." In *Cambridge Companion to Music and Digital Culture,* edited by Nicholas Cook, Monique Ingalls, and David Trippett, 178–192. Cambridge, UK: Cambridge University Press, 2019.

Sanders, Cheryl J. *Saints in Exile: The Holiness-Pentecostal Experience in African American Religion and Culture.* New York: Oxford University Press, 1996.

Schultze, Quentin J. "Evangelical Radio and the Rise of the Electronic Church, 1921–1948." *Journal of Broadcasting and Electronic Media* 32 (Summer 1988): 289–306.

———. "The Invisible Medium: Evangelical Radio." In *American Evangelicals and the Mass Media*, edited by Quentin J. Schultze, 13. Grand Rapids, MI: Academie Books, 1990.

———. "The Mythos of the Electronic Church." *Critical Studies in Mass Communication* 4 (September 1987): 245–261.

Sconce, Jeffrey. *Haunted Media: Electronic Presence from Telegraphy to Television*. Durham, NC: Duke University Press, 2000.

Sharpe, Christina. *In the Wake: On Blackness and Being*. Durham, NC: Duke University Press, 2016.

Shelemay, Kay Kaufman. *Let Jasmine Rain Down: Song and Remembrance among Syrian Jews*. Chicago: University of Chicago Press, 1998.

Shelley, Braxton D. *Healing for the Soul: Richard Smallwood, the Vamp, and the Gospel Imagination*. New York: Oxford University Press, 2021.

"Show of Faith." *Memphis Commercial Appeal*, May 30, 1999.

Sixty-second Annual Holy Convocation of the COGIC Souvenir Book and Official Program, November 4–14, 1969. Pentecostal and Charismatic Research Archive, University of Southern California Digital Library.

Smith, James K. A. *Thinking in Tongues: Pentecostal Contributions to Christian Theology*. Grand Rapids, MI: William B. Eerdmans Publishing Co., 2010.

Spaulding, Norman. "History of Black Oriented Radio in Chicago, 1929–1963." PhD dissertation. University of Illinois at Urbana-Champaign, 1981.

Spillers, Hortense. "Fabrics of History: Essays on the Black Sermon." PhD dissertation. Brandeis University, 1974.

Stanyek, Jason, and Benjamin Piekut. "Deadness: Technologies of the Intermundane." *The Drama Review* 54, no. 1 (2010): 14–38.

Sterne, Jonathan. *The Audible Past: Cultural Origins of Sound Reproduction*. Durham, NC: Duke University Press, 2003.

———. *MP3: The Meaning of a Format*. Durham, NC: Duke University Press, 2012.

Temperley, David. *The Cognition of Basic Musical Structures*. Cambridge, MA: MIT Press, 2001.

Turner, William. "The Musicality of Black Preaching: A Phenomenology." In *Performance in Preaching: Bringing the Sermon to Life*, edited by Jana Childers and Clayton Schmitt, 191–209. Grand Rapids, MI: Baker Academic, 2008.

———. *The United Holy Church of America: A Study in Black-Holiness Pentecostalism*. Piscataway, NJ: Gorgias Press, 2006.

Wacker, Grant. *Heaven Below: Early Pentecostals and American Culture*. Cambridge, MA: Harvard University Press, 2001.

Wallace, Maurice. *King's Vibrato: Modernism, Blackness, and the Sonic Life of Martin Luther King Jr.* Durham, NC: Duke University Press, 2022.

Walton, Jonathan L. *Watch This! The Ethics and Aesthetics of Black Televangelism*. New York: New York University Press, 2009.

Waters, David. "He's One of the Best Preachers in the World." *Memphis Commercial Appeal*, April 20, 1997.

Weheliye, Alexander. *Phonographies: Grooves in Sonic Afro-Modernity*. Durham, NC: Duke University Press, 2005.

White, Calvin. *The Rise to Respectability: Race, Religion, and the Church of God in Christ*. Fayetteville: University of Arkansas Press, 2012.

Wilbourne, Emily. "Demo's Stutter, Subjectivity, and the Virtuosity of Vocal Failure." *Journal of American Musicological Society* 68, no. 3 (2015): 659–662.

Williams, Syneetra A. "Bountiful Blessings COGIC Moving into New Temple." *Memphis Commercial Appeal*, May 27, 1999.

Williams-Jones, Pearl. "The Musical Quality of Religious Folk Ritual." *Spirit* 1, no. 1 (1977): 19–33.

Yong, Amos, and Estrelda Alexander, eds. *Afro-Pentecostalism: Black Pentecostal and Charismatic Christianity in History and Culture*. New York: New York University Press, 2010.

Index

Adams, Tabitha, 178
aesthetics, 12; Black, 50; musical, 20, 26; theological, 61
afro-modernism, 49; sonic, 63, 65
Afterliveness, 5, 25, 28–31, 33–5, 39, 65–67, 69, 71, 80, 87, 94, 97, 101, 114, 119, 122, 142, 145, 149, 170–171, 175–176, 178, 181, 185, 188–190
Alexander, Estrelda, 14
amplification, 34, 36, 59, 97, 105–106, 108–109, 111, 139, 159, 165
anointing, 29, 35, 148–151, 153–155, 163, 170, 175, 181, 186
antiphonal, 6, 34, 65, 76, 78, 81, 121, 130, 134–7; "antiphonal life," 7, 67, 128; call of, 68; grammar of, 115;
atmosphere. *See* antiphonal
Aytchan, Mance, 58, 60–61, 110, 118, 123, 154

Bailey, John S. (Bishop), 8
Baldwin, James, 17
Bamford, Heather, 158
baptism, 7, 24–26
Benjamin, Walter, 113
Bible, Holy Scriptures: Acts 4:12, 91; Acts 16, 79, 81; Acts 19:11–12, 152–153; Ammon, Ammonites, 50, 157; Ark of the Covenant, 111–112, 129–30; Bethlehem, 47, 99; Capernaum, 99; 2 Chronicles, 1, 3, 20, 27, 54, 64, 79, 86–89, 115, 118, 125–126, 156–157; City of David, 129; 1 Corinthians, 22; Galatians 3:26–29, 98; Ichabod, 111; Isaiah 38, 84, 96; Isaiah 41, 92; Isaiah (prophet), 59; Isaiah 59:9, 7; Jeheazial, 65; Jericho, 99; Jerusalem, 99; Jesus, 9, 23, 46–47, 49, 52, 58–62, 66, 73, 78, 80–81, 98–100, 104, 106, 108, 132–134, 137, 144, 152, 168; Judah, 1, 50–51, 112, 157–158; 2 Kings, 84, 102–103; Luke (writer), 23, 99, 105, 132; Luke 5:12–15, 98; Mark (writer), 22, 99; Mark 1:40–45, 98; Mark 4:35–41, 132; Moab, 157; Mount Seir, 157; Nazareth, 99, 152; Paul, Apostle, 48, 79–80, 87, 153, 160; Philippians 2:5–11, 92, 123; Philistines, 111; Psalm 119:59, 91; 2 Samuel 6:14, 129; Silas, 79–81, 87; Uzzah, 130; Ziz, 118
Black Entertainment Television (BET), 13, 45, 48
Blake, Charles E. (Bishop), 45–46, 48, 94
Blanton, Anderson, 14, 151, 153
blues, 32, 50, 52, 76, 83–4, 104, 124, 126, 139, 149, 166, 176
Bohme, Gernot, 137

INDEX

Bountiful Blessings. See broadcasting
Bowler, Kate, 13
Brewster, William Herbert, 134
broadcasting, 5, 34, 43, 51, 77, 87, 97, 164; aesthetics of, 118; assemblage of, 142; *Bountiful Blessings*, 4, 12, 18, 20, 40, 43, 68*fig.*, 94, 142, 150, 155-156*fig.*, 164, 170-172, 177-178, 181-183, 188-190; ecology of, 65; grammar of, 96-98; instruments of, 56, 141; radio, 15-16, 145; and religion, 5, 7, 11, 14-15, 18-19, 28, 32, 35-36, 40, 45-47, 49, 57-8, 62-3, 128, 148-149, 166, 170, 178, 181, 184, 191; sequence of, 53-54; studio for, 56; technologies of, 52, 190; televisual, 48, 144. *See also* technophilia; tuning up/tuning in
Brown, John, 153-155, 163, 175, 202n32, 206n15
Brubaker, Jed R., 171
Butler, Anthea, 14
Buttrick, David, 14
Bynum, Juanita, 12

Callas, Maria, 89
Campbell, Lucie: "He'll Understand, He'll Say Well Done" (hymn), 120
cancer: prostate, 1, 86, 89; breast, 153
Chemprali: tones of, 141
Christmas Day, 92, 144, 167-9
Chude-Sokei, Louis, 31-32; and "black technopoetics," 56, 63
church(es): Baptist Church, 8-9, 17-18, 83, 134; Bountiful Blessings Deliverance Church, Inc., 40; Calvary Episcopal Church, 15; Cathedral of Bountiful Blessings, 8; Catholic Church, 10; Church of God, 16-17; Church of God in Christ (COGIC), 1-2, 7-10, 12-13, 19, 40, 43, 45-46, 89, 91-92, 94, 128, 150, 163, 173, 178-9, 183; Foursquare Church, 152; Holiness-Pentecostal, 1, 8-9, 12, 40, 57, 111; Mount Calvary Assembly Hall of the Pentecostal Faith Church, 17; New Bethel Baptist Church, 17; New Jerusalem Church of God in Christ, 7-8; New Salem Missionary Baptist Church, 17; Temple of Deliverance, 57, 91, 117
clothing: of Patterson, 4, 148, 153-155, 159, 164, 181
Cobbs, Clarence (Rev.), 16
Columbia Broadcasting Company (CBS), 16
Congressional Black Caucus, 163

Congressional Record, 163-164, 206n22
Connerton, Paul, 141
contrafacta, contrafactum, 84, 116, 134; COGIC, 93
cosmology, 141
Crawley, Ashon, 21, 25, 31, 49, 57, 92
Crouch, Andraé: "Through It All," 123
Crouch, Samuel M. (Bishop), 16

David, King of Israel, 64, 112, 131
Detroit Bible Institute, 8
Deutsch, Diana, 109
devotional, 14, 21, 32, 35, 86, 114-115, 131, 148, 152, 154-155, 158-159, 163-164, 166, 186, 187-188, 191
Dillard, Linwood (Superintendent), 147-148, 205n1
Dixon, Calvin, 18
Dollar, Creflo, 12
Douglas, Willie, 43, 56
Dunlap, Walter, 129, 131

Easter Sunday, 60, 124
echos (ἦχος), 74-75
ecstasy, 121, 127, 136, 139, 141-142, 146; afterlife of, 127; corporeal, 132; embodied, 108; homiletic, 72; pursuit of, 119; religious, 51, 79-80, 82, 97, 109, 127-128, 141-142, 146; spiritual, 85; vocal, 140
Eidsheim, Nina, 89
Eikerenkoetter, Frederick J., II (Rev. Ike), 18; Science of Living, the, 18
Eisenlohr, Patrick, 14, 54, 114, 136
endurance, 2, 7, 15, 32, 40, 85, 87, 92-3, 115, 118, 127-8, 159, 161, 179, 184, 187
Engelke, Matthew, 14, 114
epistemology: Black Pentecostal, 21, 57, 165
evangelical, 13, 15, 18, 56
evangelist, 12, 17, 19, 25, 31, 170. *See also* televangelist

Facebook. *See* social media
Federal Communications Commission (FCC), 45
Federal Council of Churches of Christ in America, 15
Feldman, Martha, 14, 83
Feller, Gavin, 14
fidelity: audible, 127, 135; homiletic, 34, 98, 112-115, 118-119; performative, 113
Ford, L. H. (Bishop), 10
Fox, Aaron, 75

INDEX

Franklin, Clarence LaVaughn (C. L.), 17, 23, 25; *The Shadow of the Cross*, 17 (radio program)
Franklin, Aretha, 17, 180
Frederick, Marla, 13–14, 40, 188
Fuller, Charles, 16

Gabriel, Charles: "His Eye Is on the Sparrow," 72. *See also* Martin, Civillia
Gates, J. M., 18
Giggie, John, 9, 14
glossolalia, 5, 21–25, 27, 29, 184
Graham, Billy, 19, 25
Great Awakening, 15
Great Migration, 17, 100
Griffith, R. Marie, 153
Gumbrecht, Hans, 162

Hangen, Tona, 14–15
Harkness, Nicholas, 14, 22–24
Harrell, David Edwin, Jr., 14, 152
Hartman, Saidiya, 30, 67, 193n4, 198n1, 200n41
Hayes, Gillian R., 171
Hebrew, 2, 86, 112
heteroglossia, 23
Hirschkind, Charles, 14
Horn, Rose Artimus (Mother), 17; "Pray for Me Priestess," 17; "Radio Church of God of the Air," 17
Hutchins, Derrick (Bishop), 10–11

impairment: vocal, 83–84, 86, 95. *See also* voice
infrastructure, 14, 38, 47, 71, 125; broadcasting, 18, 62; denomination, 12; harmonic, 117; media, 5, 33, 40, 46, 57, 65, 68, 77, 128; metrical, 117; musical, 124, 129; sonic, 21, 34, 121, 126, 137, 166; technological, 156
Instagram. *See* social media
instrumentality, 4, 6, 20, 31; Black Pentecostal, 5, 21, 26, 28–29, 39, 63, 81, 92, 113, 117, 144, 191; sacred, 21; vocal, 24, 50, 54, 57, 64, 74, 77, 82–83, 85, 94, 167. *See also* Patterson, G. E. (Bishop); voice
intermundane, 173, 178
interpenetration, 14, 75, 78, 135, 173
Israel, Israeli, Israelite, 50, 96, 102, 110–111, 129–30

Jackson, Derrick (Brother), 100, 120–121
Jakes, TD, 12

Jehovah-Rophe, 103
Jenkins, Henry, 173
Johnson, Mark, 77
Jones, Alisha Lola, 31, 135
Jones, Charles Price, 9

Kane, Brian, 74
Kelley, Frances, 173
keys (music), 27, 34, 90, 104, 121, 123–124, 127, 130, 139–140, 142. *See also* pitch
King, Martin Luther, Jr., 30, 40, 196–197n41
Klassen, Pamela, 14

Lakoff, George, 77
language, 22, 24–25, 46, 75, 83, 94, 129, 131
Larson, Steve, 141
Lemoyne Owen College, 8
Lepore, Jill, 13
leprosy, 99–100
Lofton, Kathryn, 31
"logic of the prayer cloth." *See* clothing
logos (λόγος), 74–75, 104–105. *See also* Word of God

Mapuche (Andean-Argentinian indigenous group), 141
Martin, Civillia: "His Eye Is on the Sparrow," 72. *See also* Gabriel, Charles
Martin, Lerone, 17, 57, 196n41. *See also* King, Martin Luther, Jr.
Mason, Charles Harrison (Bishop), 7, 9, 25, 92–94, 163
McGee, F. W., 118
McLuhan, Marshall, 53–54, 57
McPherson, Aimee, 16, 155; Foursquare church radio, 152
mediation, 5–6, 29, 32–33, 39, 47, 66, 85, 114, 144, 162, 175; religious, 5, 13, 21, 27, 66, 165, 170; sonic, 118; technical, 29; technological, 33, 39, 63
Meintjes, Louise, 113
Memphis Commercial Appeal, 52, 74
Meyer, Birgit, 14, 60–61, 63, 151. *See also* Stolow, Jeremy
Michael, James O., 178
Michaux, Lightfoot Solomon (Elder), 16–17, 196n41
Mitchell, Henry, 14
modulation, 25, 34, 36, 50, 57, 71–72, 74–75, 77–78, 81, 102, 144, 166. *See also* voice

Moten, Fred, 82
Murray, Andrew: *Divine Healing*, 153
musicality, Black, 5, 20, 25, 27, 32, 63, 166, 191; homiletic, 28, 32-35, 73, 86, 90, 94, 101-102, 110, 144, 149; of Patterson, 57, 60, 97, 117-118, 127, 130, 135, 157, 165
musicking: Black, 64, 79, 92, 101, 184, 188
Muslim: Egyptian, 14; Mauritian, 13, 114

National Broadcasting Company (NBC), 15
Nelson, Alondra, 30
Newsweek, 56

Ong, Walter, 54, 119
"Oracle of Christ," 29, 53-55, 71-72, 82, 85, 101, 109
organology: vocal, 71
Osteen, Joel, 12
Owens, Chandler David (Presiding Bishop), 10

Patterson, Gilbert Earl (Bishop), 1-15, 17-18, 20-40, 43-142, 144-151, 153-173, 175-191, 193-4, 197-8, 200-211, 213-4; "After the Dust Settles," 92, 147; "All We Need Is at Home," 55; "The Arrows of the Lord's Deliverance," 102, 126; "Call His Name," 106, 108, 122, 144, 188; "A Compassionate Father," 91, 105, 123; "A Cry in Desperation," 138; "And David Recovered All," 20; "David's Day of Thanksgiving," 114, 129-130; "Dealing with Life's Battles," 27, 64, 86-88, 126, 157; "Delivered from Fear," 67; "The Departed Glory Shall Return," 58, 110-111, 114; eternal song, 1-4, 7, 26-27, 33, 64-66, 79, 87-90, 108, 115-119, 121, 125-127, 140, 157-159, 161-162, 166, 187; "The Faith of Strangers," 91; "Focusing Our Eyes upon the Lord," 2-4, 86, 88, 115, 127, 157; "Get Up, Jesus," 134; "God Can," 122; "God in Jesus Christ Made the Difference," 122; "God's Plan Can Be Altered but Not Cancelled," 122; "The God of All Supply," 79, 81, 123; "The Gospel According to John," 46, 144, 167; "Have Your Way," 92; "He Cares for You," 132, 136*fig.*, 137; "Healing in the Temple," 172; "The Healing of King Hezekiah," 83-84, 96; "Hold on! Help is on the Way!," 50, 52, 63; "The Hope of Our City," 54-55*fig.*; "How Much I Owe" (hymn), 124; "I Can't Keep It to Myself," 98, 100-101; "I don't believe in oil, I just believe in the Word," 150-156, 165-167; "I Never Shall Forget," 145, 168; "I Surrender All" (hymn), 38, 75-76; "I Thank You Jesus, I Thank You Lord," 91; "I will deliver thee" (song), 107; "The Importance of the Holy Ghost," 47-48; "Infallible Proofs," 122; "Is Your All on the Altar?" (hymn), 76; "It's Not Your Battle," 65, 157; "It's Time for You to Sing Your Song," 64, 126; "Jehosophat's Prayer and God's Answer" (sermon), 1, 3, 7, 64, 66, 80, 86, 89, 115, 127, 157-8, 160; "Jesus Breaks Every Fetter," 75, 93; "Job 42:10," 123; "Just a Little Talk with Jesus," 80-81, 87; "Learn When It's Your Mail," 122; "Lord, Let Your Glory Fill This House," 90, 122; "Living the Abundant Life," 123; "Neither Were They Thankful," 90, 122, 161, 184; "The Next Fifteen Years," 96, 123; "The Password," 85, 122, 140; "Peace Be Still" (song), 134; "The Power of Preaching," 122; "The Power of the Word," 84, 91; "praise break," 142; "Psalm 37," 122; "The Purpose of the Four Gospels," 169-170*fig.*; "The Saint's Remedy in Times of Trouble," 107, 122, 141; "A Second Touch," 123, 150; *Singing the Old Time Way*, 37-38, 52, 75, 93, 124; "Strategies for Victory," 121, 126; "There's Power in the Blood" (sermon), 78, 122; "This Is Your Year of Restoration," 138; "A Time to Remember" ("Tape no. 199"), 43; "A Vicarious Victory," 58, 61-63, 137; "We Wait for Light, but We Walk in Darkness," 7; "When the Dust Settles," 122; "Where Are Your Eyes Focused," 122; "Who Hath Bewitched You?," 8; "Will You Dare to Be Different," 91; "You Can Depend on God," 159-160; "Your Day Will Come," 138-139;
Patterson, J. O. (Bishop), 9-10, 23
Patterson, Louise (Evangelist), 18, 110, 113-114, 147, 155-156, 170, 177-183, 188-190
Patterson, Mary Louise, 7
Patterson, William Archie, Sr. (Bishop), 7
Pearson, Carlton, 19-20
pedagogy, 23
Pentecost Sunday, 21-22, 29
Pentecostalism: Black, 5-6, 20, 22, 24, 29, 49-51, 63, 69, 82, 149-150, 166-167,

176, 180, 186, 190-191; and technophilia, 5, 20-21, 30, 33, 38, 46, 57, 101, 119, 165, 185
Perry, Robert L. (Bishop), 174
Peters, John Durham, 14, 54, 125
phenomenology, 34, 122
Piekut, Benjamin, 173. *See also* Stanyek, Jason
pitch, 26-27, 32, 34-35, 72, 107, 112, 121-122, 130, 132, 138-141, 166; absolute, 141; eternal, 6-7, 27-29, 31, 35-36, 39, 65, 72, 114, 118, 128, 137, 140-142, 144-146, 149, 157, 159-163, 166, 168, 176, 187-188, 190-191; perfect, 141; stable, 141
Price, Frederick KC, 12
Prince, Ruth (Sister), 8
Protestantism: Black, 13; South Korean, 22
Pinn, Anthony, 28

Quashie, Kevin, 30

Rader, Paul, 16
radio, 4-5, 8, 23, 33, 35, 38, 53-54, 58, 66, 68, 70, 102, 140, 142, 144-145, 149, 152, 155, 161, 163-164, 167, 170, 172, 176, 185, 187; internet, 11; ministers, 16-17; religious, 15-18, 25, 39-40; station, 11, 40, 43, 45, 112, 143*fig*. *See also* broadcasting
Reckson, Lindsay V., 51
recording, 6, 19, 28, 33, 35, 38-39, 65, 67, 113-115, 148, 160, 166, 169-173, 175, 179, 188-189; archival, 37; cassette, 186; live, 19, 37-38, 52, 75, 77, 93; project, 37, 76, 116; sound, 112, 202n30; VHS, 18; video, 29
Redmond, Shana, 30, 67, 128, 193n4, 198n1, 200n41; "antiphonal life," 7; *Everything Man: The Form and Function of Paul Robeson*, 128
Reed, Anthony, 31-33, 48, 80; "black media concept," 31
Religious Right, 16
resonance, 6, 16, 36, 54, 73, 128, 145, 161, 188; aural, 81; medieval, 159; posthumous, 3, 68, 93, 95, 140, 184
reverberation, 3, 6, 39, 45, 92, 128-129
revivalist, 16, 19; Healing and Charismatic, 35, 149
rhema, 104-105
riff: bluesy, 84; Broadcast Ensemble of, 175; eternal, 7, 26-28, 65, 90-91*fig*., 92-94,
101, 104-109, 116, 118-119, 127, 140, 145, 157, 159-162, 166, 168, 187. *See also* pitch, eternal
Roberts, Oral, 12, 18-20, 151-152, 155, 166; *Healing Waters* (television broadcast), 19; Healing Revival, 152; Healing Waters (broadcast), 152; *If You Need Healing, Do These Things*, 151; Oral Roberts University, 20; "theologico-technical," 151
Robertson, Carol, 141
Robeson, Paul, 30, 67, 128
Ross, Leora, 18

sacred, 87; heart, 59; instrumentality, 21; music, 92, 101, 163; practice, 21; rhetoric, 78; singing, 1; speech, 25; text, 110, 119; word (Words), 104; writ, 55, 62, 113-114, 118-119. *See also* musicking
Salvatore, Nick, 17
Sanders, Cheryl, 14
Schultze, Quentin, 14
sermon. *See* Patterson, G. E. (Bishop)
Shelemay, Kay Kaufman, 93
Smallwood, Richard: "I Love the Lord (He Heard My Cry)," 179
Smith, Bessie, 82
Smith, James K. A., 151
Smith, Lucy (Elder), 16
Smith, Stephen (Pastor), 163, 202n32
social media, 4-5, 15, 18, 30, 33, 35, 39-40, 67-68, 70, 129, 149-150, 161-162, 164, 170-171, 173, 176, 184, 186; Facebook, 4, 13, 30, 40, 67, 160-161, 167-168, 171-173, 181, 187, 201nn46-47, 206n19, 206n21, 207nn26-27, 207nn31-32, 207nn34-36; Instagram, 4, 30, 40, 147-148, 160, 184-186*fig*., 205n1, 208n5; TikTok, 4, 30, 40, 160; YouTube, 3-4, 13, 29-30, 61, 82, 94, 115, 155, 168-170, 172-173, 180-181, 187-188, 193nn1-3, 194n18, 198n68, 202n26, 202nn30-32, 204n25, 205n22, 207n28-30, 207n33
sound, 5, 7, 14, 20-22, 26-30, 32-35, 37-39, 51-52, 54, 57-58, 61-67, 69, 72-74, 80, 82, 88, 90, 93-94, 97, 102-103, 105, 112-114, 119, 129, 131-132, 135-136, 140, 142, 144, 156, 158, 162, 175, 181, 187, 190-191; Black, 5-6, 31, 49
Stanyek, Jason, 173. *See also* Piekut, Benjamin

Sterne, Jonathan, 14, 57, 105, 112, 175
Stolow, Jeremy, 60–61. *See also* Meyer, Birgit
strike, Sanitation Workers', 40
Swaggart, Jimmy, 12
"Sweet Jesus" (praise song), 83
Synan, Vinson, 82, 202n17

tayil (vocal genre), 141
technoethics: funereal, 180
technology, 5–6, 11, 13–14, 20, 29, 31, 40, 48–49, 52, 54, 63, 69, 177, 179, 190. *See also* sound
technophilia, 56, 58, 114, 180–181. *See also* Patterson, G. E. (Bishop)
technopoetics, 31, 56, 62–63, 191
televangelist, 12, 18. *See also* evangelist
television, 4–5, 11–12, 16, 18–20, 33, 38, 40, 43, 45–46, 48–49, 52–53, 55, 58, 61, 66–68, 70, 73, 93, 118, 140, 149, 155, 161, 163–164, 167, 170, 172, 175–176, 181–182, 185, 187–189
Temperley, David, 125
Tennessee A & I State College (now Tennessee State University), 8
testimony, 23–26, 92, 99–101, 110, 153
theurgical technique, 151–152
TikTok. *See* social media
topos (τοόπος), 74–75
Tri-State Defender, 43, 150
trial, Scopes, 15
Trinity Broadcasting Network (TBN), 13, 19, 45
tuning up/tuning in, 2, 34, 51, 63, 73, 77, 97–98, 100–102, 109, 117, 119, 125, 130, 140, 146, 168, 182
Turner, William, 14
TV Guide, 43–44*fig.*

vocality, 4, 19, 21, 33, 50, 52, 71, 73–74, 77, 82, 84–85, 87, 150, 190. *See also* Patterson, G. E. (Bishop); voice

voice, voices, 16, 22, 34, 49, 66, 74, 78–79, 82–83, 90, 134, 177; bad, 33, 52, 83–85, 89; Black, 20, 49, 63; choral, 33, 78; dying, 33, 71, 85–86, 88–89; eternal, 33, 71, 89–90, 94; European American, 49; familiar, 39; homiletic, 6, 65; human, 5, 20–21, 27–29, 33, 35, 39, 50, 54, 77, 99, 149, 166, 176, 191; modulating, 33, 71–77, 81, 94; of Patterson, 4–6, 23–26, 28, 36, 38–39, 45, 49–54, 64, 68, 70–85, 87–89, 94–95, 100–102, 105, 107, 109, 111–112, 118–119, 121, 127, 130–132, 135, 139–141, 144–145, 161, 175, 186–187, 191; posthumous, 71; and Protestantism, 15; and singing, 14, 94; tired, 33. *See also* Patterson, G. E. (Bishop)

Wacker, Grant, 14
Walton, Jonathan, 12, 14, 19, 40
Waters, David, 52, 74, 137
Wesleyan Holiness movement, 9
White, Calvin, 13
White, Frank O. (Elder), 110
White, Paula, 12
The Whole Truth, 8
Wilbourne, Emily, 85
Williams-Jones, Pearl, 92
Word of God, 5, 46–47, 54, 57, 74, 76, 103–104, 110, 150–151. *See also* logos
World War I, 16
World War II, 16–17

xenolalia, 23

Yong, Amos, 14
YouTube. *See* social media

Zeitlin, Judith, 14
Zimbabwe: Apostolics, 114; Pentecostals, 14

Founded in 1893,
UNIVERSITY OF CALIFORNIA PRESS
publishes bold, progressive books and journals
on topics in the arts, humanities, social sciences,
and natural sciences—with a focus on social
justice issues—that inspire thought and action
among readers worldwide.

The UC PRESS FOUNDATION
raises funds to uphold the press's vital role
as an independent, nonprofit publisher, and
receives philanthropic support from a wide
range of individuals and institutions—and from
committed readers like you. To learn more, visit
ucpress.edu/supportus.

www.ingramcontent.com/pod-product-compliance
Lightning Source LLC
Chambersburg PA
CBHW020802230426
43666CB00007B/820